M000298504

The Quotable
Machiavelli

IL PRINCIPE DI NICCHOLO MACHIA
VELLO AL MAGNIFICO LOREN‑
ZO DI PIERO DE MEDICI.

*

LA VITA DI CASTRVCCIO CASTRA‑
CANI DA LVCCA A ZANOBI BVON‑
DELMONTI ET A LVIGI ALEMAN‑
NI DESCRITTA PER IL
MEDESIMO.

*

IL MODO CHE TENNE IL DVCA VA‑
LENTINO PER AMMAZAR VITEL
LOZO, OLIVEROTTO DA FER‑
MO IL.S.PAOLO ET IL DV
CA DI GRAVINA ORSI
NI IN SENIGAGLIA,
DESCRITTA PER
IL MEDESIMO.

❧

Con Gratie, & Priuilegi di, N.S. Clemente
VII.& altri Principi, che intra il termino di, X.
Anni non si Stampino, ne Stampati si uendino:
sotto le pene, che in essi si contengono,
M. D. XXXII.

Frontispiece. Title page from *The Prince.* Princeton University Library,
Rare Books Division, Department of Rare Books and Special Collection.

The Quotable
Machiavelli

Edited by
Maurizio Viroli

PRINCETON UNIVERSITY PRESS

PRINCETON AND OXFORD

press.princeton.edu
Jacket art: Portrait of Niccolò Machiavelli by Antonio Maria Crespi
("il Bustino"), oil on canvas. DEA/Veneranda Biblioteca Ambrosiana/
Getty Images.

Library of Congress Cataloging-in-Publication Data

Names: Machiavelli, Niccolò, 1469–1527, author. | Viroli,
Maurizio, editor.
Title: The quotable Machiavelli / edited by Maurizio Viroli.
Description: Princeton : Princeton University Press, 2016. | Includes
bibliographical references and index.
Identifiers: LCCN 2016015209 | ISBN 9780691164366
(hardcover : alk. paper)
Subjects: LCSH: Political science—Early works to 1800.
Classification: LCC JC143 .M1463 2016 | DDC 320.1—dc23
LC record available at https://lccn.loc.gov/2016015209

British Library Cataloging-in-Publication Data is available

This book has been composed in Minion Pro with
Goudy Oldstyle display

Printed on acid-free paper. ∞

Printed in the United States of America

1 3 5 7 9 10 8 6 4 2

To Philip Bobbitt, in gratitude

Contents

the French—Germany and the German Free Cities—
Italy—Julius Caesar—Livy (Roman Historian)—
Moses—Plutarch—Rome and the Roman People—
Romulus—Turks and the Turkish Empire—Venice

Introduction

Love of Politics and Love of Country

If we are to begin to understand and appreciate an author as controversial and misunderstood as Niccolò Machiavelli, a few preliminary warnings based on facts are in order. The first is that Machiavelli's main and lasting passion and vocation was politics. "Fortune has seen to it," he wrote Francesco Vettori on April 9, 1513, "that since I do not know how to talk about either the silk or the wool trade, or profits or losses, I have to talk about politics. I need either to take a vow of silence or to discuss this." Politics meant for him service for the common good in the hope of attaining lasting glory. When from 1498 to 1512 he served as Secretary of the Second Chancery and the Committee of Ten of the Republic of Florence (both committees were concerned primarily with the government of the Florentine Dominion and with foreign affairs), Machiavelli discharged his duties with impeccable honesty. "My poverty," he proudly proclaimed, "is a witness to my loyalty and honesty."[1] No one, not even his political enemies or his most severe critics, has been able to refute this assertion.

---

[1] Niccolò Machiavelli to Francesco Vettori, December 10, 1513, in Niccolò Machiavelli, *Opere*, vol. 2, ed. Corrado Vivanti (Turin: Einaudi, 1999), p. 297; Eng. trans., *Machiavelli and His Friends: Their Personal Correspondence*, ed. and trans. James B. Atkinson and David Sices (DeKalb, IL: Northern Illinois University Press, 1996), p. 265.

As he wrote in the letter that opens *The Prince*, he attained his mastery of political matters at the cost of hardships and risks. On March 1509, for instance, while the Florentine army was busy trying to conquer Pisa, the governors of Florence had considered sending him to Cascina, a much safer place behind the lines. He answered: "I am aware that that post would expose me to less danger and fatigue, but if I wanted to avoid danger and fatigue I should not have left Florence; and therefore I entreat your Lordships to allow me to remain in the camps to cooperate with the commissaries in all the measures that have to be taken. For here I can make myself useful, but at Cascina I should not be good for anything, and should die of sheer desperation."[2]

Machiavelli's political adversaries accused him of being the puppet (*mannerino*) of Piero Soderini who, as Gonfalonier of Justice, held the highest office of the Republic of Florence. Historical evidence points in a different direction. He was, to be sure, a rather unconventional Segretario: opinionated, keen to express his own judgments on political matters instead of simply reporting facts, irreverent, unable to flatter government officials, and ever ready to criticize the faults of Florentine institutions and to show his contempt for the incompetence, corruption, and meanness of many members of the political elite. He

---

[2]Niccolò Machiavelli to the Signori of Florence, April 16, 1509, in *Opere, op. cit.*; Engl. trans., *The Historical, Political, and Diplomatic Writings of Niccolò Machiavelli*, vol. 4, ed. and trans. Christian E. Detmold (Boston and New York: Houghton, Mifflin and Company, 1891), p. 173.

steered clear, however, of factional involvements.[3] It was precisely on account of his unwillingness to play the game of factional politics and serve powerful citizens that he found himself isolated when the popular government led by Piero Soderini was overthrown by the Medici and their partisans. When he asserted, "There should be no doubt about my word; for, since I have always kept it, I should not start learning how to break it now. Whoever has been honest and faithful for forty-three years, as I have, is unable to change his nature," he was being truthful.

He might have added that his loyalty to the Republic was the main cause of his political downfall. Soon after the Medici returned to Florence in September 1512, the new government under their control fired Machiavelli from office, tried him, and sentenced him to one year's confinement within the Florentine Dominion. Then, in February 1513, he was imprisoned and tortured under the charge of conspiracy against the new government. He was freed in March, after Giovanni de' Medici was elected pope with the name Leo X. Thereafter he tried hard to persuade the Medici, in Florence and in Rome, to put him back in the service of the Republic.

Yet he did not compose his most famous (or infamous) work, *The Prince*, to please them or to gain their favor. Had that been the case, he would have written a quite dif-

---

[3] See Robert Black, "Machiavelli, Servant of the Florentine Republic," and John M. Najemy, "The Controversy Surrounding Machiavelli's Service to the Republic," in Gisela Bock, Quentin Skinner, and Maurizio Viroli, eds., *Machiavelli and Republicanism* (Cambridge: Cambridge University Press, 1990), pp. 71–100 and 101–118.

ferent text, one full of praise for the Medici and for their glorious history, replete with the kind of counsel that men like Giuliano, Giulio, Lorenzo, and Leo X best liked to hear. Machiavelli knew that the most important rule of successful flattery is to say what pleases the person from whom one expects to obtain favors. In *The Prince* he did exactly the opposite. Instead of reinforcing the well-established principles that had allowed the Medici to gain control over Florence, Machiavelli gave them advice that they were not in the least able to appreciate and that would surely have irritated them, had they read the work. He was not a servant of the Medici; he wanted the Medici to follow him. But the Medici had no wish to avail themselves of a counselor like Machiavelli. They gave him some minor offices and the assignment of writing a history of Florence, and this only after 1523, when another member of the Medici family became pope (Giulio de' Medici, with the name Clement VII).

In Machiavelli's mind, love of politics and love of country were one and the same. He interpreted and practiced politics as service to his country because he loved it, and his country was Florence, and Italy. In 1521, when he was in Carpi to discharge a quite inglorious mission on behalf of the Wool Guild of Florence, he did not hesitate to explain flatly to Francesco Guicciardini, at the time governor of the papal states of Modena and Reggio, that he took his duty seriously, even if it was quite a lowly one for such a man as he, "because never did I disappoint that republic whenever I was able to help her out—if not with deeds, then with words; if not with words, then with signs—I have no intention of disappointing her now."[4] In a letter written on April 16, 1527, two months before he died, he confessed to his friend Francesco Vettori: "I love my country, more than my soul." He was not boasting. Florence had been ungrateful and unjust to him, yet he decided to remain there even when, in 1521, he was offered an excellent opportunity to move to Ragusa to be again at the service of the former Gonfalonier of the Republic, Piero Soderini.[5]

His contemporaries regarded Machiavelli as a fine observer of political life. On August, 23, 1500, his assistant in the Chancery, Biagio Buonaccorsi, wrote him: "I do not want to fail to let you know how much satisfaction your letters give everyone; and you may believe me, Niccolò, since you know that adulation is not my forte, that when I found myself reading those earlier letters of yours to certain citizens, and some of the foremost, you were most

---

[4] Niccolò Machiavelli to Francesco Guicciardini, May 17, 1521, in Niccolò Machiavelli, *Opere*, vol. 2, p. 372; Eng. trans., *Machiavelli and His Friends*, p. 336. Machiavelli stresses his love of the fatherland also in the opening of his *A Dialogue on Language* (*Discorso o dialogo intorno alla nostra lingua*), in *Opere*, vol. 3, p. 261: "Whenever I have had an opportunity of honoring my country, even if this involved me in trouble and danger, I have done it willingly, for a man is under no greater obligation than to his country; he owes his very existence, and later, all the benefits that nature and fortune offer him, to her. And the nobler one's country, the greater one's obligation. In fact he who shows himself by thought and deed an enemy of his country deserves the name of parricide, even if he has a legitimate grievance." Eng. trans., *The Literary Works of Machiavelli: With Selections from the Private Correspondence*, ed. and trans. J. R. Hale (London and New York: Oxford University Press, 1961), p. 175.

[5] Piero Soderini to Niccolò Machiavelli, April 13, 1521, in *Opere*, vol. 2, pp. 369–70; Eng. trans. *Machiavelli and His Friends*, p. 334.

highly commended by them, and I took extreme pleasure from it and strove adroitly to confirm that opinion with a few words, showing with what ease you did it." After he lost his office, on November 7, 1512, eminent friends continued to solicit his opinion on important matters of international relations. Francesco Vettori wrote to him: "Examine everything, and I know you have such intelligence that although two years have gone by since you left the shop I do not think you have forgotten the art."[6]

Francesco Guicciardini, unquestionably one of the finest political minds of Renaissance Italy, criticized Machiavelli for his inclination to interpret political events through abstract models and examples taken from antiquity. He maintained that political decisions should be made using *discrezione* (discretion)—that is, a highly refined form of political prudence that is not based on general rules, cannot be learned in books, and that very few men have by nature or are able to attain through long practice.[7] Yet Guicciardini too admired Machiavelli's judgment and wanted him as his main counselor when he had to face the tremendous task of saving the last glimmerings of Italian independence in 1525–1527.

Machiavelli's main areas of expertise and interest were international relations and military matters. What really fascinated him, however, were the founders of republics or

---

[6] Francesco Vettori to Niccolò Machiavelli, December 3, 1514, in *Opere*, vol. 2, p. 330; Eng. trans. *Machiavelli and His Friends*, p. 294.

[7] Francesco Guicciardini, *Ricordi*, C 110, in *Opere di Francesco Guicciardini*, vol. 1, ed. Emanuella Lugnani Scarano (Torino: Utet, 1983).

principalities and the redeemers of peoples from foreign domination, tyranny, and corruption. He wrote *The Prince* to give life, with his words, to a redeemer capable of arousing "obstinate faith," and "piety," and to revive the "ancient valor" in the hearts of the Italians. With the *Discourses on Livy* he hoped to shape the "spirits" of youths so that they would denounce their own times, times filled with "every extreme misery, infamy, and reproach," and emulate instead the times of antiquity, "so filled with virtue and religion."[8] In *The Art of War*, he aimed to encourage his contemporaries and posterity to "bring back" the militia into its ancient orders, restoring its age-old virtue. He lamented the fact that he himself was unable to undertake the work of redemption, but held out the hope that others, in a new age, might be able to implement his teaching.[9] All his great works were designed to shape souls, teach, revive forgotten ways of life, and resurrect ancient ideas and principles for the purpose of attaining good political constitutions and mores. He was a theorist of grand politics.

A Man of the Renaissance

Machiavelli's intellectual style exhibits a number of characteristics typical of the modern scientific mind. For example, he consistently shows remarkable intellectual courage and a penchant to challenge the most revered opinions of his time: "Contrary to the general opinion,

[8] *Discourses on Livy*, preface to Book II.
[9] *The Art of War*, VII.

then, I conclude and affirm . . ." is a phrase we find often in his writings.[10] He regularly rejects the principle of authority, including even the authority of Aristotle, still the most respected of political writers in Machiavelli's day. When Francesco Vettori cites Aristotle's *Politics* to argue that the Swiss cannot entertain expansionist ambitions, he replies: "I do not know what Aristotle says about confederated republics, but I certainly can say what might reasonably exist, what exists, and what has existed."[11]

To validate political theories and political assessments, he credits only rational considerations based on facts. "On these matters," he writes to Franceso Vettori, "I do not want to be prompted by any authority but reason."[12] He is not only aware, but quite proud of his critical and free style of thinking: "I think, and ever shall think, that it cannot be wrong to defend one's opinions with arguments founded upon reason, without employing force."[13] In *The Prince* he has penned words that might well count as the fundamental tenet of political scientists: "It seems to me proper to pursue the effective truth of the matter, rather than to indulge in mere speculation."[14]

Many passages of Machiavelli's political works exhibit a style attentive to the nuances of concepts and language,

[10] See for instance *Discourses on Livy*, I. 58 and II.10.

[11] Niccolò Machiavelli to Francesco Vettori, August 26, 1513; Eng. trans., *Machiavelli and His Friends*, p. 258.

[12] Niccolò Machiavelli to Francesco Vettori, April 29, 1523; Eng. trans., *Machiavelli and His Friends*, p. 233.

[13] *Discourses on Livy*, I. 58.

[14] *The Prince*, XV; Eng. trans., *The Historical, Political, and Diplomatic Writings of Niccolò Machiavelli, op. cit.*, vol. 2.

framing political issues in the clearest possible way: "All states and governments that have had, and have at present, dominion over men, have been and are either republics or principalities. The principalities are either hereditary or they are new. Hereditary principalities are those where the government has been for a long time in the family of the prince. New principalities are either entirely new, as was Milan to Francesco Sforza, or they are like appurtenances annexed to the hereditary state of the prince who acquires them, as the kingdom of Naples is to that of Spain. States thus acquired have been accustomed either to live under a prince, or to exist as free states; and they are acquired either by the arms of others, or by the conqueror's own, or by fortune or virtue." I am citing from the opening of *The Prince*.[15]

Yet, it would be misleading to read Machiavelli's books as the works of a modern political scientist. He was a man of the Renaissance, and he shared the period's belief in astrology and magic. He held, for instance, that "the occurrence of important events in any city or country is generally preceded by signs and portents and by men who predict them."[16] His attempt to explain this process falls well short of the scientific: "The air is peopled with spirits, who by their superior intelligence foresee future events, and out of pity for mankind warn them by such signs, so that they may prepare against the coming evils." And sure enough, he concludes, "The truth of the fact exists, that

[15] *The Prince*, I.
[16] *Discourses on Livy*, I. 56.

these portents are invariably followed by the most re-markable events."[17]

Machiavelli believed that the movements of planets and stars affect the deliberations and actions of individu-als and of peoples, and on the basis of this belief he ex-plained political facts. In the *Discourses on Livy*, for in-stance, in the context of his discussion of Roman religion, he remarks: "The heavens did not judge the laws of this prince [Romulus] sufficient for so great an empire, and therefore inspired the Roman Senate to elect Numa Pom-pilius as his successor, so that he might regulate all those things that had been omitted by Romulus."[18] Remarkable words indeed, if we consider that his source, Livy, makes no mention whatsoever of divine or celestial influence on the wise deliberations of Roman senators. The heavenly inspiration is entirely Machiavelli's idea.

Machiavelli also affirms that God intervenes in the life of peoples. In the final chapter of *The Prince* he alludes to men who seemed "*ordinati da Dio*" (ordered by God) to redeem Italy. In the *Florentine Histories* he interprets ex-traordinary natural events as signs of God's wrath. Of the fire that burned the church of Santo Spirito during the visit of the Duke of Milan in 1471, he relates, without questioning it, the popular belief that it was God's punish-ment for the corrupt customs of the Duke's court: "At that time was seen a thing never before seen in our city: this being the season of Lent, in which the Church commands

[17] Ibid.
[18] *Discourses on Livy,* I. 11.

that one fasts by not eating meat, his court, without respect to Church or God, all fed on meat. And because many spectacles were held to honor him, among which was represented the giving of the Holy Spirit to the Apostles in the church of Santo Spirito, and because that church burned down as a result of the many fires that are made in such solemnities, it was believed by many that God, angered against us, had wished to show that sign of his wrath."[19]

Like his Florentine contemporaries, Machiavelli believed in the power of prophecy and wrote prophecies of his own.[20] The outstanding example is the "exhortation to liberate Italy from the barbarians," with which he ends *The Prince*. In this text Machiavelli prophesies Italy's emancipation on the basis of signs he believes he has been able to decode: "Having now considered all the things we have spoken of, and thought within myself whether at present

---

[19]Similar considerations come into play when he describes an extraordinary storm that ravaged Tuscany: "Thereupon, when arms had been put away by men, it appeared that God wished to take them up Himself: so great was a wind storm that then occurred, which in Tuscany had effects unheard of in the past and for whoever learns of it in the future will have marvelous and memorable effects. . . . Without doubt, God wanted to warn rather than punish Tuscany; for, if such a storm had entered into a city among many and crowded houses and inhabitants, as it did enter among few and scattered oaks and trees and houses, without doubt it would have made ruin and torment greater than that which the mind can conjecture. But God meant . . . that this small example should be enough to refresh among men the memory of His power"; *History of Florence*, VI. 34, in *The Historical, Political, and Diplomatic Writings of Niccolò Machiavelli*, vol. 1, ed. and trans. Christian E. Detmold (Boston: James R. Osgood and Company, 1882), p. 314.

[20]See for instance his remarks in *History of Florence*, VI. 29.

the time was not propitious in Italy for a new prince, and if there was not a state of things which offered an opportunity to a prudent and capable man to introduce a new system that would do honor to himself and good to the mass of the people, it seems to me that so many things concur to favor a new ruler that I do not know of any time more fitting for such an enterprise." Like a prophetic poet, he unveils God's plan for Italy: "And although before now a spirit has been shown by some which gave hope that he might be appointed by God for her redemption, yet at the highest summit of his career he was thrown aside by fortune." Then, to eloquently introduce his prophecy, he cites the words of Petrarch: "Virtue will seize arms / Against furor, and the battle will be brief: / For ancient valor / Is not yet dead in Italian hearts."[21]

His examples are often more rhetorical than scientific. They do not serve the purpose of demonstrating the empirical validity of a scientific law, but are designed rather to render a piece of political advice more persuasive, and to stimulate the desire to emulate a specific way of acting: "Let no one wonder if, in what I am about to say of entirely new principalities and of the prince and his government, I cite the very highest examples. For as men almost always follow the beaten track of others, and proceed in their actions by imitation, and yet cannot altogether follow the ways of others, nor attain the high qualities of those whom they imitate, so a wise man should ever follow the ways of great men and endeavor to imitate only such as have been

[21] *The Prince*, XXVI.

most eminent; so that even if his merits do not quite equal theirs, yet that they may in some measure reflect their greatness. He should do as the skillful archer, who, seeing that the object he desires to hit is too distant, and knowing the extent to which his bow will carry, aims higher than the destined mark, not for the purpose of sending his arrow to that height, but so that by this elevation it may reach the desired aim."[22]

Only very rarely, and always as a pure intellectual exercise, does Machiavelli try to explain princes' actions by assuming that they are rational and pursue their best interest accordingly. To suppose that they made their decisions based on reason would be of little avail as he is convinced that human beings in general are not wise: "And truly, anyone wise enough to adapt to and understand the times and the pattern of events would always have good fortune or would always keep himself from bad fortune; and it would come to be true that the wise man could control the stars and the Fates. But such wise men do not exist: in the first place, men are shortsighted; in the second place, they are unable to master their own natures; thus it follows that Fortune is fickle, controlling men and keeping them under her yoke."[23] What would be the point of explaining or predicting princes' actions on the assumption that they are wise and act rationally, when in fact they are not and they do not?

[22] *The Prince*, VI.

[23] Niccolò Machiavelli to Giovan Battista Soderini, September 13–21, 1506.

Investigating Political Life

Machiavelli studied the actions of princes and the deliberations of councils in order to grasp the reasons (*ragioni*) of those actions and those deliberations. By "reasons" he means the goals that political actors intend to achieve. The first step to accomplish this task, he tells us, is to understand the passions, the humors, and the beliefs that orient the conduct of a particular prince or ruler.[24] A prince who is afraid to lose his power does not act in the same way as a prince who is confident of his ability to expand his dominions; a prince possessed by love of glory does not act like a prince whose soul is dominated by avarice; a prince who hates other princes and is consumed by envy or by the desire to avenge himself does not act like a prince who trusts his subjects and other princes and entertains no plans for revenge.

Examples abound of Machiavelli's method for deciphering the intentions of a prince by probing the geography of his passions. On December 10, 1514, for instance, he writes: "I believe that the reason why the king of England has clung to France was to avenge the insults Spain inflicted upon him during the war with France. This in-

---

[24] As Felix Gilbert has stressed in a masterful essay of 1957, in Machiavelli's time no such a thing as a scientific method to investigate political events existed. To explain and predict political events, Florentine rulers and citizens relied on the observation of the character of political leaders and on very general ideas about human nature, often couched in popular proverbs and sayings. "Florentine Political Assumptions in the Period of Savonarola and Soderini," *Journal of Warburg and Courtauld Institutes* 20 (1957), pp. 187–214. Machiavelli follows the same path.

dignation was justified, and I see no issue that might so readily eliminate this indignation and destroy the loving relationship that has formed between these two monarchs; unlike many who are influenced by the inveterate hostility between the English and French, I am not, because the people want what their kings want, not the reverse. As for the English being offended by France's power in Italy, this would inevitably have to result from either envy or fear. Envy might exist if England too were unable to find a spot for acquiring honor and were obliged to remain idle; but if he too can achieve glory for himself in Spain, the cause of the envy is removed. As for fear, you must understand that frequently one acquires territory and not armed forces; and if you think it through carefully you will realize that as far as the king of England is concerned, the king of France's acquisition of cities in Italy is one of territory, not armed forces, because with so great an army France could attack that island whether or not he had Italian territory."[25]

He interprets a republic's intentions in a similar vein. Concerning the possibility of Imperial and Swiss domination over Northern Italy, Machiavelli notes that "at first men are satisfied with being able to defend themselves and with not being dominated by others; from this point they move on to attacking others physically and seeking to dominate them. At first the Swiss were satisfied with defending themselves against the dukes of Austria; this defense began to make them appreciated at home. Then they

[25] Niccolò Machiavelli to Francesco Vettori, December 10, 1514.

were satisfied to defend themselves against Duke Charles, which gave them a renown beyond their homeland. Finally, then, they were satisfied with taking their pay from other people so that they could keep their youth ready for warfare and do them honor. This process has given them more renown and, for having observed and become familiar with more and more regions and people, made them more audacious; it has also instilled in their minds an aspiring spirit and a will for soldiering on their own."[26]

To decipher princes' passions, and on those grounds predict and interpret their behavior, Machiavelli very often turns to history. He is confident of his ability to understand the behavior of princes or peoples of his time by identifying pertinent analogies with past events that historians reported as having happened in comparable circumstances, and with similar protagonists. It was for this reason that he wanted to consult Plutarch's *Parallel Lives* when he was assigned the mission to uncover Duke Cesare Borgia's intentions.[27] Niccolò's skill at divining the meaning of princes' actions, words, gestures, and beliefs gained him his reputation as a true master of the art of the state.

Because he was a true master of the *arte dello stato*, and not an amateur, Machiavelli was well aware that political life does not lend itself to the sort of scientific examination that aspires to find demonstrable truths. In fact, he often presented his views as conjectures and tentative assess-

---

[26] Niccolò Machiavelli to Francesco Vettori, August 10, 1513.
[27] Niccolò Machiavelli to Biagio Buonaccorsi, October 21, 1502.

ments, openly recognizing the limits of his own capacity to understand the significance of the events that were unfolding before his eyes. To interpret the intent of *political* actors was particularly difficult, he knew, because they always cover their real plans. In the fifteen years that he spent in the apprenticeship of the art of the state, Machiavelli had many opportunities to observe this distinctive quality of princes. "As I have many times written to you," he reported to the government of Florence, "this Lord is very secretive, and I do not believe that what he is going to do is known to anybody but himself. And his chief secretaries have many times asserted to me that he does not tell them anything except when he orders it. . . . Hence I beg Your Lordships will excuse me and not impute it to my negligence if I do not satisfy Your Lordships with information, because most of the time I do not satisfy even myself" (from Cesena, December 22, 1502).

Evaluations about princes' actions can never be final because there is no judge to whom one can appeal for a conclusive verdict (*non è iudizio da reclamare*).[28] Moreover, each student of political affairs judges the outcome from his or her own perspective, guided or misguided by his or her passions and beliefs.[29] Interpretive work is valuable, but hardly conclusive. The best one can hope for is to come up with convincing narratives and plausible advice, and that will nonetheless be questioned by others who come up with different narratives and different counsel.

[28] *The Prince*, XVIII.
[29] See for instance Niccolò Machiavelli to Francesco Vettori, August 10, 1513.

Politics is largely irrational because of the pervasive power of passions. But there is a way, Machiavelli maintains, to shed some light on it. This way is his interpretive method.

A Teacher of Wisdom

Machiavelli owes his fame to his political works. A large body of this book is accordingly taken from them. Yet he also wrote on human passions, on vices and virtues, on human beings' position and destiny within the larger cosmos, on history, on life, and on death. His reflections on these broader issues offer us, as I hope this selection will at least suggest, some quite remarkable wisdom on how we should conduct our lives so as to fully develop our best qualities and face with courage the misfortunes, the agonies, and the sorrows that afflict our world.

The guiding principle behind Machiavelli's wisdom is that the right way of living one's own life is to accommodate both gravity and lightness, the serious and the playful, reason and passions. His letter to Francesco Vettori of January 31, 1515 makes this point with considerable eloquence: "Anyone who might see our letters, honorable *compare*, and see their variety, would be greatly astonished, because at first it would seem that we were serious men completely directed toward weighty matters and that no thought could cascade through our heads that did not have within it probity and magnitude. But later, upon turning the page, it would seem to the reader that we—still the very same selves—were petty, fickle, lascivious, and were directed toward chimerical matters. If to some this behavior seems contemptible, to me it seems laudable, because we are imitating nature, which is changeable; whoever imitates nature cannot be censured."

Loyal to this philosophy of life, Machiavelli at times completely devotes himself to grand and important political matters; while at other times he lets himself be carried off by the passion of love: "I have met a creature," he writes Vettori on August 3, 1514, "so gracious, so refined, so noble—both in nature and in circumstance—that never could either my praise or my love for her be as much as she deserves. I ought to tell you, as you did me, how this love began, how Love ensnared me in his nets, where he spread them, and what they were like; you would realize that, spread among the flowers, these were nets of gold woven by Venus, so soft and gentle that even though an insensitive heart could have severed them, nevertheless I declined to do so. . . . And even though I may now seem to have entered into great travail, I nevertheless feel so great a sweetness in it, both because of the delight that rare and gentle countenance brings me and because I have laid aside all memory of my sorrows, that not for anything in the world would I desire my freedom, even if I could have it. I have renounced, then, thoughts about matters great and grave. No longer do I delight in reading about the deeds of the ancients or in discussing those of the moderns: everything has been transformed into tender thoughts, for which I thank Venus and all of Cyprus."[30]

[30] Niccolò Machiavelli to Francesco Vettori, August 3, 1514.

When fortune or the malignity of men hits us hard, irony and laughter offer some consolation, if not a complete remedy. In the darkest years of his life, between 1514 and 1520, Machiavelli composed his finest comedy, *Mandragola*, for the purpose of making people, including himself, laugh. It is the laughter of a defeated and disconsolate man.[31] But it helps one to carry on in the hope that better times will come. They will not come, however, if one does nothing but wait. Malignant fortune can be defeated, perhaps, but only if human beings keep fighting and do not give up: "I repeat, then, as an incontrovertible truth, proved by all history, that men may second Fortune, but cannot oppose her; they may develop her designs, but cannot defeat them. But men should never despair on that account; for, not knowing the aims of Fortune, which she pursues by dark and devious ways, men should always be hopeful, and never yield to despair, whatever troubles or ill fortune may befall them."[32]

When Machiavelli passed away, on June 21, 1527, Fortune had defeated him. He had failed to achieve the political goals he had been struggling for all his life long: Italy was under foreign domination; the new popular government instituted in 1527 did not give him back his post as Segretario; moral and political corruption was triumphant all over Italy. But his books, in which he had infused his political and moral wisdom, began to be read, and slowly they helped peoples to gain their independence

[31] See the prologue to *Mandragola*.
[32] *Discourses on Livy*, II. 29.

and establish good republican governments, endowed with good laws, good armies, and good examples of political leadership. Here, the people of the United States of America deserve a special mention. We know for a fact that almost all of the Founding Fathers knew, directly or indirectly, Machiavelli's works, and they had absorbed and reworked his ideas.[33] His posthumous glory is the reward for his determination not to surrender to the malignity of men and times. His philosophy of life is a lesson for all times, but above all for dark times.

A Quotable Author

Niccolò Machiavelli's works lend themselves well to publication in the form of excerpts. In 1578 the Italian writer Francesco Sansovino filled his *Concetti politici* with maxims taken from Machiavelli's main political and historical works: 108 from the *Discourses on Livy*, 29 from *The Prince*, 4 from the *Art of War*, and 25 from *The Florentine Histories*.[34] In 1590 Sansovino's selections were translated into English with the title *The Quintesence of Wit*; in 1619 another English edition was published in London, titled *Archaio-ploutos: Containing, ten following bookes to the*

---

[33] See for instance C. Bradley Thompson, "John Adams's Machiavellian Moment," *Review of Politics* 57 (1995), pp. 389–417. See also Karl Walling, "Was Alexander Hamilton a Machiavellian Statesman?" *Review of Politics* 57 (1995), pp. 419–447; and Brian Danoff, "Lincoln, Machiavelli, and American Political Thought," *Presidential Studies Quarterly* 30 (2000), pp. 290–310.

[34] Francesco Sansovino, *Concetti politici*, published by Giovanni Antonio Bertano in Venice, 1578.

former Treasurie of auncient and moderne times. Being the learned collections, iudicious readings, and memorable observations: not onely divine, morall, and philosophicall; but also poeticall, martiall, politicall, historical, astrologicall.[35]

Over a century later, in 1771, the Italian jurist Stefano Bartolini published in Rome a selection of political maxims taken from Machiavelli's works (though the author's name was never mentioned). Another edition appeared in the same year in Lausanne, with the addition of a phony letter alleged to be from Machiavelli to his son Bernardo.[36] Three editions of the same work came out in 1797, and in 1891 an English edition was published with the title *Thoughts of a Statesman*. The editors included the evidently forged letter of Niccolò Machiavelli to his firstborn

---

[35] *The quintesence of wit.* Being a corrant comfort of conceites, maximies, and poleticke deuises, selected and gathered together by Francisco Sansouino. Wherein is set foorth sundrye excellent and wise sentences, worthie to be regarded and followed. Translated out of the Italian tung, and put into English for the benefit of all those that please to read and vnderstand the works and worth of a worthy writer; London, Edward Allde, 1590; *Archaio-ploutos*: Containing, ten following bookes to the former Treasurie of auncient and moderne times. Being the learned collections, iudicious readings, and memorable observations: not onely divine, morall, and philosophicall; but also poeticall, martiall, politicall, historical, astrologicall, &c. Translated out of that worthy Spanish gentleman, Pedro Mexia, and m. Francesco Sansovino, that famous Italian: As also, of those honourable Frenchman, Anthony du Verdier, lord of Vaupriuaz: Loys Guyon, sieur de la Nauche, counsellour vnto the King: Claudius Gruget, Parisian, &c; London: Printed by William Iaggard, 1619.

[36] *La mente d' un uomo di stato. Forma mentis aeterna Tacit. Vit. Agricol.*, in Roma MDCCLXXI, a spese di Gaetano Quojani mercante libraro al Corso vicino S. Marcello. Con licenza de' Supariori; *La mente d'un uomo di stato, Forma mentis aeterna. Tacit. Vit. Agrico.* Losanna, 1771.

son Bernardo, with a note explaining the history of the text: "This collection of maxims, extracted from the works of Machiavelli, was made by an eminent Italian jurist and man of letters, who selected and arranged them to show the injustice of the charges against the writings of Machiavelli, resulting from an unfair prejudice and imperfect understanding of his sentiments. The little book was printed in Rome, with the entire approval of the Papal censors, in the year 1771. Subsequently a corrected edition was printed at Lausanne in Switzerland, enriched with a polished dedicatory letter, pretending to have been written by Machiavelli himself to his son. This letter was so exactly in the style of Machiavelli that it deceived the public, and even those best acquainted with his writings. To give it still more a varnish of authenticity, a little note was added to the letter intended to make it appear that it had been found amongst the papers of Francesco Del Nero [an eminent Florentine statesman of the fifteenth century]."[37]

The purpose of the forged letter was to dispel the many and strong negative feelings that were still common in the eighteenth-century learned community. Under the heading "Religion," for instance, we read: "All enterprises to be undertaken should be for the honor of God and the general good of the country; the fear of God facilitates every enterprise undertaken by governments . . . ; the non-observance of religion and of laws are vices that are the more detestable as they are caused by those who govern; it

---

[37] *The Historical, Political, and Diplomatic Writings of Niccolo Machiavelli*, vol. 2, ed. and trans. Christian E. Detmold (Boston and New York: Houghton, Mifflin and Company, 1891).

is impossible that he who governs should himself be respected by those who disregard the Deity; in well-constituted governments the citizens fear more to break their oaths than the laws, because they esteem the power of God more than that of men; governments that wish to maintain themselves incorrupt must above all else maintain religious ceremonies uncorrupted, and hold them always in the highest veneration; if in all the governments of the Christian republic religion were maintained as it was instituted by its Divine Founder, the state and the Christian republics would be much more united and happy than what they are now; to show little reverence to God, and still less to the Church, is not the act of a free man, but of one that is dissolute, and more inclined to evil than to good; the disregard of all devotion and of all religion brings with it many troubles and infinite disorders; . . . it is not proper that men should pass their holidays in idleness and in places of pleasure; among all the qualities that distinguish a citizen in his country is his being above all other men liberal and munificent, especially in the construction of public edifices, such as churches, monasteries, and retreats for the poor, for the infirm, and for pilgrims; the good citizen, although constantly spending money in the building of churches and in charities, yet complains that he has never been able to spend so much in honor of God but what he finds himself His debtor on his books; it is proper to thank God, when in his infinite goodness he deigns to accord to a state or to a citizen some mark of approval, which the one has merited by its greatness, and the other by his rare virtues and wisdom."[38]

Also well adapted to American ideas of republican government were Machiavelli's maxims on the rule of law: "We ought to attach little value to living in a city where the laws are less powerful than men; that country only is desirable where you can enjoy your substance and your friends in security, and not that where your property can be easily taken away from you, and where your friends, for fear of their own property, abandon you in your greatest need; a state cannot exist securely unless it has bound itself by many laws, in which the security of all its population is comprised; whoever is not restrained by the laws commits the same error as an unrestrained mob; the power of the law is capable of overcoming every obstacle, even that of the nature of the territory; as the preservation of good morals needs good laws, so the laws, to maintain themselves, require good morals; to prevent good morals from being corrupted and changed into bad morals, the legislator must restrain the human passions and deprive men of all hope of being able to trespass with impunity; it is the laws that make men good; good laws give rise to good education; good education produces good examples; in a well-constituted government the laws are made for the public good, and not to satisfy the ambition of a few; to despoil any one of his goods by new laws, at a time

[38] "Thoughts of a Statesman," in *The Historical, Political, and Diplomatic Writings of Niccolo Machiavelli*, vol. 2, pp. 437–38.

when he claims them with justice before the tribunals, is a wrong that will bring with it the greatest dangers to the legislator."[39]

Attractive and familiar as they might be, these "Machiavellian" sentences correspond only vaguely to Machiavelli's texts. In this volume I have instead tried to faithfully present Machiavelli's ideas, however provocative or distant or obsolete they may appear to contemporary readers. I have also endeavored to preserve the flavor of his unique prose, checking and, when necessary, amending existing translations, or translating the original Italian text when that seemed appropriate. I wish to thank Professor Pasquale Stoppelli for his precious comments.

[39] "Thoughts of a Statesman," in *The Historical, Political, and Diplomatic Writings of Niccolo Machiavelli*, pp. 444–445.

Chronology

1469	Niccolò di Bernardo Machiavelli is born in Florence on May 3. His mother is Bartolomea de' Nelli; his father is Bernardo di Bernardo.
1476	Niccolò attends grammar school.
1481	He studies Latin under the guidance of Paolo da Ronciglione.
1486	Bernardo Machiavelli brings home a copy of Livy's *History of Rome*, on which Niccolò will base his *Discourses on Livy*.
1498	Machiavelli is appointed Head of the Second Chancery of the Republic of Florence; he then also becomes Secretary to the Ten of Liberty and Peace. His main duty is to assist the Signoria in matters of international affairs and the dominion. He is very close to Gonfalonier Piero Soderini, the highest officer of the Florentine Republic.
1499	Mission to Forlì, where he meets the Duchess Caterina Sforza.
1500	Niccolò's father Bernardo passes away on May 19; he completes his first diplomatic mission to France, where he meets King Louis XII and George d'Amboise, Cardinal of Rouen.
1501	He marries Marietta di Luigi Corsini, who will give him seven children: Primerana, Bernardo, Lodovico, Piero, Guido, Bartolomea (or Baccia or Baccina), and Totto.
1502–1503	He helps to make the office of Gonfalonier a lifetime appointment. (The Gonfalonier was

the highest magistrate of the Republic with powers of representation and coordination of the various institutions of the Florentine government.) He composes an oration for the purpose of raising funds to provide Florence with adequate military defense (*Words to Speak on Providing Money*). Diplomatic missions to Cesare Borgia, the very ambitious and able son of Pope Alexander VI, who wanted to establish a principality in central Italy and then fell from power after the death of his father.

1504   Second mission to France to meet with King Louis XII. He composes the *First Decennial*, a history in verse of Florence and Italy from 1494. Diplomatic missions to Mantua and Siena.

1506   He is sent on a diplomatic mission to Pope Julius II.

1506   He organizes the first installment of a Florentine militia, composed of soldiers from the *contado*, and writes the poem "Of Fortune."

1507–1508   He undertakes a mission to the Emperor Maximilian.

1509   Florentine troops attack Pisa; Machiavelli heads the negotiations that lead to the city's surrender.

1510–1511   Two missions to the Court of France to discuss the issue of the schismatic Gallican Council, held first in Pisa and then in Milan.

1512   After the sack of Prato by Spanish and papal armies, Soderini's republic is overthrown and the Medici return to power in Florence.

1513   Machiavelli is dismissed from his office, tried,

sentenced to one year's confinement within the Florentine Dominion, then imprisoned and tortured under the charge of conspiracy against the newly restored Medicean government. He is freed in March, after Giovanni de' Medici is elected pope under the name Leo X. He retires to his family's country properties in Sant'Andrea in Percussina, where he works on the *Discourses on Livy* and completes *De Principatibus*, a short work destined to become famous as *The Prince*.

1515–1516   He writes *The [Golden] Ass*, an unfinished poem, and frequents the Orti Oricellari, a gathering of young Florentine aristocrats, where he discusses his ideas on the imitation of Roman republican politics.

1514–1519   He composes a comedy, *Mandragola*, an instant success and one of the greatest works of Italian theater.

1519   Publication of *Mandragola*.

1520   Having composed *The Life of Castruccio Castracani*, a captain of Lucca (1281–1328), he receives from Cardinal Giulio de' Medici (later Pope Clement VII) the commission to write a history of Florence. He also composes, again by invitation of Cardinal Giulio de' Medici, a proposal for a new constitution to ensure Florence's peaceful transition from the Medicis' regime to a republican government (*Discourse on Remodeling the Government of Florence after the Death of the Junior Lorenzo*).

1521   The government of Florence sends Machiavelli to Carpi to settle matters concerning jurisdiction over the monasteries of the Minor Friars.

There he befriends Francesco Guicciardini. He publishes *The Art of War*, a dialogue in which he encourages a return to the ancient Roman military orders and to the spirit they exhibited. It is the only one of his political or historical works to appear in print during his lifetime, although all his writings were circulated in manuscript copies.

1525 He composes another comedy, *Clizia*, and a *Discourse* or *Dialogue on Our Language*. His authorship of this work has been disputed. He presents the *Florentine Histories* to Pope Clement VII.

1526 He composes the fable *Belfagor, The Devil Who Married*.

1527 He composes a sermon to a lay religious confraternity (*An Exhortation to Penitence*). Spanish and German soldiers sack Rome. In Florence the Medici are overthrown and the republican government restored. Machiavelli dies on June 21 and is buried in Santa Croce.

1531 Posthumous publication of the *Discourses on Livy*, which required the permission of the papal court.

1532 Posthumous publication of *The Prince*, again with the permission of the papal court.

1559 Machiavelli's works are placed on the papal court's Index of Prohibited Books. They can no longer be sold, read, or quoted, and Machiavelli's name cannot be cited in books.

1640 First English translation of *The Prince*, by Edward Dacres.

Note on the Texts

For Machiavelli's works I have used Niccolò Machiavelli, *Opere*, a cura di Corrado Vivanti, 4 vols, Turin: Einaudi, 1999–2005.

ENGLISH TRANSLATIONS:

Machiavelli and His Friends: Their Personal Correspondence, trans. and ed. James B. Atkinson and David Sices, DeKalb, IL: Northern Illinois University Press, 1996.

The Historical, Political, and Diplomatic Writings of Niccolò Machiavelli, ed. and trans. Christian E. Detmold, vols. 1 and 3. Boston: James R. Osgood Company, 1882; vols. 2 and 4, Boston and New York: Houghton, Mifflin and Company, 1891.

An Exhortation to Penitence, in *Machiavelli: The Chief Works and Others*, trans. Allan Gilbert, vol. 1, Durham and London: Duke University Press, 1989.

The Art of War; Belfagor, the Devil Who Married; Discourse on Remodeling the Government of Florence; Mandragola; Tercets on Ambition; Tercets on Ingratitude or Envy; Tercets on Fortune; The [Golden] Ass; "By the Hermits," in *The Chief Works and Others*, trans. Allan Gilbert, vol. 2, Durham and London: Duke University Press, 1989.

Words to Be Spoken on the Law for Appropriating Money, in *The Chief Works and Others*, trans. Allan Gilbert, vol. 3, Durham and London: Duke University Press, 1989.

All other translations are my own.

The Quotable
Machiavelli

I
Machiavelli on Himself, His Family, and Friends

Figure 1. Portrait of Niccolò Machiavelli. Private Collection/Bridgeman Images.

As for turning my face toward Fortuna, I should like you to get this pleasure from these troubles of mine,* that I have borne them so bravely that I am proud of myself for it and consider myself more of a man than I believed I was.

Machiavelli to Francesco Vettori,† March 18, 1513

Fortune has seen to it that since I do not know how to discuss either the silk or the wool trade, or profits or losses, I have to talk about the state. I must either take a vow of silence or discuss this. Niccolò Machiavelli, former Secretary.

Machiavelli to Francesco Vettori, April 9, 1513

Therefore, if at times I laugh or sing, I do so because I have no other way than this to give vent to my bitter tears.

Machiavelli to Francesco Vettori, April 16, 1513

The story is called *Mandragola*. You will see the reason when it is acted, I foretell. The writer is not very famous, yet if you do not laugh, he will be ready to pay for your wine. A doleful lover, a judge by no means shrewd, a friar living wickedly, a parasite the darling of Malice will be sport for you today.

And if this material—since really it is slight—does not befit a man who likes to seem wise and dignified, make this excuse for him, that he is striving with these trifling thoughts to make his wretched life more pleasant, for otherwise he doesn't know where to turn his face, since he has

---

* Machiavelli had lost his post as Secretary of the Republic in November 1512; in February 1513, he was imprisoned under the charge of conspiracy against the Medici. He got out of prison on around March 13.

† Francesco Vettori (1474–1539), Florentine diplomat.

been cut off from showing other powers with other deeds, there being no pay for his labors.

Prologue to *Mandragola*

Since your departure I have had so much trouble that it is no wonder I have not written to you. In fact, if anything, it is a miracle that I am alive, because my post was taken from me and I was about to lose my life, which God and my innocence have preserved for me. I have had to endure all sorts of other evils, both prison and other kinds. But, by the grace of God, I am well and I manage to live as I can—and so I shall strive to do, until the heavens show themselves to be more kind.

Machiavelli to his nephew Giovanni Vernacci,

June 26, 1513

I know this letter is going to seem disordered to you, not of the consistency you might have expected. Excuse me for being alien in spirit to all these political discussions, removed from any human face and ignorant of matters going on around me, as my being restricted to my farm bears witness. Thus I am obliged to discourse in the dark; I have based everything on the information you have given me. Therefore I implore you to consider me excused.

Machiavelli to Francesco Vettori, April 29, 1513

I do not think the moon is made of green cheese, and in these matters I do not want to be persuaded by any authority lacking reason.

Machiavelli to Francesco Vettori, April 29, 1513

Magnificent ambassador. Your very kind letter has made me forget all my past suffering; and although I was more than certain of the love that you bear me, this letter has been most welcome to me. I thank you as much as I can and pray God that, to your advantage and benefit, He will give me the power to be able to give you satisfaction for it, because I can say that all that is left to me of my life I owe to the Magnificent Giuliano and your Paolo.* And if these new masters of ours see fit not to leave me lying on the ground, I shall be happy and believe that I shall act in such a way that they too will have reason to be proud of me. And if they should not, I shall get on as I did when I came here: I was born in poverty and at an early age learned how to scrimp rather than to thrive. If you stay there, I shall come and spend some time with you when you tell me that it is all right. And, to cut this short, I send you and Paolo my regards; I am not writing to him because I do not know what else to say.

Machiavelli to Francesco Vettori, March 18, 1513

I am living on my farm, and since my latest disasters, I have not spent a total of twenty days in Florence. Until now, I have been catching thrushes with my own hands. I would get up before daybreak, prepare the birdlime, and go out with such a bundle of birdcages on my back that I looked like Geta when he came back from the harbor with

---

*Giuliano de' Medici (1479–1516), son of Lorenzo de' Medici (the Magnificent); Paolo Vettori (1477–1526), Florentine politician, brother of Francesco Vettori.

Amphitryon's books. I would catch at least two, at most six, thrushes. And thus I passed the entire month of November. Eventually this diversion, albeit contemptible and foreign to me, became impossible—to my regret. I shall tell you about my life. I get up in the morning with the sun and go into one of my woods that I am having cut down; there I spend a couple of hours inspecting the work of the previous day and talking with the woodsmen, who always have some dispute on their hands, either among themselves or with their neighbors. I could tell you a thousand good stories about these woods and my experiences, and about Frosino da Panzano and other men who wanted some of this firewood. In particular, Frosino sent for some loads of wood without saying a word to me; when it came time to settle, he wanted to withhold ten lire that he said he had won off me four years ago when he beat me at *cricca* at Antonio Guicciardini's house. I started to raise hell; I was going to call the wagoner who had come for the wood a thief, but Giovanni Machiavelli *eventually* stepped in and got us to agree. Once the north wind started blowing, Battista Guicciardini, Filippo Ginori, Tommaso del Bene, and some other citizens all ordered a load from me. I promised some to each one; I sent Tommaso a load, which turned into half a load in Florence because he, his wife, his children, and the servants were all there to stack it—they looked like Gaburra on Thursdays when he and his crew flay an ox. Consequently, once I realized who was profiting, I told the others that I had no more wood; all of them were angry about it, especially Battista, who includes this among the other calamities of Prato. . . . Then I make my way along the road toward the inn, I chat with passersby, I ask news of their regions, I learn about various matters, I observe mankind: the variety of its tastes, the diversity of its fancies. By then it is time to eat; with my household I eat what food this poor farm and my minuscule patrimony yield. When I have finished eating, I return to the inn, where I find the company usually of the innkeeper, a butcher, a miller, and a couple of kilnworkers. I idle away the time with them for the rest of the day playing *cricca* and backgammon: these games lead to thousands of squabbles and endless insults and vituperations. More often than not we are wrangling over a penny; but nonetheless people can hear us yelling even in San Casciano. Thus, having been cooped up among these vermin, I get the mold out of my brain and let out the malice of my fate, content to be ridden over roughshod in this fashion, if only to discover whether or not my fate is ashamed of treating me so!

Machiavelli to Francesco Vettori, December 10, 1513

When evening comes, I return home and enter my study; on the threshold I take off my workday clothes, covered with mud and dirt, and put on the garments of court and palace. Fitted out appropriately, I step inside the venerable courts of the ancients, where, solicitously received by them, I nourish myself on that food that *alone* is mine and for which I was born; where I am unashamed to converse with them and to question them about the motives for their actions, and they, out of their human kindness, answer me. And, for four hours at a time, I feel no boredom, I forget my troubles, I do not dread poverty, and I am not terrified by death. I lose myself in them completely.

Machiavelli to Francesco Vettori, December, 10, 1513

Besides, there is my desire that these Medici princes should begin to engage my services, even if they should start out by having me roll a stone [like Sisyphus]. For then, if I could not win them over, I should have only myself to blame. And through this study of mine, were it to be read, it would be evident that during the fifteen years I have been studying the art of the state I have neither slept nor squandered my time, and anyone ought to be happy at the chance to make use of someone who has had so much experience at the expense of others. There should be no doubt about my word; for, since I have always kept it, I would not start learning how to break it now. Whoever has been honest and faithful for forty-three years, as I have, is unable to change his nature; my poverty is a witness to my loyalty and honesty.

Machiavelli to Francesco Vettori, December 10, 1513

May your Magnificence [Lorenzo de' Medici, Duke of Urbino]* then accept this little gift in the same spirit in which I send it; and if you will read and consider it well, you will recognize in it my desire that you may attain that

---

* Lorenzo de' Medici, Duke of Urbino (1492–1519), son of Piero de' Medici.

greatness which fortune and your great qualities promise. And if your Magnificence will turn your eyes from the summit of your greatness toward those low places, you will know how undeservedly I have to bear the great and continued malice of fortune.

Dedicatory letter to *The Prince*

In this city of ours—a magnet for all the world's pitchmen—there is a friar of Saint Francis, who is half hermit, and who to increase his standing as a preacher professes to be a prophet; and yesterday morning in Santa Croce, where he preaches, he said many things great and wonderful: That before much time elapses, so that whoever is ninety years of age will live to see it, there will be an unjust pope created against a just pope, and the unjust pope will have false prophets with him, he will create cardinals, and he will divide the Church. The king of France is to be crushed and someone from the House of Aragon will be master of Italy. Our city will go up in flames and be sacked, the churches be abandoned and crumble, the priests dispersed, and we will have to do without divine services for three years. There will be pestilence and widespread famine; in the city not ten men will remain; on farms, not two. He said that for eighteen years there has been a devil in a human body—and he has said mass. That well over two million devils were unleashed in order that they might oversee all of this; they would enter into many dying bodies and not allow those bodies to putrefy, so that false prophets and clerics might resuscitate the dead and be believed. These activities so demoralized me yesterday that

although I was supposed to go this morning to see La Riccia, I did not go; I am not at all sure whether, had I been supposed to go see Riccio, I would have been concerned.*
I myself did not hear the sermon, for I do not observe such practices, but I have heard it told about in this manner throughout all of Florence.

Machiavelli to Francesco Vettori, December 19, 1513

Fortune truly has brought me to where I may be justly able to requite you, for while in the country I have met a creature so gracious, so refined, so noble—both in nature and in circumstance—that never could either my praise or my love for her be as much as she deserves. I ought to tell you, as you did me, how this love began, how Love ensnared me in his nets, where he spread them, and what they were like. You would realize then that, spread among the flowers, these were nets of gold woven by Venus, so soft and gentle that even though an insensitive heart could have severed them, nevertheless I declined to do so. For a while I reveled within them, until their tender threads hardened and locked into knots that could not be loosed. And do not think Love employed ordinary means to capture me, because aware that they would be inadequate, he resorted to extraordinary ones about which I was ignorant and against which I declined to protect myself. Suffice it to say that although I am approaching my fiftieth year, neither does the heat of the sun distress me,

---

*Machiavelli is playing with words here. La Riccia was a florentine courtesan and a lover of Machiavelli; il Riccio was a young homosexual offering his services to adult males.

nor do rough roads wear me out, nor do the dark hours of the night terrify me. Everything seems easy to me: I fall in with her every whim, even those that seem different from and contrary to what my own will ought to be. And even though I may now seem to have entered into great travail, I nevertheless feel so great a sweetness in it, both because of the delight that rare and gentle countenance brings me and because I have laid aside all memory of my sorrows, that not for anything in the world would I desire my freedom—even if I could have it. I have renounced, then, thoughts about matters great and grave. No longer do I delight in reading about the deeds of the ancients or in discussing those of the moderns: everything has been transformed into tender thoughts, for which I thank Venus and all of Cyprus.

Machiavelli to Francesco Vettori, August 3, 1514

So I am going to stay just as I am amid my vermin, unable to find any man who recalls my service or believes I might be good for anything. But I cannot possibly go on like this for long, because I am rotting away, and I can see that if God does not show a more favorable face to me, one day I shall be forced to leave home and to place myself as a tutor or secretary to a governor, if I cannot do otherwise, or to plant myself in some forsaken spot to teach reading to children and leave my family here to count me dead. They would do much better without me. I am causing them expense, for I am used to spending and cannot do without spending. I am writing you this not because I want you to go to any trouble for me or to worry about me, but simply to get it off my chest, and I will not write any more about this matter. It is as odious to me as a subject can be.

Machiavelli to Francesco Vettori, June 10, 1514

Dearest Giovanni,* I have written to you twice during the last four months, and I am sorry that you have not received my letters, because it occurs to me that you will think I do not write because I have forgotten you. That is not true at all: Fortune has left me nothing but my family and my friends, and I make capital out of them—and particularly out of those who are closest to me, as are you.

Machiavelli to Giovanni Vernacci, November 19, 1515

As for me, I have become useless to myself, to my family, and to my friends, because my doleful fate has willed it to be so. The best I can say is that all I have left is my own good health and that of all my family. I bide my time so that I may be ready to seize good Fortune should she come; should she not come, I am ready to be patient.

Machiavelli to Giovanni Vernacci, February 15, 1516

But since the adversities that I have suffered, and still am suffering, have reduced me to living on my farm, I sometimes go for a month at a time without thinking about myself—so it is not surprising if I neglect to answer you.

Machiavelli to Giovanni Vernacci, June 8, 1517

Lately I have been reading Ariosto's *Orlando Furioso*; the entire poem is really fine, and many passages are marvelous. If he is there with you, give him my regards and tell

---

* Machiavelli's nephew.

him that my only complaint is that in his mention of so many poets he has left me out like some prick and that he has done to me in his *Orlando* what I shall not do to him in my *Ass*.

Machiavelli to Lodovico Alamanni, December 17, 1517[*]

Nevertheless, so that we can appear to be alive, Zanobi Buondelmonti, Amerigo Morelli, Battista della Palla, and I sometimes get together and discuss that excursion to Flanders with so much energy that we dream we are already on the road—so that it seems we have already used up half of the pleasures we might have been able to have. In order that we may plan for it more systematically, we shall make a small trial run the last Thursday of Carnival by going as far as Venice; we cannot make up our minds, however, whether we should set off early and go down there [to Rome] for you or wait for you to come here so we can go straight to Venice.

Machiavelli to Lodovico Alamanni, December 17, 1517

While in many matters I may have made mistakes, at least I have not been mistaken in choosing you [Zanobi Buondelmonti and Cosimo Rucellai] before all others as the persons to whom I dedicate these *Discourses*; both because I seem to myself, in doing so, to have shown a little gratitude for kindness received, and at the same time to have departed from the hackneyed custom which leads many authors to inscribe their works to some prince, and

[*] Prominent Florentine aristocrat.

blinded by hopes of favor or reward, to praise him as possessed of every virtue; whereas with more reason they might reproach him as contaminated with every shameful vice. To avoid which error I have chosen, not those who are, but those who from their infinite merits deserve to be princes; not such persons as have it in their power to load me with honors, wealth, and preferment, but such as, though they lack the power, have all the will to do so. For men, if they would judge justly, should esteem those who are, and not those whose means enable them to be generous; and in like manner those who know how to govern kingdoms, rather than those who possess the government without such knowledge.

Preface to the *Discourses on Livy*

I was completely absorbed in imagining the style of preacher I should wish for Florence: he should be just what would please me, because I am going to be as pigheaded about this idea as I am about my other ideas. And because never did I disappoint that republic whenever I was able to help her out—if not with deeds, then with words; if not with words, then with signs—I have no intention of disappointing her now. In truth, I know that I am at variance with the ideas of her citizens, as I am in many other matters. They would like a preacher who would teach them the way to Paradise, and I should like to find one who would teach them the way to go to the Devil. Furthermore, they would like their man to be prudent, honest, and genuine, and I should like to find one who would be madder than Ponzo, wilier than Fra Girolamo, and more hypocritical than Frate Alberto, because I think it would be a fine thing—something worthy of the goodness of these times—should everything we have experienced in many friars be experienced in one of them. For I believe that the following would be the true way to go to Paradise: learn the way to Hell in order to steer clear of it. Moreover, since I am aware how much belief there is in an evil man who hides under the cloak of religion, I can readily conjure up how much belief there would be in a good man who walks in truth, and not in pretense, tramping through the muddy footprints of Saint Francis.

Machiavelli to Francesco Guicciardini, May 17, 1521

As for the lies of these citizens of Carpi, I can beat all of them at that, because I have long been a doctor of this art—and good enough . . . so, for some time now I have never said what I believe and never believed what I said; and if indeed I do sometimes tell the truth, I hide it behind so many lies that it is hard to find.

Machiavelli to Francesco Guicciardini, May 17, 1521

If my virtue / Were as immense as my desire, / Pity now still asleep, awake would be. / But since desire and strength / Do not go well together, / Suffer I must the length / Of all my woes, my lord. / And you I do not blame / I blame myself for this: / Great beauty wants / I see and I confess / a much greener age.

"Alla Barbera" (sonnet)

To My Dear Son Guido di Niccolò Machiavelli.
In Florence.

My dearest son Guido. I received a letter from you that has given me the greatest pleasure, especially since you write that you have quite recovered; I could not have had better news. If God grants you and me life, I believe that I may make you a man of good standing, if you are willing to do your share. For, besides the influential friendships I have now, I have made a new one with Cardinal Cibo so close that I am astonished at it myself—that will prove to be opportune for you. But you must study and, since you no longer have illness as an excuse, take pains to learn letters and music, for you are aware how much distinction is given me for what little ability I possess. Thus, my son, if you want to please me and to bring profit and honor to yourself, study, do well, and learn, because everyone will help you if you help yourself.

Since the young mule has gone mad, it must be treated just the reverse of the way crazy people are, for they are tied up, and I want you to let it loose. Give it to Vangelo and tell him to take it to Montepugliano and then take off its bridle and halter and let it go wherever it likes to regain its own way of life and work off its craziness. The village is big and the beast is small; it can do no one any harm. Thus, we can observe what it wants to do without causing ourselves any problems, and whenever it comes to its senses, you will be on the spot to catch it again. As for the rest of the horses, do whatever Lodovico has told you to do. Thank God he has recovered and that he has sold

them. Since he has sent some money, I know he has profited, but I am surprised and saddened that he has not written. Greet Madonna Marietta* for me, and tell her I have
been expecting—and still do—to leave here any day; I
have never longed so much to return to Florence as I do
now, but there is nothing else I can do. Simply tell her that,
whatever she hears, she should be of good cheer, since I
shall be there before any danger comes. Kiss Baccina,
Piero, and Totto, if he is there; I would dearly appreciate
hearing whether his eyes are any better. Live in happiness
and spend as little as you can. And remind Bernardo,
whom I have written to twice in the last two weeks and
received no reply, that he had better behave himself.
Christ watch over you all.

Machiavelli to his son Guido, April 2, 1527

And I repine at Nature, who either should have made me
such that I could not see this or should have given me the
possibility for putting it into effect. Since I am an old man,
I do not imagine today that I can have opportunity for it.
Therefore I have been liberal of it with you who, being
young and gifted, can at the right time, if the things I have
said please you, aid and advise your princes to their
advantage.

The Art of War VII

I love Messer Francesco Guicciardini, I love my fatherland
more than my own soul.

Machiavelli to Francesco Vettori, April 16, 1527

---

* Marietta Corsini, Machiavelli's wife.

II
Machiavelli Described by His Relatives, Friends, and Lovers

Figure 2. Portrait of Niccolò Machiavelli. Private Collection/Bridgeman Images.

Machiavelli is poor and good, whatever others might think, this is the plain truth, I can testify in faith. He has been imposed too heavy taxes, has very small patrimony and no money, and many children.

From a letter of Francesco Vettori, in Roberto Ridolfi,
The Life of Niccolò Machiavelli

I read your entire letter to Signor Marcello,[*] two other chancellors, and Biagio, who are all seized by a marvelous desire to see you. For your amusing, witty, and pleasant conversation, while it echoes about our ears, relieves, cheers, and refreshes us, who are spent and flagging from constant work.

Agostino Vespucci[†] to Machiavelli,
October 20–29, 1500

So you see where that spirit of yours, so eager for riding, wandering, and roaming about, has gotten us. Blame yourself and not others if anything adverse happens. I wish that no one except you were standing by me and was my superior in the Chancery, although you attempt and dare all the things which that most poisonous viper attacks me, pursues me, and cuts me to bits for, about which that terrible man, worthless and contentious, gives me orders. But that is all water under the bridge. Biagio likewise, besides hating you on account of such things, blabbers on, reviles you with insults, damning and cursing

[*] Marcello di Virgilio Andriani, Secretary of the First Chancery of the Republic of Florence.

[†] Machiavelli's assistant in the Chancery.

you, says and cares for nothing, reckoning all things worthless.

> Agostino Vespucci to Machiavelli, October 14, 1502

I am managing this office as well as I can, at your command, and so I go wallowing about and I am waiting for you, by God, very anxiously, and I just can't wait. Madonna Marietta is cursing God, and she feels she has thrown away both her body and her possessions. For your own sake, arrange for her to have her dowry like other women, otherwise we won't hear the end of it.

> Biagio Buonaccorsi* to Machiavelli,
> December 21, 1502

Suffice it to say that I have had good luck with your affairs, although I do not know how I have done with my own. But I am afraid that your indemnity is going to the dogs, because here the cry among these chancellors is that you are a cold fish and you never acted pleasantly toward them. I, who want to cleanse you of any infamy that might befall you, will carry it out with them at your expense and right in your face. So go and retch if you are not satisfied, that is the way it has to be.

> Biagio Buonaccorsi to Machiavelli, December 21, 1502

This absence of yours from among the dotards here has clearly shown the people that you are the root of all evil. It is evident that you inherited your customs and manners completely from Tommaso del Bene; because now that

---

* Machiavelli's assistant in the Chancery.

you are not here, nothing is heard either of gambling or of taverns or of any other little thing. And thus we can tell whence all ill originated. . . . I would not hold back; but most of the time either the place or the writings or a third person is lacking, and someone to bring the band together is always lacking because you are not here.

Filippo de' Nerli to Machiavelli, September 6, 1525

My dearest Niccolò, you make fun of me, but you are not right to, for I would be flourishing more if you were here. You know very well how happy I am when you are not down there; and all the more so now, as I have been told that there is so much disease there. Just think how I must feel, for I find no rest either day or night. That is the happiness I get from the baby. So I pray you to send me letters a little more often than you do, for I have had only three of them. Do not be surprised if I have not written you, because I have not been able to. I have had a fever up to now; I am not angry. For now the baby is well, he favors you: he is white as snow, but his head looks like black velvet, and he is hairy like you. And since he looks like you, he seems beautiful to me. He is so lively, as if he had been in the world for a year already; he opened his eyes when he was scarcely born and filled the whole house with noise. But our daughter is not feeling well. Remember to come back home. Nothing else. God be with you, and keep you. I am sending you a doublet and two shirts and two kerchiefs and a towel, which I am sewing for you.

Marietta Corsini to Machiavelli,

November 24, 1503

When I am in Florence, I divide my time between Donato del Corno's shop and La Riccia; I think I am getting on both their nerves because he calls me "Shop Pest" and she calls me "House Pest." Yet both of them value me as an adviser, and so far this reputation has stood me in such good stead that Donato has let me warm myself by his fire and she sometimes lets me kiss her on the sly. I believe this good will not last long, since I have given both of them some tidbits of advice that have never panned out; just today La Riccia said to me in a certain conversation she feigned to be having with her maid, "Wise men, oh these wise men, I don't know what they have upstairs; it seems to me they get everything wrong."

Machiavelli to Francesco Vettori, February 4, 1514

But you tell me something that astonishes me: you have found so much faith and so much compassion in La Riccia[*] that, I swear to you, I was partial to her for your sake, but now I have become her slave, because most of the time women are wont to love Fortune and not men, and when Fortune changes, to change as well. I am not surprised about Donato, because he is a man of faith, and in addition to this he continually experiences the same as you.

Francesco Vettori to Machiavelli, January 16, 1515

Madonna Marietta wrote to me via her brother to ask when you will be back; she says she does not want to write, and she is making a big fuss, and she is hurt because you

---

[*] A Florentine courtesan with whom Machiavelli had a long relationship.

promised her you would stay 8 days and no more. So come back, in the name of the devil, so the womb doesn't suffer.

> Biagio Buonaccorsi to Machiavelli,
> October 15–18, 1502

Madonna Marietta is angry and does not want to write to you. I cannot do anything else.

> Biagio Buonaccorsi to Machiavelli,
> November 26, 1502

Niccolò, this is a time when if ever one was wise it should be now. I do not believe your ideas will ever be accessible to fools, and there are not enough wise men to go around: you understand me, even if I am not putting it very well. Every day I discover you to be a greater prophet than the Hebrews or any other nation ever had.

> Filippo Casavecchia to Machiavelli,
> June 17, 1509

I know you have such intelligence that although two years have gone by since you left the shop, I do not think you have forgotten the craft.

> Francesco Vettori to Machiavelli, December 3, 1514

My very dear Machiavelli. It was certainly good judgment on the part of our reverend consuls of the Wool Guild to have entrusted you with the duty of selecting a preacher, not otherwise than if the task had been given to Pacchierotto, while he was alive, or to Ser Sano* to find a beauti-

---

* Pacchierotto and Ser Sano were two Florentine homosexuals.

ful and graceful wife for a friend. I believe you will serve them according to the expectations they have of you and as is required by your honor, which would be stained if at this age you started to think about your soul, because, since you have always lived in a contrary belief, it would be attributed rather to senility than to goodness. I remind you to take care of this matter as swiftly as possible, because in staying there long you run two risks: one, that those holy friars might pass some of their hypocrisy on to you; the other, that the air of Carpi might turn you into a liar, because that has been its influence, not only in the present age but also for centuries gone by. If by ill chance you were to be lodged in the house of some Carpian, your case would be beyond remedy.

Francesco Guicciardini to Machiavelli, May 17, 1521

III
Man and Cosmos

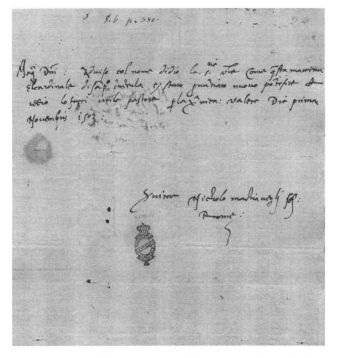

Figure 3. Machiavelli Papers, 1 C. 24r. Biblioteca Nazionale Centrale di Firenze.

Devils and Hell

He who sees the devil in very truth, sees him with smaller horns and not so black.

"By the Hermits"

But then on the other hand, the worst that can happen to you is to die and go off to Hell! How many others have died! And how many excellent men have gone to Hell! Why should you be ashamed to go there, too?

Mandragola, Act 4, Scene 1

Calling them therefore to council, Pluto spoke to this effect: My dear friends, even though by Heaven's decrees and by decision of Fate, entirely beyond repeal, I possess this kingdom, and for it I cannot be under obligation to any judgment, either heavenly or earthly, yet, since it is the highest prudence for those who are most powerful to be most subject to the laws and most to esteem the judgment of others, I have determined in an affair that might result in some shame to our empire to get your advice on how I ought to conduct myself. Because, since the souls of all the men who come to our kingdom say that their wives caused it, and since this seems to us impossible, we fear that if we pronounce judgment in accord with this tale, we shall be slandered as too credulous, and if we do not pronounce it, as not severe enough and hardly lovers of justice. And because the first sin is that of light-minded men and the second of unjust ones, and since we wish to escape the reproaches that might result from either one, but have not found a way to do it, we have summoned you that you might aid us with your counsel and be the reason why this kingdom, as in the past it has been without infamy, may continue in the same way in the future.

> Speech delivered by Pluto, the king of Hell, before his
> counselors, in *Belfagor, the Devil Who Married*

BY THE DEVILS DRIVEN OUT FROM HEAVEN

Once we were—but now no longer are—blessed spirits; because of our pride we all were driven from Heaven; and in this city of yours we have seized the rule, because here we find confusion and sorrow greater than in Hell.

And hunger and war and blood and ice and fire little by little we have brought into the world upon each mortal; and in this carnival we come to be with you, because of each ill we have been and will be decreed the beginning.

This is Pluto and that is Proserpina placing herself by his side—a woman beautiful above all earthly women. Love conquers all things; hence it conquered him, who never rests in his attempt to make all others do what he has done himself.

All pleasures and displeasures of Love by us are begotten, both weeping and laughter and joy and sorrow. All those who are in love should follow our will, and they will be pleased because in doing every evil we take delight.

> *Machiavelli: The Chief Works and Others,*
> trans. Allan Gilbert, vol. 2, p. 878.

Fortune

By many this goddess is called omnipotent, because who-ever / comes into this life either late or early feels her power. / She often keeps the good beneath her feet; the wicked she raises / up; and if ever she promises you any-thing, never does she keep / her promise.

Tercets on Fortune, lines 25–30

And truly, anyone wise enough to adapt to and under-stand the times and the pattern of events would always have good fortune or would always keep himself from bad fortune; and it would come to be true that the wise man could control the stars and the Fates. But such wise men do not exist: in the first place, men are shortsighted; in the second, they are unable to master their own natures; thus it follows that Fortune is fickle, controlling men and keep-ing them under her yoke.

Machiavelli to Giovan Battista Soderini, September 13–21, 1506[*]

Men can second fortune but not oppose it, they can weave its warp but not break it. They should indeed never give up for, since they do not know its end and it proceeds by oblique and unknown ways, they have always to hope and, since they hope, not to give up in whatever fortune and in whatever travail they may find themselves.

Discourses on Livy, II. 27

[*] Giovan Battista Soderini, nephew of Piero Soderini, Gonfalonier of the Republic of Florence.

I am well aware that many have held and still hold the opinion that the affairs of this world are so controlled by Fortune and by the Divine Power that human wisdom and foresight cannot modify them; that, in fact, there is no remedy against the decrees of fate, and that therefore it is not worthwhile to make any effort, but to yield unconditionally to the power of Fortune. This opinion has been generally accepted in our times, because of the great changes that have taken place, and are still being witnessed every day, and are beyond all human conjecture. In reflecting upon this, I am myself at times inclined to that belief; nevertheless, as our free will is not entirely destroyed, I judge that it may be assumed as true that Fortune to the extent of one half is the arbiter of our actions, but that she permits us to direct the other half, or perhaps a little less, ourselves. I compare this to a swollen river, which in its fury overflows the plains, tears up the trees and buildings, and sweeps the earth from one place and deposits it in another. Every one flies before the flood and yields to its fury, unable to resist it; and notwithstanding this state of things men do not when the river is in its ordinary condition provide against its overflow by dikes and walls, so that when it rises it may flow either in the channel thus provided for it, or that at any rate its violence may not be entirely unchecked, nor its effects prove so injurious. It is the same with Fortune, who displays her power where there is no organized valor to resist her, and where she knows that there are no dikes or walls to control her.

The Prince, XXV

I conclude, then, inasmuch as Fortune is changeable, that men who persist obstinately in their own ways will be successful only so long as those ways coincide with Fortune's ways; for whenever these two differ, they fail. But, on the whole, I judge impetuosity to be better than caution; for Fortune is a woman, and if you wish to master her, you must strike and beat her, and you will see that she allows herself to be more easily vanquished by the rash and the violent than by those who proceed more slowly and coldly. And therefore, as a woman, she ever favors youth more than age, for youth is less cautious and more energetic, and commands Fortune with greater audacity.

The Prince, XXV

God's and the Heavens' Influence on Human Affairs

Not yet has Heaven altered its opinion, nor will alter it, while / the Fates keep toward you their hard purpose. / And those feelings which you have found, so hostile and so / adverse, not yet, not yet are purged; / but when their roots are dry, and the Heavens show themselves / gracious, times happier than ever before will return; / and so pleasant and delightful will they be that you will have joy / from the memory of both past and future affliction.

The Golden Ass, lines 100–110

God, who in similar extremities has always taken the city of Florence under his special protection, caused an unexpected event, which gave the pope and the kings as well as the Venetians more important things to think of than the affairs of Florence.

History of Florence, VIII. 9

Among all these changes not the least one was that of religion; for combating the habit of the ancient faith with the miracles of the new gave rise to the gravest tumults and discords among men, and even if the Christian religion had been a united one, its introduction would nevertheless have been followed by minor discords; but the Greek Church, opposing those of Rome and Ravenna together, and the heretical sects being in conflict with the Catholics, caused infinite misery in the world: of which Africa furnishes us proof, for she had to endure far more troubles from the sect of the Arians, to which the Vandals adhered, than she suffered from their cruelty and rapacity. Men thus living in the midst of so many persecutions bore the terror of their souls written in their eyes; for, besides the infinite evils which they had to endure, they were deprived in great measure of the ability to seek a refuge in the help of God, which is the hope of the wretched; for the greater portion of them, being uncertain as to what God they should fly to for refuge, died miserably, bereft of all help and all hope.

History of Florence, I. 5

Then was seen a thing which in our day had never yet been witnessed; for it being Lent, when the Church commands us to fast and eat no flesh, this court, regardless of the ordinances of the Church and of God, feasted daily upon meat. Many spectacles were gotten up in honor of the Duke, among them one in the church of San Spirito, where was represented the descent of the Holy Spirit upon the Apostles; and, in consequence of the many lights on that occasion, the entire church was burnt, which was regarded by many as a manifestation of the wrath of the Almighty in his indignation against us for our misconduct. And if the Duke of Milan found in Florence abundance of courtly pleasures and extravagant customs, he left there many more than he found; so that the good citizens deemed it necessary to restrain and put bounds to them by sumptuary laws against extravagance in dress, feastings, and funerals.

On the visit of the Duke of Milan in 1471;
History of Florence, VII. 28

No greater gift, then, does Heaven give to a man, nor can Heaven show him a more glorious road than this. So of all the many blessings God has given to your House and to Your Holiness in person, this is the greatest: that of giving you power and material for making yourself immortal, and for surpassing by far in this way your father's and your grandfather's glory. Heaven cannot give a man a greater gift than this or point him a more glorious way.

Discourse on Remodeling the Government of Florence

God's Mercy

Since this evening, honored fathers and superior brothers, I am to speak to Your Charities, in order to obey my superiors, and am to say something on penitence, it has seemed to me good to begin my exhortation with words of that teacher of the Holy Spirit, David the Prophet, so that those who have sinned with him may, according to his words, hope they can receive mercy from God all powerful and all merciful. And that they can obtain it, since David obtained it, they should not fear, because neither greater transgression nor greater penitence for a man than in his instance can be conceived, nor in God can greater generosity to pardon be found.

"Exhortation to Penitence"

Good and Evil

Virtue makes countries tranquil, / and from Tranquility, Laziness next emerges, / and Laziness burns the towns and villages. / Then, after a country has for a time been subject to lawlessness, / Ability often returns to live there once again. / Such a course she who governs us permits and requires, so that / nothing beneath the sun ever will or can be firm. / And it is and always has been and always will be, that evil / follows after good, good after evil.

The Golden Ass, lines 94–104 (translation modified)

Prophecies

Whence it happens I know not, but it is seen from examples both ancient and recent, that no grave calamity has ever befallen any city or country which has not been foretold by vision, by augury, by portent, or by some other Heaven-sent sign. . . . The causes of such manifestations ought, I think, to be inquired into and explained by someone who has a knowledge, which I have not, of causes natural and supernatural. It may, however, be, as certain wise men say, that the air is filled with intelligent beings, to whom it is given to forecast future events; who, taking pity upon men, warn them beforehand by these signs to prepare for what awaits them. Be this as it may, certain it is that such warnings are given, and that always after them new and strange disasters befall nations.

Discourses on Livy, I. 56

Purgatory

WOMAN: Take this florin, then, and you're to say the requiem mass every Monday for two months, for the soul of my late husband. Even though he was a terrible man, still, flesh is flesh; I can't help feeling that whenever I remember him. But do you think he is really in Purgatory?

TIMOTEO: Absolutely!

Mandragola, Act 3, Scene 3

Return to Beginnings

There is nothing more true than that all the things of this world have a limit to their existence; but those only run the entire course ordained for them by Heaven that do not allow their body to become disorganized, but keep it unchanged in the manner ordained, or if they change it, so do it that it shall be for their advantage, and not to their injury. And as I speak here of mixed bodies, such as republics or religious sects, I say that those changes are beneficial that bring them back to their original principles.

Discourses on Livy, III. 1

For in nature as in simple bodies, when there is an accumulation of superfluous matter, a spontaneous purgation takes place, which preserves the health of that body. And so it is with that compound body, the human race; when countries become overpopulated and there is no longer any room for all the inhabitants to live, nor any other places for them to go to, these being likewise all fully occupied,—and when human cunning and wickedness have gone as far as they can go,—then of necessity the world must relieve itself of this excess of population by one of those three causes; so that mankind, having been chastised and reduced in numbers, may become better and live with more convenience.

Discourses on Livy, II. 5

The Universe, Its Hidden Power

Hardly had God created stars and light, / Heaven and elements and man / (the one He made lord over all such beauties bright); / And hardly had He thrown out of His home / Proud Angels, out of Eden impious Adam, / Who with his mate had dared to taste the apple; / Then ah, it was at the time Abel and Cain / Toiled with their father at their daily work, / Happy indeed in their poor home place, / A hidden power which up above is nurtured, / Among the stars that circle in the sky, / And is not friendly to the human kind, / But gives us war and strips us of sweet peace, / To take all happiness and calm away, / Unleashed two furies, sent them down to dwell with us.

Tercets on Ambition, lines 16–29

The World and Its Eternity

To those philosophers who maintain that the world has existed from eternity, we might reply, that, if it were really of such antiquity, there would reasonably be some record beyond five thousand years, were it not that we see how the records of time are destroyed by various causes, some being the acts of men and some of Heaven. Those that are the acts of men are the changes of religion and of language; for when a new sect springs up, that is to say a new religion, its first effort is (by way of asserting itself and gaining influence) to destroy the old or existing one; and when it happens that the founders of the new religion speak a different language, then the destruction of the old religion is easily effected. . . . As to causes produced by Heaven, they are such as destroy the human race, and reduce the inhabitants of some parts of the world to a very few in number; such as pestilence, famine, or inundations. Of this the latter are the most important, partly because they are most universal, and partly because the few that escape are chiefly ignorant mountaineers, who, having no knowledge of antiquity themselves, cannot transmit any to posterity. And should there be among those who escape any that have such knowledge, they conceal or pervert it in their own fashion, for the purpose of gaining influence and reputation; so that there remains to their successors only just so much as they were disposed to write, and no more. And that such inundations, pestilences, and famines occur cannot be doubted, both because all history is full of accounts of them, and because we see the effects of them in the oblivion of things, and also because it seems reasonable that they should occur.

Discourses on Livy, II. 5

IV
The Human Condition

Figure 4. Machiavelli's summer home. Photo by Vignaccia76.

Antiquity and the Ancients

When we consider the near universal respect for antiquity, and how often—to name but one example—a great price is paid for some fragments of an antique statue, which we are anxious to own as an ornament for our home, or so that artists may strive to imitate them in their own works; and then, too, when we see the wonderful examples that the histories of ancient kingdoms and republics present to us, the prodigies of virtue and of wisdom displayed by their kings, commanders, citizens, and legislators who have sacrificed themselves for their country—when, as I say, we see all these, more admired than imitated (for too often not the least trace of such ancient virtue remains), we cannot but be at the same time as much surprised as afflicted. The more so as in the differences that arise between citizens, or in the maladies to which they are subjected, we see these same people take recourse to the judgments and the remedies prescribed by the ancients. Our civil laws are in fact nothing but decisions given by their jurists, and which, reduced to a system, direct our modern jurists in their decisions. And what is the science of medicine but the experience of ancient physicians, which their successors have taken for their guide? And yet when it comes to founding a republic, maintaining a state, governing a kingdom, organizing an army, conducting a war, dispensing justice, and expanding an empire, you will find neither prince, nor republic, nor captain, nor citizen who has recourse to the examples of antiquity!

Discourses on Livy, Preface to Book I

Avarice

In concluding, then, this discourse, I say that, as the vice of ingratitude is usually the consequence of either avarice or fear, it will be seen that the peoples never fall into this error from avarice, and that fear also makes them less liable to it than princes, inasmuch as they have less reason for fear, as we shall show further on.

Discourses on Livy, I. 29

Thence comes that avarice which we see so common among the citizens, and that craving, not for true glory, but for those false honors from which flow hatreds, enmities, dissensions, and factions, which, in turn, produce murders, exiles, and the afflictions of the good and the elevation of the wicked. For the good, confiding in their innocence, do not, like the wicked, seek extraordinary means for their defense, and to obtain honors; and thus are they ruined, undefended, and unhonored.

History of Florence, III. 5

The children succeeded their fathers, and, ignorant of the changes of fortune, having never experienced its reverses, and indisposed to remain content with this civil equality, they in turn gave themselves up to avarice, ambition, libertinage, and violence and soon caused the aristocratic government to degenerate into an oligarchic tyranny, regardless of all civil rights.

Discourses on Livy, I. 2

For when a people or a prince has sent a general on some important expedition where by his success he acquires great glory, the prince or people is in turn bound to reward him. But if instead of such reward they dishonor and wrong him, influenced thereto by avarice, then they are guilty of an inexcusable wrong, which will involve them in eternal infamy.

Discourses on Livy, I. 29

I say that, as the vice of ingratitude is usually the consequence of either avarice or fear, it will be seen that the peoples never fall into this error from avarice, and that fear also makes them less liable to it than princes, inasmuch as they have less reason for fear.

Discourses on Livy, I. 29

I set out by saying that the vice of ingratitude springs either from avarice or fear.

Discourses on Livy, I. 29

For a people suffers more from the avarice of its magistrates than from the rapacity of an enemy, for of the latter you may sooner or later hope for an end, but of the former never.

History of Florence, V. 8

Beasts

Chance has given birth to these different kinds of governments among men; for at the beginning of the world the inhabitants were few in number, and lived for a time dispersed, like beasts.

Discourses on Livy, I. 2

You must know, therefore, that there are two ways of carrying on a contest; the one by law, and the other by force. The first is practiced by men, and the other by animals; and as the first is often insufficient, it becomes necessary to resort to the second. A prince then should know how to employ the nature of man, and that of the beasts as well. This was figuratively taught by ancient writers, who relate how Achilles and many other princes were given to Chiron the centaur to be nurtured, and how they were trained under his tutorship; which fable means nothing else than that their preceptor combined the qualities of the man and the beast; and that a prince, to succeed, will have to employ both the one and the other nature, as the one without the other cannot produce lasting results. It being necessary then for a prince to know well how to employ the nature of the beasts, he should be able to assume both that of the fox and that of the lion; for whilst the latter cannot escape the traps laid for him, the former cannot defend himself against the wolves. A prince should be a fox, to know the traps and snares; and a lion, to be able to frighten the wolves; for those who simply hold to the nature of the lion do not understand the matter.

The Prince, XVIII

We do not want to behave like beasts. Doesn't she have to hear the nuptial mass?

Clizia, Act 3, Scene 7

Bloodshed

The French are more eager for money than for blood, and
are liberal only in fine speeches.

Of the Nature of the French

One man cannot live long enough to have time to bring
back to good habits a people which for any length of time
has indulged in evil ones. Or if one of extreme long life, or
two contiguous virtuous successors, do not restore the
state, it will quickly lapse into ruin, no matter how many
dangers and how much bloodshed have been incurred in
the effort to restore it.

Discourses on Livy, I. 17

For the power of the adversaries of the law had increased
twofold in the meantime, and its revival excited such feelings of hatred between the people and the Senate, that it
led to violence and bloodshed beyond the boundaries of
civil life.

Discourses on Livy, I. 37

Compassion

An act of humanity and benevolence will at all times have
more influence over the minds of men than violence and
ferocity.

Discourses on Livy, III. 20

Our city above all, despite the old examples to the contrary, can maintain itself not only united, but can reform
its manners and institutions, provided you, Signori, are

resolved to have it so. And to this we advise you, moved by compassion for our country, and not by any private passions. Although the corruption of the city is great, yet we implore you at once to destroy the evil that afflicts her, the madness that consumes her, and the passions that kill her.

History of Florence, III. 5

Women are the most compassionate creatures in the world, and also the most exasperating. If you avoid them, you avoid the annoyance and the benefit; if you accommodate them, you have the annoyance and the benefit at the same time. But it has always been true that you can't have honey without the bees.

Mandragola, Act 3, Scene 4

I know very well that there are a lot of people who let you talk, pretending they feel compassionate, and then laugh at you behind your back.

Clizia, Act 1, Scene 1

Those who lack compassion are inimical to human beings.

Exhortation to Penitence

Those who are not full of religion cannot be compassionate.

Exhortation to Penitence

Concealment

If under their distinguished acts there was concealed an ambition common to usefulness, or (as some say) contrary to it, I, who do not know it, am not bound to de-

scribe it; for in all my narrative I have never attempted to
cover a dishonest act with honest reasons, nor have I ever
dimmed a praiseworthy act by representing it as having
been done for a contrary purpose.

History of Florence, Dedicatory letter to Clement VII[*]

Influenced therefore by his restless and ambitious spirit,
he [Corso Donati] sought to cloak his dishonest intentions with an honest pretext, and falsely charged a number
of citizens who had administered the public funds with
having misappropriated them to private purposes, and
demanded their trial and punishment.

History of Florence, II. 21

Confession

[Saint Francis and Saint Dominic] continued themselves
to live in poverty; and by means of confessions and
preachings they obtained so much influence with the people, that they were able to make them understand that it
was wicked even to speak ill of wicked rulers, and that it
was proper to render them obedience and to leave the
punishment of their errors to God. And thus these wicked
rulers do as much evil as they please, because they do not
fear a punishment which they do not see nor believe.

Discourses on Livy, III. 1

FRATE TIMOTEO: If you want to confess, I'm at
your service.

---

[*] Born Giulio de' Medici, was pope from 1523 to 1534.

WOMAN: Not today. Somebody's waiting for me, and it's enough for me to have let out a bit right here like this. Have you said those masses of Our Lady?

FRATE: Yes, madam.

WOMAN: Now take this florin, and every Monday for two months say the mass of the dead for the soul of my husband. And though he was a bad one, yet the flesh does pull. I can't help mourning when I think about him. But do you believe he's in Purgatory?

FRATE: There's no doubt of it.

WOMAN: I'm not at all sure he is. You know what he did to me sometimes. Oh, how much I complained about him to you! I kept away from him as much as I could, but he was so pressing. Oh, good Lord!

FRATE: Have no fears. The mercy of God is great; if a man doesn't lack the will, time for repentance won't be lacking.

WOMAN: Do you believe the Turk is coming over into Italy this year?

FRATE: Yes, if you don't say your prayers.

Mandragola, Act 3, Scene 3

Conscience

I have already told you, and I'll say it again: if Friar Timoteo tells you there will be no burden on your conscience, then you can do it without any qualms.

Mandragola, Act 3, Scene 10

As far as conscience is concerned, you must follow this rule: where there is a certain good and an uncertain evil, you must never abandon that good for fear of the evil.

Mandragola, Act 3 , Scene 11

I swear to you, my lady, by this consecrated breast, that there is as much burden to your conscience in disobeying your husband in this case as there is in eating meat on Wednesday, and that is a sin that a little holy water can wash away.

Mandragola, Act 3, Scene 11

Nor could they believe that he had refrained from doing this either from goodness or scruples of conscience; for no sentiment of piety or respect could enter the heart of a man of such vile character as Giovanpaolo Baglioni, who had dishonored his sister and murdered his nephews and cousins for the sake of obtaining possession of the state; but they concluded that mankind was neither utterly wicked nor perfectly good, and that when a crime has in itself some grandeur or magnanimity they will not know how to attempt it.

Discourses on Livy, I. 27

These false apprehensions are not to be disregarded and should be carefully considered, the more so as it is very easy to be surprised by them; for a man who has a guilty conscience readily thinks that everybody is speaking of him. You may overhear a word spoken to someone else that will greatly disturb you, because you think it has reference to you, and may cause you either to discover the conspiracy by flight, or embarrass its execution by hastening it before the appointed time. And this will happen the more easily the more accomplices there are in the conspiracy.

Discourses on Livy, III. 6

It really grieves me that many of you should from mere conscience repent of your past acts, and be resolved to abstain from new ones. Certainly, if this be true, then you are not the men I took you to be; for neither conscience nor infamy should frighten you; victory never brings shame, no matter how obtained. Of conscience you should make no account at all; for where there is, as in your case, the fear of hunger and prisons, you cannot and should not be restrained by the fear of hell.

Speech of a rebellious plebeian,
in *History of Florence*, III. 13

I remind you of the advice that Romeo gave the duke of Provence, who had four daughters; he urged him to make a distinguished marriage for the eldest, pointing out that she would provide an example and precedent for the rest. So he married her to the king of France and gave him half of Provence as dowry. Once he did this, he married the others off to three kings.

Machiavelli to Francesco Guicciardini,
December 19, 1525

Courage (Animo)

The Duke [Cesare Borgia] meantime allows himself to be carried away by his sanguine confidence, believing that the word of others is more to be relied upon than his own.

Machiavelli to the Signoria of Florence, November 4, 1503

The Venetian and papal armies did meet, but two of the most important premises just mentioned did not come about because the Swiss did not come and the people of Milan were useless. Hence, once we appeared before Milan, the people did not stir; since we were minus the Swiss, we did not have the courage to stay there and we withdrew to Marignano.

Machiavelli to Bartolomeo Cavalcanti, October 6, 1526

Cowardice

In short, with mercenaries the danger lies in their cowardice and bad faith; whilst with auxiliaries their valor constitutes the danger.

The Prince, XIII

A prince who disarms his subjects will at once offend them, by thus showing that he has no confidence in them, that he suspects them either of cowardice or want of loyalty, and this will cause them to hate him.

The Prince, XX

With the customary impetuosity that characterized all his acts, Julius placed himself with only a small guard in the hands of his enemy Baglioni, whom he nevertheless carried off with him, leaving a governor in his stead to administer the state in the name of the Church. Sagacious men who were with the Pope observed his temerity and the cowardice of Baglioni, and could not understand why the latter had not by a single blow rid himself of his enemy, whereby he would have secured for himself eternal fame and rich booty, for the Pope was accompanied by all the cardinals with their valuables.

Discourses on Livy, I. 27

Want of firmness in the execution arises either from respect, or from the innate cowardice of him who is to commit the act. Such is the majesty and reverence that ordinarily surrounds the person of a prince, that it may easily mitigate the fury of a murderer, or fill him with fear.

Discourses on Livy, III. 6

No commander, therefore, need despair of forming good troops so long as he does not lack men; and a prince who has plenty of men, and yet has not good soldiers, has to blame only his own indolence and want of skill, and not the cowardice of the men.

Discourses on Livy, III. 38

It was this that produced the unfavorable opinion in Rome of Fabius Maximus, who could not persuade the people of Rome that it would be advantageous for that republic to proceed slowly with the war, and to bear the assaults of Hannibal without engaging in battle with him; because the Roman people considered this course as cowardly, and did not see the advantages that would be gained by it, and Fabius had not the faculty of demonstrating these to them.

Discourses on Livy, I. 53

Of such idle and indolent princes, therefore, and of these most cowardly armies, my history will be full; but before I descend to these, I shall, in accordance with my promise in the beginning, relate the origin of Florence, to explain fully to the understanding of everyone what the condition of that city was in those days, and how she arrived at it in the midst of all the troubles that had befallen Italy for a thousand years.

History of Florence, I. 39

Cruelty

Some may wonder how it was that Agathocles,* and others like him, after their infinite treason and cruelty, could live for any length of time securely in the countries whose sovereignty they had usurped, and even defend themselves successfully against external enemies, without any attempts on the part of their own citizens to conspire against them; whilst many others could not by means of cruelty maintain their state even in time of peace, much less in doubtful times of war. I believe that this happened according as the cruelties were well or ill applied; we may call cruelty well applied (if indeed we may call that "well" which in itself is evil) when it is committed once from

---

* Greek tyrant of Syracuse (317–289 BC) and king of Sicily (304–289 BC).

necessity for self-protection, and afterwards not persisted in, but converted as far as possible to the public good. Ill-applied cruelties are those which, though at first but few, yet increase with time rather than cease altogether. Those who adopt the first practice may remedy their condition before God, as had been done by Agathocles; but those who adopt the latter course will not possibly be able to maintain themselves in their state.

The Prince, VIII

Every prince ought to desire the reputation of being merciful, and not cruel; at the same time, he should be careful not to misuse that mercy.

The Prince, XVII

Cesare Borgia was reputed cruel, yet by his cruelty he reunited the Romagna to his states, and restored that province to order, peace, and loyalty; and if we carefully examine his course, we shall find it to have been really much more merciful than the course of the people of Florence, who, to escape the reputation of cruelty, allowed Pistoia to be destroyed. A prince, therefore, should not mind the ill repute of cruelty, when he can thereby keep his subjects united and loyal; for a few displays of severity will really be more merciful than to allow, by an excess of clemency, disorders to occur, which are apt to result in rapine and murder; for these injure a whole community, whilst the executions ordered by the prince fall only upon a few individuals.

The Prince, XVII

Among the many admirable qualities of Hannibal, it is related of him that, having an immense army composed of a very great variety of races of men, which he led to war in foreign countries, no quarrels ever occurred among them, nor were there ever any dissensions between them and their chief, either in his good or in his adverse fortunes; which can only be accounted for by his extreme cruelty.

The Prince, XVII

Hannibal, on the contrary, conducted himself in Italy with violence, cruelty, rapine, and every kind of perfidy. Yet he obtained the same success that Scipio had in Spain.

Discourses on Livy, III. 21

As to Hannibal, there is no particular instance where his cruelty and perfidy caused him any immediate injury; but we may well presume that Naples and many other cities remained faithful to Rome solely from fear of Hannibal's cruelty.

Discourses on Livy, III. 21

Discussing now . . . the qualities of Commodus, Severus, Antoninus, Caracalla, and Maximinus, we find them to have been most cruel and rapacious; and that, for the sake of keeping the soldiers satisfied, they did not hesitate to commit every kind of outrage upon the people; and that all of them, with the exception of Septimius Severus, came to a bad end.

The Prince, XIX

Thus conspiracies against several persons at the same time should be avoided; they do no good to the conspirators, nor to the country, nor to anyone, but rather cause the tyrants that survive to become more cruel and insupportable than before, as was the case with those of Florence, Athens, and Heraclea. . . .

Discourses on Livy, III. 6

Death

Had the Duke Cesare Borgia been in health at the time of Alexander's [Pope Alexander VI, the Duke's father] death, everything would have gone well with him; for he said to me on the day when Julius II was created Pope, that he had provided for everything that could possibly occur in case of his father's death, except that he never thought that at that moment he should himself be so near dying.

The Prince, VII

In doubtful times there will ever be a lack of men whom he can trust. Such a prince cannot depend upon what he observes in ordinary quiet times, when the citizens have need of his authority; for then everybody runs at his bidding, everybody promises, and everybody is willing to die for him, when death is very remote. But in adverse times, when the government has need of the citizens, then but few will be found to stand by the prince.

The Prince, IX

Princes cannot always escape assassination when [the assassin is] prompted by a resolute and determined spirit; for any man who himself despises death can always inflict it upon others.

The Prince, XIX

The death of Virginia had caused the Roman people to retire, armed, to the Mons Sacer.

Discourses on Livy, I. 44

CALLIMACO: I realize you're right. But what can I
do? What plans can I make? Where can I turn?
I absolutely have to try something, whether it is
noble, dangerous, drastic, or vile. It's better to
die than to live like this. If I could only sleep at
night, if I could eat, if I could talk with people,
if I could enjoy anything at all anymore, I would
be patient and bide my time. But there is no
cure; and if my hope isn't kept alive by some
plan or other, I will surely die. So, seeing that I'll
die anyway, I have to do something; and I won't
stop at anything, no matter how brutal, cruel, or
foul.

Mandragola, Act 1, Scene 3

CALLIMACO: Oh God! What have I done to deserve such a reward? I'm ready to die for joy.
LIGURIO: What kind of people are these? For joy or
for sorrow, one way or another he wants to die!

Mandragola, Act 4, Scene 2

The Death Penalty

The constitution of Rome was excellent upon this point, for there an appeal to the people was the ordinary practice, and when an important case occurred, where it would have been perilous to delay execution by such an appeal, they had recourse to the dictator, who had the right of immediate execution; this, however, was resorted to only in cases of extreme necessity. But in Florence, and in other cities that like her had their origin in servitude, the power of life and death was lodged in the hands of a stranger, sent by the prince to exercise that power. When these cities afterwards became free, they left that power in the hands of a foreigner, whom they called "the Captain." But the facility with which he could be corrupted by the powerful citizens made this a most pernicious system; and in the course of the mutations of their governments that system was changed, and a council of eight citizens was appointed to perform the functions of the Captain; which only made matters worse, for the reason which we have given elsewhere, that a tribunal of a few is always under the control of a few powerful citizens.

Discourses on Livy, I. 49

Deceit

Having thus reestablished his reputation, and trusting no longer in the French or any other foreign power, [the Duke Cesare Borgia] had recourse to deceit, so as to avoid putting them to the test.

The Prince, VII

It must be evident to everyone that it is more praiseworthy for a prince always to maintain good faith, and practice integrity rather than craft and deceit. And yet the experience of our own times has shown that those princes have achieved great things who made small account of good faith, and who learned to circumvent the intelligence of others and that in the end they got the better of those whose actions were dictated by loyalty and good faith.

The Prince, XVIII

It is true that in the execution of a conspiracy against one's country there are greater difficulties and dangers to surmount. For it is very rare that the forces of a conspirator suffice against so many; and it is not everyone that controls an army like Caesar, or Agathocles, or Cleomenes, and the like, who by a single blow made themselves masters of their country. For such men the execution is sure and easy, but others who have not the support of such forces must employ deceit and cunning, or foreign aid.

Discourses on Livy, III. 6

As to the employment of deceit and cunning [I give the following instance]. Pisistratus, after the victory which he had gained over the people of Megara, was greatly beloved by the people of Athens. One morning he went forth from his house wounded, and charged the nobility with having attacked him from jealousy, and demanded permission to keep a guard of armed followers for his protection, which was accorded him. This first step enabled him easily to attain such power that he soon after made himself tyrant of Athens.

Discourses on Livy, III. 6

Although deceit is detestable in all other things, yet in the conduct of war it is laudable and honorable; and a commander who vanquishes an enemy by stratagem is equally praised with one who gains victory by force.

Discourses on Livy, III. 40

I do not confound such deceit with perfidy, which breaks pledged faith and treaties; for although states and kingdoms may at times be won by perfidy, yet will it ever bring dishonor with it.

Discourses on Livy, III. 40

The lieutenant, wondering at their presumption, which did not seem reasonable to him, suspected and discovered the deceit, and thus defeated the design of the Tuscans. This instance will serve to show that the commander of an army should always mistrust any manifest error which he sees the enemy commit, as it invariably conceals some stratagem.

Discourses on Livy, III. 48

Nor do I believe that there was ever a man who from obscure condition arrived at great power by merely employing open force; but there are many who have succeeded by fraud alone, as, for instance, Giovanni Galeazzo Visconti in taking the state and sovereignty of Lombardy from his uncle, Messer Bernabò.

Discourses on Livy, II. 13

And as Rome employed every means, by chance or choice, to promote her aggrandizement, so she also did not hesitate to employ fraud; nor could she have practiced a greater fraud than by taking the course we have explained above of making other peoples her allies and associates, and under that title making them slaves, as she did with the Latins and other neighboring nations.

Discourses on Livy, II. 13

Decline

But the very reverse happens where there is a prince whose private interests are generally in opposition to those of the city, whilst the measures taken for the benefit of the city are seldom deemed personally advantageous by the prince. This state of things soon leads to a tyranny, the least evil of which is that it checks the advance of the city in its career of prosperity, so that it grows neither in power nor wealth, but on the contrary rather declines.

Discourses on Livy, II. 2

Desire

Those who desire to win the favor of princes generally endeavor to do so by offering them those things which they themselves prize most, or such as they observe the prince to delight in most.

Dedicatory letter to *The Prince*

The desire for conquest is certainly most natural and common among men, and whenever they yield to it and are successful, they are praised; but when they lack the means, and yet attempt it anyhow, then they commit an error that merits blame.

The Prince, III

He [a prince] should do as the skillful archer, who, seeing that the object he desires to hit is too distant, and knowing the extent to which his bow will carry, aims higher than the destined mark, not for the purpose of sending his arrow to that height, but so that by this elevation it may reach the desired aim.

The Prince, VI

Such a selection of site would doubtless be more useful and wise if men were content with what they possessed, and did not desire to exercise command over others.

Discourses on Livy, I. 1

And, truly, whoever weighs all these reasons accurately may well remain in doubt which of the two classes he would choose as the guardians of liberty, not knowing which would be least dangerous—those who seek to acquire an authority which they have not, or those who desire to preserve that which they already possess. After the nicest examination, this is what I think may be concluded from it. The question refers either to a republic that desires to extend its empire, as Rome, or to a state that confines itself merely to its own preservation. In the first case Rome should be imitated, and in the second the example of Sparta and Venice should be followed.

Discourses on Livy, I. 5

The reason of this is that nature has created men so that they desire everything, but are unable to attain it; desire being thus always greater than the faculty of acquiring, discontent with what they have and dissatisfaction with themselves result from it. This causes the changes in their fortunes; for as some men desire to have more, whilst others fear to lose what they have, enmities and war are the consequences; and this brings about the ruin of one province and the elevation of another.

Discourses on Livy, I. 37

Despair

I know that encampment [behind the lines in the siege the Florentines mounted against Pisa] would be less dangerous and less strenuous, but had I not wanted danger and hard work, I would not have left Florence. So, may it please Your Lordships, let me stay here in these camps and work with the commissioners on the events that may occur: here I can be of some good use; there I should be of no good use at all and I would die of despair.

Machiavelli to the Ten of War, April 16, 1509

The reward which Antonius received for this service was that Mutianus deprived him of the command of the army, and gradually reduced his authority in Rome to nothing; so that Antonius, indignant, went to see Vespasian, who was still in Asia, who received him in such manner that, being soon after deprived of all rank, he died almost in despair.

Discourses on Livy, I. 29

Men should never despair . . . for, not knowing the aims of Fortune, which she pursues by dark and devious ways, men should always be hopeful, and never yield to despair, whatever troubles or ill fortune may befall them.

Discourses on Livy, II. 29

For although the wing commanded by Brutus had been victorious, yet Cassius thought that it had been defeated, and that consequently the whole army was beaten; so that, despairing of his safety, he killed himself.

Discourses on Livy, III. 18

As stated above, the Roman Consul and his army were shut in by the Samnites, who proposed to him the most ignominious conditions, such as to pass under a yoke, and to send the army back to Rome disarmed; which filled the Consul and the army with despair.

Discourses on Livy, III. 41

> NICOMACO: What do you want with a wife? You are already thirty-eight, and a young girl is no good for you. It stands to reason that, after she was with you for a few months, she would look for a man younger than you, and you would become desperate. And then I couldn't have confidence in you anymore. You would lose your standing, you would become a pauper, and the two of you would go begging.
> *Clizia*, Act 3, Scene 5

Discourse

If you find that discoursing upon matters bores you because you realize that they frequently turn out differently from the opinions and ideas we have, you are right—because the same thing has happened to me.

Machiavelli to Francesco Vettori, April 9, 1513

Disease

Your Lordships will see that it was fifteen days ago today that they [the army of German pikemen that eventually conquered and sacked Rome in early May 1527] decided to pass, but they have not yet been able to do it; so that we may reasonably hope that the same causes may keep them fifteen days more, if not here where they are, at least this side of the mountains. But it behooves us, as I have said, to employ this time well, otherwise our ruin will only have been postponed, and will be the greater, the same as bodies that have been enfeebled by long disease are less able to support it than they were in its beginning.

Machiavelli to Francesco Guicciardini, March 30, 1527

It is like a consuming disease to be obliged to withdraw the troops from the places we have left behind for the purpose of placing them as garrisons in those that are before us; otherwise, we should not be in time to do it, and disorders and inconveniences would arise that would be apt to prove our ruin.

Machiavelli to Francesco Guicciardini,

April 11, 1527

Dishonesty

Whereupon Aristides reported to the people [of Athens] that the proposed plan of Themistocles was highly advantageous but most dishonest, and therefore the people absolutely rejected it; which would not have been done by

Philip of Macedon, nor many other princes, who would only have looked to the advantages, and who have gained more by their perfidy than by any other means.

Discourses on Livy, I. 40

Before Pope Alexander VI had crushed the petty tyrants that ruled the Romagna, that country presented an example of all the worst crimes. The slightest causes gave rise to murder and every species of rapine; and this was due exclusively to the wickedness of the princes, and not to the evil nature of the people, as alleged by the former. For these princes, being poor, yet wishing to live in luxury like the rich, were obliged to resort to every variety of robbery. And among other dishonest means which they employed was the making of laws prohibiting some one thing or another; and immediately after, they were themselves the first to encourage their non-observance, leaving such transgressions unpunished until a great number of persons had been guilty of them, and then suddenly they turned to prosecute the transgressors; not from any zeal for the law, but solely from cupidity, in the expectation of obtaining money for commuting the punishment.

Discourses on Livy, III. 29

The End Result

Everybody sees what you seem to be, but few really feel what you are; and these few dare not oppose the opinion of the many, who are protected by the majesty of the state;

for the actions of all men, and especially those of princes, are judged by the result, where there is no other judge to whom to appeal.

The Prince, XVIII

Besides that, we must always consider the end result. Your end is to fill a seat in Heaven and to make your husband happy.

Mandragola, Act 3, Scene 11

It was not wise to judge of things only by their results, for it often happened that the best-considered undertakings did not come to a good end, whilst the most ill-advised were frequently successful. And were we to approve evil counsels because of the good which occasionally has attended them, we should virtually be encouraging error, which might result disastrously for the republic; for certainly evil counsels do not always produce happy results. And in the same way it would be an error to blame a judicious enterprise because it had had an unsuccessful issue; for such a course would discourage the citizens from giving the city the benefit of their counsels, and to say that which they thought.

Speech of Rinaldo degli Albizzi, in the
History of Florence, IV. 7

Error

Although at the beginning of the growth of their dominion on land they had no occasion to have any serious apprehensions of their commanders, because their own reputation was great and their possessions on land small, yet when they extended these, which happened under the captaincy of Carmignuola, they became sensible of their error.

The Prince, XII

Messer Agnolo Acciaiuoli was Archbishop of Florence at that time. In his preaching he had magnified the doings of the Duke, and had won for him great favor with the people. But when he afterwards saw him as lord of Florence, and perceived his tyrannical conduct, he became convinced that he had misled his country; and to make good the error which he had committed, he could think of no other remedy than that the same hand that had inflicted the wound should also heal it; and therefore he placed himself at the head of the first and most powerful conspiracy, in which there were also the Bardi, the Rossi, the Frescobaldi, Scali, Altoviti, Magalotti, Strozzi, and the Mancini.

History of Florence, II. 36

Fault

As regards faults committed from ignorance, there is not a more striking example than that of Varro, whose temerity caused the defeat of the Romans by Hannibal at Cannae, which exposed the republic to the loss of her liberty. Nevertheless, as it was from ignorance, and not from evil intention, they not only did not punish him, but actually rendered him honors; and on his return, the whole order of Senators went to meet him, and, unable to congratulate him on the result of the battle, they thanked him for having returned to Rome, and for not having despaired of the cause of the republic.

Discourses on Livy, I. 31

Fear

This, then, gives rise to the question whether it be better to be beloved than feared, or to be feared than beloved. It will naturally be answered that it would be desirable to be both the one and the other; but as it is difficult to be both at the same time, it is much safer to be feared than to be loved, when you have to choose between the two. For it may be said of men in general that they are ungrateful and fickle, dissemblers, avoiders of danger, and greedy of gain. So long as you shower benefits upon them, they are all yours; they offer you their blood, their substance, their lives, and their children, provided the necessity for it is far off; but when it is near at hand, then they revolt. And the prince who relies upon their words, without having otherwise provided for his security, is ruined; for friendships that are won by rewards, and not by greatness and nobility of soul, although deserved, yet are not real, and cannot be depended upon in time of adversity. Besides, men have less hesitation in offending one who makes himself beloved than one who makes himself feared; for love holds by a bond of obligation which, as mankind is bad, is broken on every occasion whenever it is in the interest of the obliged party to break it. But fear holds by the apprehension of punishment, which never leaves men.

The Prince, XVII

In the second place, men are prompted in their actions by two main motives, namely, love and fear; so that he who makes himself beloved will have as much influence as he who makes himself feared, although generally he who makes himself feared will be more readily followed and obeyed than he who makes himself beloved.

Discourses on Livy, III. 21

Flattery

For you must caress men, or you must make sure of them in some other way, but never reduce them to the alternative of having either to destroy you or perish themselves.

Discourses on Livy, III. 6

Fraud

In like manner, Venice, having obtained possession of a great part of Italy, and the most of it not by war but by means of money and fraud, when occasion came for her to give proof of her strength, she lost everything in a single battle.

Discourses on Livy, I. 6

When the citizens had become corrupt, this system became the worst possible, for then only the powerful proposed laws, not for the common good and the liberty of all, but for the increase of their own power, and fear restrained all the others from speaking against such laws; and thus the people by force and fraud made to resolve upon their own ruin.

Discourses on Livy, I. 18

After Rome had expelled her kings she was no longer exposed to the dangers which we have spoken of above as resulting from a succession of feeble or wicked kings; for the sovereign authority was vested in the Consuls, who obtained that authority not by inheritance, or fraud, or violent ambition, but by the free suffrages of the people, and were generally most excellent men.

Discourses on Livy, I. 20

If you note the conduct of men, you will see that all who achieve great riches and power obtain them either by force or by fraud; and then they conceal the abomination of their acquisitions by falsely calling them gain, so as to make it appear that they have come by them honestly. And those who from too little prudence, or too great stupidity, avoid these modes of gain, will always grovel in servitude and poverty; for the faithful servants always remain servants, and the good men ever remain poor. None ever escape from servitude except the unfaithful and the audacious, and none from poverty except the fraudulent and the rapacious.

History of Florence, III. 13

Glory

And thus he will have the double glory of having established a new principality, and of having strengthened and adorned it with good laws, good armies, good allies, and good examples. And in the same way will it be a double shame to a hereditary prince, if through want of prudence and ability he loses his state.

The Prince, XXIV

Goals

More unhappy still is that republic which from the first has diverged from a good constitution. And that republic is furthest from it whose vicious institutions impede her progress, and make her leave the right path that leads to a good end; for those who are in that condition can hardly ever be brought into the right goal.

Discourses on Livy, I. 2

The Good and Goodness

As the reformation of the political condition of a state presupposes a good man, whilst the making of himself prince of a republic by violence naturally presupposes a bad one, it will consequently be exceedingly rare that a good man should be found willing to employ wicked means to become prince, even though his final object be good; or that a bad man, after having become prince, should be willing to labor for good ends, and that it should enter his mind to use for good purposes that authority which has been acquired by evil means.

Discourses on Livy, I. 18

However strong a new prince may be in troops, yet will he always have need of the good will of the inhabitants, if he wishes to enter into firm possession of the country.

The Prince, III

Of the twenty-six emperors who reigned from the time of Caesar to that of Maximinius, sixteen were assassinated, and ten only died a natural death; and if, among those who were killed, there were one or two good ones, like Galba and Pertinax, their deaths were the consequence of the corruption which their predecessors had engendered among the soldiers.

Discourses on Livy, I. 10

All the emperors that succeeded to the throne by inheritance, except Titus, were bad, and those who became emperors by adoption were all good, such as the five from Nero to Marcus Aurelius; and when the Empire became hereditary, it came to ruin.

Discourses on Livy, I. 10

And surely, if he be a man, he will be shocked at the thought of reenacting those evil times, and be fired with an intense desire to follow the example of the good.

Discourses on Livy, I. 10

He who for a time has seemed good, and for purposes of his own wants to become bad, should do it gradually, and should seem to be brought to it by the force of circumstances; so that, before his changed nature deprives him of his former friends, lies may have gained him new ones, and that his authority may not be diminished by the change. Otherwise his deception will be discovered, and he will lose his friends and be ruined.

Discourses on Livy, I. 41

A licentious and mutinous people may easily be brought back to good conduct by the influence and persuasion of a good man, but an evil-minded prince is not amenable to such influences, and therefore there is no other remedy against him but cold steel.

Discourses on Livy, I. 58

Reflecting now upon the course of human affairs, I think that, as a whole, the world remains very much in the same condition, and the good in it always balances the evil: but the good and the evil change from one country to another, as we learn from the history of those ancient kingdoms that differed from each other in manners, whilst the world at large remained the same.

Discourses on Livy, Preface to Book II

It is the duty of a good man to teach others that good which the malignity of the times and of fortune has prevented his doing himself; so that among the many capable ones whom he has instructed, someone perhaps, more favored by Heaven, may perform it.

Discourses on Livy, Preface to Book II

A good and wise prince, desirous of maintaining that character, and to avoid giving the opportunity to his sons to become oppressive, will never build fortresses, so that they may place their reliance upon the good will of their subjects, and not upon the strength of citadels.

Discourses on Livy, II. 24

The matter is about even; for if either one of the two, the army or the commander, be good, they will be apt to make the other good likewise. But a good army without an able commander often becomes insolent and dangerous, as was the case with the Macedonian army after the death of Alexander, and with the veteran troops in the civil wars of Rome. And therefore I am disposed to believe that you can more safely rely upon a good general, who has the time to instruct his men and the facilities for arming them, than upon an insolent army with a chief tumultuously chosen by them.

Discourses on Livy, III. 13

The manner in which men live is so different from the way in which they ought to live, that he who leaves the common course for that which he ought to follow will find that it leads him to ruin rather than to safety. For a man who, in all respects, will carry out only his professions of good, will be apt to be ruined among so many who are evil. A prince therefore who desires to maintain himself must learn to be not always good, but to be so or not as necessity may require.

The Prince, XV

A sagacious prince then cannot and should not fulfill his pledges when their observance is contrary to his interest, and when the causes that induced him to pledge his faith no longer exist. If men were all good, then indeed this precept would be bad; but as men are naturally bad, and will not observe their faith toward you, you must, in the same way, not observe yours to them; and no prince ever yet lacked legitimate reasons with which to color his want of good faith.

The Prince, XVIII

A prince, and especially one who has but recently acquired his state, cannot perform all those things which cause men to be esteemed as good; he being often obliged, for the sake of maintaining his state, to act contrary to humanity, charity, and religion. And therefore is it necessary that he should have a versatile mind, capable of changing readily, according as the winds and changes of fortune bid him; and, as has been said above, not to deviate from the good if possible, but to know how to enter into evil if forced by necessity.

The Prince, XVIII

Hatred may be caused by good as well as by evil works, and therefore a prince who wants to preserve his state is often obliged not to be good; for when the mass of the people or of the soldiery, or of the nobles, whose support is necessary for him, is corrupt, then it becomes the interest of the prince to indulge and satisfy their humor; and it is under such circumstances that good works will be injurious to him.

The Prince, XIX

Let us come now to Alexander, who was so good that, among other merits, it was said of him that during the fourteen years of his reign not one person was put to death by him without regular judicial proceedings. But being regarded as effeminate, and as allowing himself to be governed by his mother, he fell into disrespect, and the soldiery conspired against him and killed him.

The Prince, XIX

Men will always naturally prove bad, unless some necessity constrains them to be good. Whence we conclude that good counsels, no matter whence they may come, result wholly from the prince's own sagacity; but the wisdom of the prince never results from good counsels.

The Prince, XXIII

As for the dangers to which he [the Duke of Athens, who intended to establish a tyrannical rule in Florence] would expose himself by this step, he did not regard them, for it was not the practice of a good man to be deterred by fear from doing a good act, and only a coward desisted from a glorious enterprise because its issue was involved in doubt. And . . . he believed his conduct would be such that in a short time they would find out that they had trusted him too little and feared him too much. . . .

History of Florence, II. 35

The Signori, frightened and covered with shame, retired to their own houses; the palace was sacked by the Duke's adherents, the gonfalon of the people was torn down, and the Duke's standard raised instead. All of which caused immeasurable grief and regret to all the good citizens, and much joy to those who had consented to it from malice or ignorance.

History of Florence, II. 35

Before his departure Messer Benedetto [Alberti] called all his relatives together, and seeing them sad and weeping, he addressed them as follows: "Fathers and seniors, you see how fortune has ruined me and threatened you, at which I am not surprised, nor should you be; for such is ever the fate of those who, among the many wicked, wish to remain good, and who desire to sustain that which the majority seek to destroy."

History of Florence, III. 22

All who have recorded the events of these times agree that, if Messer Veri's [Veri de' Medici] ambition had exceeded his goodness, he might without hindrance have made himself prince of the city.

History of Florence, III. 25

On the other hand, it is true that when by good fortune some wise, good, and powerful citizen arises in the republic (which, however, seldom happens), who establishes laws that will quell the factious spirit of the nobles and of the people and restrain it so that it can do no harm, then I say that city may call herself truly free, and such a state may be considered firm and stable.

History of Florence, IV. 1

He believed it is the duty of a good and wise citizen not to change the established institutions of the city, as there was nothing so injurious as such frequent changes, which always gave offense to many; and where so many remained discontented, there was cause for apprehending every day some unhappy occurrence.

History of Florence, IV. 10

But suppose that you were to succeed in driving him out, which might well be, having a Signoria well-disposed to it, how can you ever prevent his return, when so many of his friends remain here, who will labor most ardently for his return? You will find it impossible to guard against this danger, for his friends are so numerous and have the support and good will of the masses. And the more of his avowed friends you expel, the greater number of enemies will you make yourselves; so that in a little while he will be recalled in spite of you, and all you will have gained will be that you have driven him out a good man and that he returns a bad one; for his nature will be corrupted by those who will have recalled him, and whom he could not oppose being under such obligations to them.

Speech of Niccolò da Uzano, against the expulsion
of Cosimo de' Medici from Florence, in the
History of Florence, IV. 27

Every case that came before the magistrates, even the smallest, became a cause of contention; secrets were divulged, and the good and evil alike became objects of favor or disfavor; good men and wicked were assailed alike, and no magistrate performed his duty.

> *History of Florence*, IV. 28

It has ever been less painful for good and wise men to hear of the misfortunes of their country than to witness them; and it has ever been deemed more glorious to be reputed an honorable rebel than an enslaved citizen.

> Speech of Rinaldo degli Albizzi, in the
> *History of Florence*, IV. 32

No good man will ever find fault with anyone who seeks to defend his country, in whatever way he may deem it proper to do so.

> Speech of Rinaldo degli Albizzi, in the
> *History of Florence*, V. 8

Nor should anyone who raises arms against his country be condemned under all circumstances; for cities, although they are complex bodies, yet very much resemble individual bodies. And as these are often afflicted with infirmities that can only be cured with fire and steel, so in the former likewise similar troubles frequently occur, which any good and devoted citizen would sin more by leaving uncured than by curing them, though it be with fire and steel.

> Speech of Rinaldo degli Albizzi, in the
> *History of Florence*, V. 8

Greatness of Soul

Such were the beginning and causes of disorders, conspiracies, and plots against the sovereigns set on foot not by the feeble and timid, but by those citizens who, surpassing the others in greatness of soul, in wealth, and in courage, could not submit to the outrages and excesses of their princes.

Discourses on Livy, I. 2

Growth

Florence, thus built under the Roman Empire, could in the beginning have no growth except what depended on the will of its master.

Discourses on Livy, I. 1

All the beginnings of religions, republics and monarchies must have within themselves some goodness, by means of which they obtain their first growth and reputation, and as in the process of time this goodness becomes corrupted, it will of necessity destroy the body unless something intervenes to bring it back to its normal condition.

Discourses on Livy, III. 1

Hatred

A prince, however, should make himself feared in such a manner that, if he has not won the affections of his people, he shall at least not incur their hatred; for the being feared, and not hated, can go very well together, if the prince abstains from taking the substance of his subjects, and leaves them their women. And if you should be obliged to inflict capital punishment upon anyone, then be sure to do so only when there is manifest cause and proper justification for it; and, above all things, abstain from taking people's property, for men will sooner forget the death of their fathers than the loss of their patrimony. Besides, there will never be any lack of reasons for taking people's property, and a prince who once begins to live by rapine will ever find excuses for seizing other people's property. On the other hand, reasons for taking life are not so easily found, and are more readily exhausted.

The Prince, XVII

History

As regards the exercise of the mind, the prince should read history, and therein study the actions of eminent men, observe how they bore themselves in war, and examine the causes of their victories and defeats, so that he may imitate the former and avoid the latter. But above all should he follow the example of whatever distinguished man he may have chosen for his model; assuming that someone has been specially praised and held up to him as glorious, whose actions and exploits he should ever bear in mind.

The Prince, XIV

Honesty

When these republics [free German cities] have occasion to spend any considerable amount of money for public account, their magistrates or councils, who have authority in these matters, impose upon all the inhabitants a tax of one or two per cent of their possessions. When such a resolution has been passed according to the laws of the country, every citizen presents himself before the collectors of this impost, and, after having taken an oath to pay the just amount, deposits in a strong-box provided for the purpose the sum which according to his conscience he ought to pay, without any one's witnessing what he pays. From this we may judge of the extent of the probity and religion that still exist among those people. And we must presume that everyone pays the true amount, for if this were not the case the impost would not yield the amount intended according to the estimates based upon former impositions; the fraud would thus be discovered, and other means would be employed to collect the amount required. This honesty is the more to be admired as it is so very rare that it is found only in that country.

Discourses on Livy, I. 55

Horror

And having observed that the past rigor of Ramiro had engendered some hatred, the Duke wished to show to the people, for the purpose of removing that feeling from their minds, and to win their entire confidence, that, if any cruelties had been practiced, they had not originated with him, but had resulted altogether from the harsh nature of his minister. He therefore took occasion to have Messer Ramiro put to death and his body cut into two parts and exposed in the marketplace of Cesena one morning, with a block of wood and a bloody cutlass left beside him. The horror of this spectacle caused the people to remain for a time stupefied and satisfied.

The Prince, VII

Humility

We often see that humility not only is of no service, but is actually hurtful, especially when employed toward insolent men, who from jealousy or some other motive have conceived a hatred against you.

Discourses on Livy, II. 14

Imitation

Let no one wonder if, in what I am about to say of entirely new principalities and of the prince and his government, I cite the very highest examples. For as men almost always follow the beaten track of others, and proceed in their actions by imitation, and yet cannot altogether follow the ways of others, nor attain the high qualities of those whom they imitate, so a wise man should ever follow the ways of great men and endeavor to imitate only such as have been most eminent; so that even if his merits do not quite equal theirs, yet that they may in some measure reflect their greatness. He should do as the skillful archer, who, seeing that the object he desires to hit is too distant, and knowing the extent to which his bow will carry, aims higher than the destined mark, not for the purpose of sending his arrow to that height, but so that by this elevation it may reach the desired aim.

The Prince, VI

Infamy

Those are doomed to infamy and universal execration who have destroyed religions, who have overturned republics and kingdoms, who are enemies of virtue, of letters, and of every art that is useful and honorable to mankind.

Discourses on Livy, I. 10

Ingratitude

When the stars, when the heavens were indignant at human / pride, for man's abasement Ingratitude then was born in the world. / Of Avarice she was the daughter and of Suspicion; she was / nursed in the arms of Envy; in the breasts of princes and kings she lives. / There as in her chief abode she makes her nest; from thence she anoints the hearts of all other men with the poison of her treachery. / Thus in all places this evil is felt, because everything is pierced and bitten by her nurse's envenomed tooth. / And if any man early enrolls himself among the fortunate, / through Heaven's good wishes and her joyous aid, in no long time afterward he unsays his words, / when, wearied out, he sees his blood and his sweat and his life of good service repaid with injury and calumny.

Tercets on Ingratitude, lines 22–37

Among the latter was Michele di Lando, who was not saved from the fury of the party by all the services he had rendered, and to which he owed his authority at a time when an unbridled mob was destroying the city. His country showed him little gratitude for all his good deeds; an error often committed by princes and republics, and one which often causes those who are alarmed by such examples to injure their princes before they have experienced their ingratitude.

History of Florence, III. 22

Men in general are ungrateful and fickle, dissemblers, avoiders of danger, and greedy of gain. So long as you shower benefits upon them, they are all yours; they offer you their blood, their substance, their lives, and their children, provided the necessity for it is far off; but when it is near at hand, then they revolt.

The Prince, XVIII

In reading the history of republics we find in all of them a degree of ingratitude to their citizens; this, however, seems to have been the case to a lesser extent in Rome than in Athens, and perhaps less even than in any other republic. In seeking for the reason of this difference, so far as Rome and Athens are concerned, I believe it was because Rome had less cause for mistrusting her citizens than Athens. In fact, from the time of the expulsion of the kings until Sylla and Marius, no Roman citizen ever attempted to deprive his country of her liberty; so that, there being no occasion to suspect her citizens, there was consequently no cause for offending them inconsiderately. The very contrary happened in Athens, for Pisistratus had by fraud robbed her of her liberty at the very time of her highest prosperity; so soon as she afterwards recovered her freedom, remembering the injuries received and her past servitude, she resented with the utmost harshness, not only all faults, but the mere semblance of faults, on the part of her citizens.

Discourses on Livy, I. 28

It seems to me proper here, in connection with the above subject, to examine whether the people or a prince is more liable to the charge of ingratitude; and by way of illustrating this question the better, I set out by saying that the vice of ingratitude springs either from avarice or fear. For when a people or a prince has sent a general on some important expedition where by his success he acquires great glory, the prince or people is in turn bound to reward him. But if instead of such reward they dishonor and wrong him, influenced thereto by avarice, then they are guilty of an inexcusable wrong, which will involve them in eternal infamy. . . . But when they fail to reward, or rather when they offend, not from avarice, but from suspicion and fear, then the people or the prince have some excuse for their ingratitude. . . . In concluding, then, this discourse, I say that, as the vice of ingratitude is usually the consequence of either avarice or fear, it will be seen that the peoples never fall into this error from avarice, and that fear also makes them less liable to it than princes, inasmuch as they have less reason for fear.

Discourses on Livy, I. 29

A prince, to avoid the necessity of living in constant mistrust or of being ungrateful, should command all his expeditions in person, as the Roman Emperors did in the beginning, and as the Sultan does at the present time, and as in fact all valiant princes ever have done and will do. For if victorious, all the glory and fruits of their conquests will be theirs; but if they are not present themselves at the action, and the glory of victory falls to the share of another, then it will seem to them that the conquest will not profit them unless they extinguish that glory of another which they have failed to achieve themselves. Thus they become ungrateful and unjust, and in that way their loss will be greater than their gain. . . . A republic that wishes to avoid the vice of ingratitude cannot employ the same means as a prince; that is to say, she cannot go and command her own expeditions, and is obliged therefore to confide them to some one of her citizens. But it is proper that I should suggest as the best means to adopt the same course that Rome did, in being less ungrateful than others, and which resulted from her institutions.

Discourses on Livy, I. 30

Insolence

The Veienti began with insults and attacks to abuse and offend the Romans, with such a degree of temerity and insolence that it caused the Romans to forget their dissensions and to become united; so that when it came to a regular battle between them and the Veienti and Tuscans, the Romans completely defeated and routed them.

Discourses on Livy. II. 25

When the Spaniards had arrived in the plains of Florence, they found no one coming to their support, and having run out of provisions they attempted to open negotiations; but the citizens of Florence had become insolent, and declined all terms. The loss of Prato and the ruin of their own state were the consequence of this conduct.

Discourses on Livy, II. 27

A good army without an able commander often becomes insolent and dangerous, as was the case with the Macedonian army after the death of Alexander, and with the veteran troops in the civil wars of Rome.

Discourses on Livy, III. 13

Rome and Venice furnish us an example of this [that great men and powerful republics preserve an equal dignity and courage in prosperity and adversity]. No ill fortune ever made the former abject, nor did success ever make her insolent.

Discourses on Livy, III. 31

Love

How beautiful is love in the youthful heart! / by so much it beseems not one / who has passed the flower of his years. / Love has power befitting the years, / and in early life it is greatly honored but in late has little worth or none. / So, you old men in love, / it is best to leave that undertaking to ardent youths, who, eager for heavier toil, / can do more generous honor to their lord.

Clizia, Act 2, Scene 5

He who makes no test, oh Love, / of your great power, / must hope in vain ever to have true faith in Heaven's highest worth. / He does not know how at the same time / one can live and die, how one can search for ill and run away from good, / how one can love oneself less than some other, how often the heart is frozen and melted by fear and hope; / he does not know how men and gods in equal measure / dread the weapons with which you're armed.

Clizia, Act 1, Scene 3

Certainly the man who said that the lover and the soldier are alike told the truth. The general wants his soldiers to be young; women don't want their lovers to be old. It's a repulsive thing to see an old man a soldier; it's most repulsive to see him in love. Soldiers fear their commander's anger; lovers fear no less that of their ladies. Soldiers sleep on the ground out of doors; lovers on the wall ledges. Soldiers pursue their enemies to the death; lovers, their rivals. Soldiers on the darkest nights in the dead of winter go through the mud, exposed to rain and wind, to carry out some undertaking that will bring them victory; lovers attempt in similar ways and with similar sufferings, and greater, to gain those they love. Equally in war and in love, secrecy is wanted, and fidelity and courage. The dangers are alike, and most often the results as well. The soldier dies in a ditch and the lover in despair.

Clizia, Act 1, Scene 2

And since my own precedent causes you dismay, remembering what Love's arrows have done to me, I am obliged to tell you how I have handled myself with him. As a matter of fact, I have let him do as he pleases and I have followed him through hill and dale, wood and plain; I have discovered that he has granted me more charms than if I had tormented him. So then, take off the saddle packs, remove the bridle, close your eyes, and say, "Go ahead, Love, be my guide, my leader; if things turn out well, may the praise be yours; if they turn out badly, may the blame be yours, I am your slave."

Machiavelli to Francesco Vettori, February 4, 1514

I have no response to your letter, except that you should give your love full rein and that whatever pleasure you seize today may not be there for you to seize tomorrow; if things still stand as they did when you wrote, I envy you more than the king of England. I beg you to follow your star; do not let things slide—not even a jot—for anything in the world, because I believe now, I have always believed, and I shall continue to believe that what Boccaccio says is true: it is better to act and to regret it than not to act and to regret it.

Machiavelli to Francesco Vettori, February 25, 1514

As for your love affair, let me remind you that Love tortures only those who attempt to clip his wings or to fetter him whenever he flies into their laps. Because he is a young, fickle boy, he gouges out the eyes, livers, and hearts of such people. But those who rejoice at his arrival and pamper him, and then let him go whenever he wants, gladly welcoming his return visits—those he always reveres and cherishes: under his command they triumph. Consequently, my dear friend, do not try to control one who flies or clip one who grows a thousand feathers for every one lost, and you will be happy.

Machiavelli to Francesco Vettori, June 10, 1514

The youthful archer many times had tried / To wound me in the breast with his arrows; He takes his pleasure thus— spite for all / And harm to everyone is his delight. / Though no diamond exists that might withstand / His arrowheads brutal and keen, / Yet now they've struck an obstacle so strong / It took little account of all their power. / So, full of rage and anger, in order / To demonstrate his consummate skill, / He made a change of quiver, bow, and shaft; / With such great force he let one fly, / That I feel its painful wound still; / thus I Confess and recognize his power.

Poem in a letter to Francesco Vettori, January 31, 1515

I should not know how otherwise to reply to your last letter about lust with words that seem to me more on target than with this sonnet; from it you will realize to what extent that little thief, Love, has gone in order to bind me with his fetters. Those with which he has bound me are so strong that I am in absolute despair of my liberty and I am unable to conceive of any means of unfettering myself; and even if fate or some other human stratagem should open a path for me to get out of them, perhaps I should not wish to go down it; so do I find these fetters—now sweet, now light, now heavy—and they make such a tangle that I believe I cannot live happily without this kind of life.

Machiavelli to Francesco Vettori, January 31, 1515

The natural prince has less cause and less necessity for irritating his subjects, whence it is reasonable that he should be more beloved. And unless extraordinary vices should cause him to be hated, he will naturally have the affection of his people.

The Prince, II

The Mind

There are three sorts of mind: the one understands things by its own quickness of perception; another understands them when explained by someone else; and the third understands them neither by itself nor by the explanation of others. The first is the best, the second very good, and the third useless.

The Prince, XXII

Miracles

Such was, in fact, the practice observed by sagacious men; which has given rise to the belief in the miracles that are celebrated in religions, however false they may be. For sagacious rulers have given these miracles increased importance, no matter whence or how they originated; and their authority afterwards gave them credence with the people. Rome had many such miracles; and one of the most remarkable was that which occurred when the Roman soldiers sacked the city of Veii. Some of them entered the temple of Juno, and, placing themselves in front of her statue, said to her, "Will you come to Rome?" Some imagined that they observed the statue make a sign of assent, and others pretended to have heard her reply, "Yes." Now these men, being very religious, as reported by Titus Livius, and having entered the temple quietly, they were filled with devotion and reverence, and might really have believed that they had heard a reply to their question, such as perhaps they could have presupposed. But this opinion and belief was favored and magnified by Camillus and the other Roman chiefs.

Discourses on Livy, I. 12

New Ways, New Continents

Although the envious nature of men, so prompt to blame and so slow to praise, makes the discovery and introduction of any new principles and systems as dangerous almost as the exploration of unknown seas and continents, yet, animated by that desire which impels me to do what may prove for the common benefit of all, I have resolved to open a new route, which has not yet been followed by anyone, and may prove difficult and troublesome, but may also bring me some reward in the approbation of those who will kindly appreciate my efforts.

Introduction to Book I of the *Discourses on Livy*

Old Times

Men ever praise the olden time, and find fault with the present, though often without reason. They are such partisans of the past that they extol not only the times which they know only from the accounts of them left by historians, but, having grown old, they also laud all they remember to have seen in their youth. Their opinion is generally erroneous in that respect, and I think the reasons which cause this illusion are various. The first I believe to be the fact that we never know the whole truth about the past, and very frequently writers conceal such events as would reflect disgrace upon their century, whilst they magnify and amplify those that lend luster to it. The majority of authors obey the fortune of conquerors to the degree that, by way of rendering their victories more glorious, they exaggerate not only the valiant deeds of the victor, but also of the vanquished; so that future generations of the countries of both will have cause to wonder at those men and times, and be obliged to praise and admire them to the utmost.

Introduction to Book II of the *Discourses on Livy*

Opportunity

To come now to those who by their courage and virtue, and not by fortune, have risen to the rank of rulers, I will say that the most eminent of such were Moses, Cyrus, Romulus, Theseus, and the like. And although we may not discuss Moses, who was a mere executor of the things ordained by God, yet he merits our admiration, if only for that grace which made him worthy to hold direct communion with the Almighty. But if we consider Cyrus and others who have conquered or founded empires, we shall find them all worthy of admiration; for if we study their acts and particular ordinances, they do not seem very different from those of Moses, although he had so great a teacher. We shall also find in examining their acts and lives, that they had no other favor from fortune but opportunity, which gave them the material which they could mold into whatever form seemed to them best; and without such opportunity the great qualities of their souls would have been wasted, whilst without those great qualities the opportunities would have been in vain.

The Prince, VI

I have heard about the disturbances in Lombardy, and we are all aware of how easy it would be to drag those scoundrels out of that region. For the love of God let us not lose this opportunity and remember that Fortune, our bad counsel, and the worst kinds of captains would have driven not only the king but even the pope to prison; the bad advice of others and this same Fortune have taken him out.

Machiavelli to Francesco Guicciardini, May 17, 1526

Order and Disorder

The general course of changes that occur in states is from a condition of order to one of disorder, and from the latter they pass again to one of order. For as it is not the fate of mundane affairs to remain stationary, so when they have attained their highest state of perfection, beyond which they cannot go, they of necessity decline. And thus again, when they have descended to the lowest, and by their disorders have reached the very depth of debasement, they must of necessity rise again, inasmuch as they cannot go lower. And thus they always decline from good to bad, and from bad they rise again to good. For virtue brings peace, and peace leisure, and leisure begets disorder, and this in turn brings ruin; and in like manner from ruin springs order, from order virtue, and from that glory and good fortune.

History of Florence, V. 1

Passions and Their Remedies

Whoever considers the past and the present will readily observe that all cities and all peoples are and ever have been animated by the same desires and the same passions; so that it is easy, by diligent study of the past, to foresee what is likely to happen in the future in any republic, and to apply those remedies that were used by the ancients, or, not finding any that were employed by them, to devise new ones from the similarity of the events. But as such considerations are neglected or not understood by most of those who read, or, if understood by these, are unknown by those who govern, it follows that the same troubles generally recur in all republics.

Discourses on Livy, I. 39

Wise men say, and not without reason, that whoever wishes to foresee the future must consult the past; for human events ever resemble those of preceding times. This arises from the fact that they are produced by men who have been, and ever will be, animated by the same passions, and thus they must necessarily have the same results. It is true that men are more or less virtuous in one country or another, according to the nature of the education by which their manners and habits of life have been formed.

Discourses on Livy, III. 43

Patriotism

Love of country had more power over the Romans than any other sentiment; and they thought so much more of [Rome's] present dangers, to which the ambition of Manlius exposed them, than of his past services, that they saw no other way of relieving themselves of those dangers than by his death.

Discourses on Livy, III. 8

Love of country should make a good citizen forget private wrongs.

Discourses on Livy, III. 47

Peace

Among other praises that have been accorded by different writers to Philopoemen, prince of the Achaians, was that in time of peace he devoted himself constantly to the study of the art of war. A wise prince then should act in like manner, and should never be idle in times of peace, but should industriously lay up stores of which to avail himself in times of adversity; so that, when Fortune abandons him, he may be prepared to resist her blows.

The Prince, XIV

Hence kings, if they wish to live securely, make up their infantry of men who, when it is time to make war, gladly for love of them go into it, and when peace comes, more gladly return home—which will always happen when a king selects men who know how to live by some other profession than this. So he must see to it that when peace comes his chief men return to rule their peoples, his gentlemen to the management of their property, and the infantry to their individual occupations. Each one of these will gladly make war in order to have peace, and will not seek to disturb the peace in order to have war.

The Art of War, I

Prudence

Thus in all these cases the Romans did what all wise princes ought to do; namely, not only to look to all present troubles, but also to those of the future, against which they provided with the utmost prudence. For it is by foreseeing difficulties from afar that they are easily provided against; while, if we await their near approach, remedies are no longer in time, for the malady has become incurable. It happens in such cases, as the doctors say of consumption, that in the early stages it is easy to cure, but difficult to recognize; whilst in the course of time, the disease not having been recognized and cured in the beginning, it becomes easy to know, but difficult to cure.

The Prince, III

Nor is it to be supposed that a state can ever adopt a course that is entirely safe; on the contrary, a prince must make up his mind to take risks in all manner of doubts and uncertainties; for such is the order of things that one inconvenience cannot be avoided except at the risk of being exposed to another. And it is the province of prudence to discriminate among these inconveniences, and to accept the least evil for good.

The Prince, XXI

It was not wisdom always to desire the final victory, and it was not prudent to drive men to desperation, for he who had no hope of good also had no fear of evil.

History of Florence, II. 14

Punishment

The Romans . . . were not only less ungrateful than other republics, but were also more lenient and considerate in the punishment of the generals of their armies. For if their misconduct was intentional, they punished them humanely; and if it was caused by ignorance, they not only did not punish them, but rewarded and honored them nevertheless. This mode of proceeding had been well considered by them; for they judged that it was of the greatest importance for those who commanded their armies to have their minds entirely free and unembarrassed by any anxiety other than how best to perform their duty, and therefore they did not wish to add fresh difficulties and dangers to a task in itself so difficult and perilous, being convinced that, if this were done, it would prevent any general from operating virtuously.

Discourses on Livy, I. 31

Rebirth (Renaissance)

By Italy's condition I do not wish you to be dismayed or terrified, because this land seems born to resurrect dead things, as she has in poetry, in painting, and in sculpture.

The Art of War, VII

It needed, then, this blow from without to revive the observance of all the institutions of the state, and to show to the Roman people not only the necessity of maintaining religion and justice, but also of honoring their good citizens. . . .

Discourses on Livy, III. 1

Such a return to first principles in a republic is sometimes caused by the simple virtues of one man, without depending upon any law that incites him to the infliction of extreme punishments; and yet his good example has such an influence that good men strive to imitate him, and the wicked are ashamed to lead a life so contrary to his example.

Discourses on Livy, III. 1

Religion and the Reform of Religions

Princes and republics that wish to maintain themselves free from corruption must, above all things, preserve the purity of religious observances and treat them with proper reverence; for there is no greater indication of the ruin of a country than to see its religion contemned.

Discourses on Livy, I. 12

If the Christian religion had from the beginning been maintained according to the principles of its founder, the Christian states and republics would have been much more united and happy than they are. Nor can there be a greater proof of its decadence than to witness the fact that the nearer people are to the Church of Rome, which is the head of our religion, the less religious they are. And whoever examines the principles upon which that religion is founded, and sees how widely different from those principles its present practices and applications are, will judge that her ruin or chastisement is near at hand. But as there are some of the opinion that the well-being of Italian affairs depends upon the Church of Rome, I will present such arguments against that opinion as occur to me; two of which are most important, and cannot according to my judgment be controverted. The first is that the evil example of the court of Rome has destroyed all piety and religion in Italy, which brings in its train infinite improprieties and disorders; for as we may presuppose all good where religion prevails, so where it is wanting we have the right to suppose the very opposite.

Discourses on Livy, I. 12

Reflecting now as to whence it came that in ancient times the people were more devoted to liberty than in the present, I believe that it resulted from this, that men were stronger in those days, which I believe to be attributable to a difference of education, founded upon the difference between their religion and ours. For, as our religion teaches us the truth and the true way of life, it causes us to attach less value to the honors and possessions of this world; whilst the Pagans, esteeming those things as the highest good, were more energetic and ferocious in their actions. We may observe this also in most of their institutions, beginning with the magnificence of their sacrifices as compared with the humility of ours, which are gentle solemnities rather than magnificent ones, and have nothing of energy or ferocity in them, whilst in theirs there was no lack of pomp and show. . . . Besides this, the Pagan religion deified only men who had achieved great glory, such as commanders of armies and chiefs of republics, whilst ours glorifies more the humble and contemplative men than the men of action. Our religion, moreover, places the supreme happiness in humility, lowliness, and a contempt for worldly objects, whilst the other, on the contrary, places the supreme good in grandeur of soul, strength of body, and all such other qualities as render men formidable; and if our religion claims of us fortitude of soul, it is more to enable us to suffer than to achieve great deeds. These principles seem to me to have made men feeble, and caused them to become an easy prey to evil-minded men, who can control them more securely, seeing that the great body of men, for the sake of gaining Paradise, are more disposed to endure injuries than to avenge them. And although it would seem that the world has become effeminate and Heaven disarmed, yet this arises unquestionably from the baseness of men, who have interpreted our religion according to the promptings of indolence rather than those of virtue. For if we were to reflect that our religion permits us to exalt and defend our country, we should see that according to it we ought also to love and honor our country, and prepare ourselves so as to be capable of defending her.

Discourses on Livy, II. 2

Now with regard to religions we shall see that revivals are equally necessary, and the best proof of this is furnished by our own [religion], which would have been entirely lost had it not been brought back to its pristine principles and purity by Saint Francis and Saint Dominic; for by their voluntary poverty and the example of the life of Christ, they revived the sentiment of religion in the hearts of men, where it had become almost extinct. The new orders which they established were so austere and powerful that they became the means of saving religion from being destroyed by the licentiousness of the prelates and heads of the Church. They continued themselves to live in poverty; and by means of confessions and preachings they obtained so much influence with the people that they were able to make them understand that it was wicked even to speak ill of wicked rulers, and that it was proper to render them obedience and to leave the punishment of their errors to God. And thus these wicked rulers do as much evil as they please, because they do not fear a punishment that they neither see nor believe in. This revival of religion then by Saint Francis and Saint Dominic has preserved it and maintains it to this day.

Discourses on Livy, III. 1

As all religion and the fear of God is dead in all their [the Florentines'] hearts, they value an oath or a pledge only so far as it may be useful to themselves. Men employ them, not for the purpose of observing them, but solely as a means to enable them more easily to deceive; and just as this deceit succeeds more easily and securely, so much greater is the praise and glory derived from it; and therefore are dangerous men praised as being ingenious, and good men derided for being dupes.

History of Florence, III. 5

It remains now only to speak of ecclesiastical principalities, in the attainment of which all difficulties occur beforehand. To achieve them requires either virtue or good fortune; but they are maintained without either the one or the other, for they are sustained by the ancient ordinances of religion, which are so powerful and of such quality that they maintain their princes in their position, no matter what their conduct or mode of life may be. These are the only princes who have states without the necessity of defending them, and subjects without governing them; and their states, though undefended, are not taken from them, whilst their subjects are indifferent to the fact that they are not governed, and have no thought of the possibility of alienating themselves from their princes.

The Prince, XI

Saints

The war [between Florence and the Pope] lasted three years, and was terminated only by the death of the Pope; it had been conducted with so much virtue, and gave such general satisfaction, that the Eight were continued in office from year to year. They were called "Saints" although they had paid but little regard to the censure [of the Pope], despoiled the churches of their goods, and forced the clergy to perform the holy offices. Thus did those citizens at that time love their country more than their souls.

History of Florence, III. 7

Science

Among other essentials for a general is a knowledge of localities and countries, for without . . . [that] knowledge he cannot successfully undertake any enterprise. And although the acquirement of every science demands practice, yet to possess this one perfectly requires more than any other. This practice, or rather this special knowledge of localities, is better acquired by the chase than in any other exercise. And therefore the ancient writers say of those heroes who in their day ruled the world, that they were nursed in the forests and brought up to the chase. For, besides this special knowledge of localities, the chase also teaches many other things that are necessary in war.

Discourses on Livy, III. 39

And because Dante says that no one produces science unless he retains what he has understood, I have jotted down what I have profited from [in conversation with the ancients] and composed a short study, *The Prince*, in which I delve as deeply as I can into ideas related to this topic, discussing the definition of a princedom, the categories of

princedoms, how they are acquired, how they are retained, and why they are lost.

Machiavelli to Francesco Vettori, December 10, 1513

Severity

But he who has to command subjects, such as Tacitus
speaks of, should employ severity rather than gentleness,
lest these subjects should become insolent and trample his
authority under foot, because of too great indulgence.
This severity, however, should be employed with modera-
tion, so as to avoid making oneself odious, for no prince is
ever benefited by making himself hated.

Discourses on Livy, III. 19

Sin

FATHER TIMOTEO: I want to go back to what I said
earlier. You must, as to conscience, accept this
rule: where a good is certain and an evil uncertain, you ought never to give up the good for
fear of the evil. Here you have a certain good,
that you will become pregnant, gain a soul for
the Lord. The uncertain evil is that the man
who lies with you after you take the medicine
may die; yet there are also those who don't die.
But because the matter is uncertain, it's not a
good thing for Messer Nicia to run this risk. As
to the action, the notion that it's a sin is a fairy
story, because the will is what sins, not the body,

and what would make it a sin would be your husband's displeasure, but you will be pleasing him; or if you should take pleasure in it, but you will get displeasure from it. Besides this, one's purpose must be considered in everything; your purpose is to fill a seat in paradise, to please your husband. The Bible says that Lot's daughters, thinking that they alone were left in the world, slept with their father, and because their intention was good, they did not sin.

LUCREZIA: What are you persuading me to?

SOSTRATA [MOTHER OF LUCREZIA]: Be persuaded, my child. Don't you see that a woman who doesn't have any children doesn't have any home? When her husband dies, she is left wretched, deserted by everybody.

FRATE: I swear to you, Madam, by this consecrated breast, that submitting to your husband in this affair is as much a matter of conscience as eating meat on Wednesday, which is a sin that goes away with holy water.

Mandragola, Act 3, Scene 11

Let not princes complain of the faults committed by the people subjected to their authority, for they result entirely from their own negligence or bad example. In examining the people who in our day have been given to brigandage and other vices of that kind, we see that these arise entirely from the faults of their rulers, who were guilty of similar abuses.

Discourses on Livy, III. 29

Stupidity

Everybody knows how happy he is
who is born stupid and believes everything.
Ambition does not disturb him,
fear does not upset him
those two that ever are the seeds
of pain and discontent.
This judge of yours,
in hope to have children,
will believe that an ass can fly;
and everything else he has wholly forgotten,
and only on this has set his desire.

    Mandragola (after the second act)

Suspicion

But when [citizens] fail to reward, or rather when they offend, not from avarice, but from suspicion and fear, then the people or the prince have some excuse for their ingratitude. We read of many instances of this kind; for the general who by his valor has conquered a state for his master, and won great glory for himself by his victory over the enemy, and has loaded his soldiers with rich booty, acquires necessarily with his own soldiers, as well as with those of the enemy and with the subjects of the prince, so high a reputation, that his very victory may become distasteful, and a cause for apprehension to his prince. For as the nature of men is ambitious as well as suspicious, and puts no limits to one's good fortune, it is not impossible that the suspicion that may suddenly be aroused in the mind of the prince by the victory of the general may have been aggravated by some haughty expressions or insolent acts on his part; so that the prince will naturally be made to think of securing himself against the ambition of his general. And to do this, the means that suggest themselves to him are either to have the general killed, or to deprive him of that reputation which he has acquired with the prince's army and the people, by using every means to prove that the general's victory was not due to his skill and courage, but to chance and the cowardice of the enemy, or to the sagacity of the other captains who were with him in that action.

Discourses on Livy, I. 29

Virtue

When we see, on the other hand, the wonderful examples which the history of ancient kingdoms and republics presents to us, the prodigies of virtue and of wisdom displayed by the kings, commanders, citizens, and legislators who have sacrificed themselves for their country—when, as I say, we see all these, more admired than imitated (for too often not the least trace of such ancient virtue remains), we cannot but be at the same time as much surprised as afflicted.

Proem to Book I of the *Discourses on Livy*

As to the idleness which the fertility of a country tends to encourage, the laws should compel men to labor if the sterility of the soil does not do so; as [is shown by the example of] those skillful and sagacious legislators who have inhabited very agreeable and fertile countries, such as are apt to make men idle and unfit for virtuous exercises. These, by way of an offset to the pleasures and softness of the climate, imposed upon their soldiers the rigors of a strict discipline and severe exercises, so that they became better warriors than what nature produces in the harshest climates and most sterile countries.

Discourses on Livy, I. 1

Kingdoms which depend entirely upon the virtue of one man endure but for a brief time, for his virtue passes away with his life, and it rarely happens that it is renewed in his successor.

Discourses on Livy, I. 11

Whence we may note that a successor of less virtue than the first king may yet be able to maintain a state established by the virtue of his predecessor, and may enjoy the fruits of his labors. But if it should happen that his life be a long one, or that his successor should not have the same virtue as the first king, then the government will necessarily go to ruin. And so, on the contrary, if one king succeeds another of equally great virtue, then it will often be seen that they achieve extraordinary greatness for their state, and that their fame will rise to the very heavens.

Discourses on Livy, I. 19

Two continuous successions of able and virtuous princes will achieve great results; and as well-constituted republics have, in the nature of things, a succession of virtuous rulers, their acquisitions and extension will consequently be very great.

Discourses on Livy, I. 20

For if in a republic a noble youth is seen to rise, who is possessed of some extraordinary virtue, the eyes of all citizens quickly turn to him, and all hasten to show him honor, regardless of consequences; so that, if he is in any way ambitious, the gifts of nature and the favor of his fellow-citizens will soon raise him to such a height that, when the citizens become sensible of the error they have committed, they have no longer the requisite means for checking him, and their efforts to employ such as they have will only accelerate his advance to power.

Discourses on Livy, I. 33

We see from the course of history that the Roman Republic, after the plebeians became entitled to the consulate, admitted all its citizens to this dignity without distinction of age or birth. In truth, age was never a necessary qualification for public office; virtue was the only consideration, whether found in young or old men.

Discourses on Livy, I. 60

All the virtues that first found a place in Assyria were thence transferred to Media, and afterwards passed to Persia, and from there they came into Italy and to Rome. And if after the fall of the Roman Empire none other sprang up that endured for any length of time, where the aggregate virtues of the world were kept together, we nevertheless see them scattered among many nations, as, for instance, in the kingdom of France, the Turkish empire, or that of the Sultan of Egypt, and nowadays the people of Germany, and before them those famous Saracens who achieved such great things and conquered so great a part of the world after having destroyed the Roman Empire of the East. The different peoples of these several countries, then, after the fall of the Roman Empire have possessed and possess still in great part that virtue which is so much lamented and so sincerely praised.

Introduction to Book II of the *Discourses on Livy*

The Romans found everywhere a league of republics, well armed for the most obstinate defense of their liberties, showing that it required the rare ability and extreme virtue of the Romans to subjugate them.

Discourses on Livy, II. 2

The Romans acted like a good husbandman, who for the purpose of strengthening a tree and making it produce more fruit and mature in better form, cuts off the first shoots it puts out, so that by retaining its virtue in the trunk the tree may afterwards put forth more abundant branches and fruit.

Discourses on Livy, II. 3

The Romans then were victorious in these three most perilous wars; and it required all their virtue to enable them to be successful; for we see that when their armies afterwards lost their ancient virtue, the Roman Empire was destroyed by . . . hordes, such as the Goths, Vandals, and others, who made themselves masters of the whole Western Empire.

Discourses on Livy, II. 8

Titus Livius is also of the same opinion; and represents the two armies to have been in all respects equal as regards numbers, discipline, virtue, and obstinacy, the only difference having been in the commanders, those of the Roman army having displayed more virtue than those of the Latins.

Discourses on Livy, II. 16

If [military] men nowadays give less proof of virtue than formerly, it is not chargeable to the introduction of artillery, but to bad discipline and the feebleness of the armies, which being in the aggregate deficient in virtue, cannot show it in their individual parts. . . . I will conclude this chapter, therefore, by saying that artillery is useful in an army when the soldiers are animated by the same virtue as that of the ancient Romans, but without that it is perfectly inefficient, especially against virtuous troops.

Discourses on Livy, II. 17

[For] whilst the Romans built no fortresses, the Spartans not only refrained from doing so, but even did not permit their city to be protected by walls, for they wanted to rely solely upon the virtue of their men for their defense, and upon no other means.

Discourses on Livy, II. 24

If so virtuous a general as Hannibal, with his army intact, sought peace rather than risk a battle, seeing that his defeat would expose his country to enslavement, what should less virtuous and less experienced generals do?

Discourses on Livy, II. 27

Republics and princes that are really powerful do not purchase alliances by money, but by their virtue and the reputation of their armies. . . . In consequence of this we daily see remarkable losses, and still more wonderful conquests; for where men have but little virtue, Fortune more signally displays her power.

Discourses on Livy, II. 30

So that on the whole we shall find many instances of battles won solely by the virtue of the soldiers, and many others where the same result was achieved by the virtue of the general alone. So that we may conclude that they are equally dependent one upon the other.

Discourses on Livy, III. 13

In times of difficulty men of virtue are sought after, but in easy times it is not men of virtue but such as have riches and powerful relations that are most in favor.

Discourses on Livy, III. 16

It matters little, therefore, to any general by which of these two systems he proceeds, provided he be a man of sufficient virtue to have made a great reputation for himself. For when this is as great as was the case with Hannibal and Scipio, it cancels all the errors which a general may commit, either by an excess of gentleness or by too great severity.

Discourses on Livy, III. 21

I say then that a new prince in an entirely new principality will experience more or less difficulty in maintaining himself, according as he has more or less virtue. And as such an event as to become a prince from a mere private individual presupposes either great virtue or rare good fortune, it would seem that one or the other of these two causes ought in a measure to mitigate many of these difficulties.

The Prince, VI

To come now to those who by their virtue, and not by fortune, have risen to the rank of rulers, I will say that the most eminent of such were Moses, Cyrus, Romulus, Theseus, and the like.

The Prince, VI

But such were the Duke's ferocity and virtue, and so well did he know how men are either won or destroyed, and so solid were the foundations which he had in so brief a time laid for his greatness, that if he had not had these two armies upon his back, and had he been in health, he would have sustained himself against all difficulties.

The Prince, VII

And yet we cannot call it virtue to massacre one's fellow-citizens, to betray one's friends, and to be devoid of good faith, mercy, and religion; such means may enable a man to achieve empire, but not glory. Still, if we consider the virtue of Agathocles in encountering and overcoming dangers, and his invincible courage in supporting and mastering adversity, we shall find no reason why he should be regarded inferior to any of the most celebrated captains. But with all this, his outrageous cruelty and inhumanity, together with his infinite crimes, will not permit him to be classed with the most celebrated men. We cannot therefore ascribe to either virtue or fortune the achievements of Agathocles, which he accomplished without either the one or the other.

> *The Prince*, VIII

Nor need the prince care about incurring censure for such vices, without which the preservation of his state may be difficult. For, all things considered, it will be found that some things that seem like virtue will lead you to ruin if you follow them; whilst others, that apparently are vices, will, if followed, result in your safety and well-being.

> *The Prince*, XV

Septimius Severus possessed such virtue that, although he imposed heavy burdens upon the people, yet, by keeping the soldiers his friends, he was enabled to reign undisturbed and happily; for his virtue caused him to be so much admired by the soldiers and the people that the latter were in a manner stupefied and astounded by it, whilst it made the former respectful and satisfied.

> *The Prince*, XIX

That defense alone is effectual, sure, and durable which depends upon yourself and your own virtue.

> *The Prince*, XXIV

NICEA: In this town [Florence] there's nothing but a bunch of shit-asses; nobody esteems virtue.

Mandragola, Act 2, Scene 3

It is better to lose everything virtuously than to lose a part ignominiously, and a part cannot be lost without shaking the whole.

Machiavelli to Francesco Vettori, December 10, 1514

Women

SOSTRATA: Listen to him, my dear. Don't you see that a woman without children is a woman without a home? If her husband dies, she is left like an animal, abandoned by everybody.

Mandragola, Act 3, Scene 11

MESSER NICIA: And I'm going to give them the key of the room on the ground floor in the loggia, so they can come there when it's convenient, because they don't have women at home and live like beasts.

Mandragola, Act 5, Scene 6

[W]e see that women have been the cause of great dissensions and much ruin to states, and have caused great damage to those who govern them.

Discourses on Livy, III. 26

Words

The Signori therefore deemed it well to call together a number of citizens who with good words should quiet the excited anger of the populace.

History of Florence, IV. 7

For a licentious and mutinous people may easily be brought back to good conduct by the words of a good man, but an evil-minded prince is not amenable to such influences, and therefore there is no other remedy against him but cold steel.

Discourses on Livy, I. 58

V
Political Life

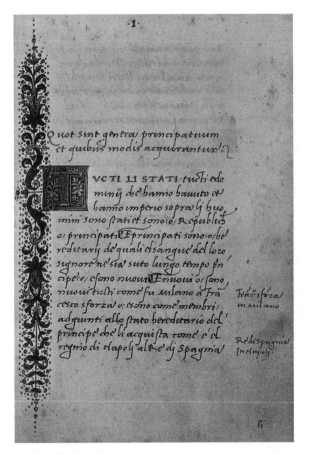

Figure 5. Illuminated page from *The Prince*. De Agostini Picture Library/Bridgeman Images.

Accusations and Calumnies

[The story of the Roman consul Manlius Capitolinus] shows how much detested calumnies are in republics, as well as under any other government, and that no means should be left unemployed to repress them in time. Now, there is no more effectual way for putting an end to calumnies than to introduce the system of legal accusations, which will be as beneficial to republics as calumnies are injurious. On the other hand, there is this difference, namely, that calumnies require neither witnesses, nor confrontings, nor any particulars to prove them, so that every citizen may be calumniated by another, whilst accusations cannot be lodged against anyone without being accompanied by positive proofs and circumstances that demonstrate the truth of the accusation. Accusations must be brought before the magistrates, or the people, or the councils, whilst calumnies are spread in public places as well as in private dwellings; and calumnies are more practiced where the system of accusations does not exist, and in cities whose constitution does not admit of them. The lawgiver of a republic, therefore, should give every citizen the right to accuse another citizen without fear or suspicion; and this being done, and properly carried out, he should severely punish calumniators, who would have no right to complain of such punishment, it being open to them to bring charges against those whom they had in private calumniated. And where this system is not well established there will always be great disorders, for calumnies irritate but do not chastise men; and those who have been thus irritated will think of strengthening themselves, hating more than fearing the slanders spread against them.

Discourses on Livy, I. 8

Agrarian Law

Such was the beginning and the end of the agrarian law. And as I have demonstrated elsewhere that the differences between the Senate and the people had been instrumental in preserving liberty in Rome, because they had given rise to the enactment of laws favorable to liberty, therefore the results of this agrarian law may seem in contradiction with that previous conclusion. But I do not on that account change my opinion, for the ambition of the nobles is so great, that, if it is not repressed by various ways and means in any city, it will quickly bring that city to ruin. So that if the contentions about the agrarian law needed three hundred years to bring Rome to a state of servitude, she would have been brought there much quicker if the people, by these laws and other means, had not for so great a length of time kept the ambition of the nobles in check.

Discourses on Livy, I. 37

Ambition

But when they began to make sovereignity hereditary and non-elective the children quickly degenerated from their fathers and, so far from trying to equal their virtues, they

considered that a prince had nothing else to do than to
excel all the rest in luxury, indulgence, and every other
variety of pleasure. The prince consequently soon drew
upon himself the general hatred. An object of hatred, he
naturally felt fear; fear in turn dictated him precautions
and wrongs, and thus tyranny quickly developed.

Discourses on Livy, I. 2

Every free state ought to afford the people the opportunity
of giving vent, so to say, to their ambition; and above all
those republics which on important occasions have to
avail themselves of this very people.

Discourses on Livy, I. 4

It was a saying of ancient writers, that men afflict themselves in evil, and become weary of the good, and that
both these dispositions produce the same effects. For
when men are no longer obliged to fight from necessity,
they fight from ambition, which passion is so powerful in
the hearts of men that it never leaves them, no matter to
what height they may rise. The reason of this is that nature
has created men so that they desire everything, but are
unable to attain it; desire being thus always greater than
the faculty of acquiring, discontent with what they have
and dissatisfaction with themselves result from it.

Discourses on Livy, I. 37

The Roman people were not content with having secured
themselves against the nobles by the creation of the Tribunes, to which they had been driven by necessity. Having

obtained this, they soon began to fight from ambition, and wanted to divide with the nobles their honors and possessions, being those things which men value most.

Discourses on Livy, I. 37

For although it is the nature of the nobility to desire to dominate, yet those who have no share in such domination are the enemies of the tyrant, who can never win them all over to him, because of their extreme ambition and avarice, which are so great that the tyrant can never have riches and honors enough to bestow to satisfy them all.

Discourses on Livy, I. 40

The object of those who make war, either from choice or ambition, is to conquer and to maintain their conquests, and to do this in such a manner as to enrich themselves and not to impoverish the conquered country.

Discourses on Livy, II. 6

But the ambition of men is such that, to gratify a present desire, they think not of the evils which will in a short time result from it. Nor will they be influenced by the examples of antiquity, which I have cited upon this and other points; for if they were, they would see that the more liberality they show to their neighbors, and the less desire they manifest to rob them of their territory, the more readily will those neighbors throw themselves into their arms.

Discourses on Livy, II. 20

You must expect therefore either to hold this city by violence, for which the citadels and their garrisons and foreign allies are generally insufficient, or you must be content with the authority which we have conferred upon you, and to this we would advise you, reminding you that that dominion only is desirable which is borne willingly. Do not attempt then, under the promptings of your ambition to place yourself where you can neither remain nor rise higher, and whence you would of necessity fall, with equal injury to yourself and ourselves!

History of Florence, II. 34

The ambitious citizens of a republic seek in the first instance to make themselves sure against the attacks not only of individuals, but even of the magistrates. To enable them to do this, they seek to gain friends, either by apparently honest ways, or by assisting men with money, or by defending them against the powerful; and as this seems virtuous, almost everybody is readily deceived by it, and therefore no one opposes it, until the ambitious individual has, without hindrance, grown so powerful that private citizens fear him and the magistrates treat him with consideration. And when he has risen to that point, no one at the beginning having interfered with his greatness, it becomes in the end most dangerous to attempt to put him down, for the reasons I have given above when speaking of the danger of trying to abate an evil that has already attained a considerable growth in a city; so that in the end the matter is reduced to this, that you must endeavor to destroy the evil at the risk of sudden ruin, or, by allowing it to go on, submit to manifest servitude, unless the death of the individual or some other accident intervenes to rid the state of him.

Discourses on Livy, I. 46

You will see how Ambition results in two kinds of action: one / party robs and the other weeps for its wealth ravaged and scattered. / Let him turn his eyes here who wishes to behold the sorrows of others, and let him consider if ever before now the sun has / looked upon such savagery. / A man is weeping for his father dead and a woman for her husband; another man, beaten and naked, you see driven in sadness from his own dwelling. / Oh how many times, when the father has held his son tight in his arms, a single thrust has pierced the breasts of them both! / Another is abandoning his ancestral home, as he accuses cruel and ungrateful gods, with his brood overcome with sorrow. / Oh, strange events such as never have happened before in the / world! Every day many children are born through sword cuts / in the womb. / To her daughter, overcome with sorrow, the mother says: "For / what an unhappy marriage, for what a cruel husband have I / kept you!" / Foul with blood are the ditches and streams, full of heads, of / legs, of arms, and other members gashed and severed. / Birds of prey, wild beasts, dogs are now their family tombs / Oh / tombs repulsive, horrible and unnatural! / Always their faces are gloomy and dark, like those of a man / terrified and numbed by new injuries or sudden fears. / Wherever you turn your eyes, you see the earth wet with tears / and blood, and the air full of screams, of sobs, and sighs. / If from others a man will deign to learn the ways of Ambition, / the sad example of these wretches can teach him.

Tercets on Ambition, lines 127–161

The Aristocracy

Aristocracy degenerates into oligarchy.

Discourses on Livy, I. 2

All principalities of which we have any accounts have been governed in one of two ways; viz., either by one absolute prince, to whom all others are as slaves, some of whom, as ministers, by his grace and consent, aid him in the government of his realm; or else by a prince and nobles, who hold that rank, not by the grace of their sovereign, but by the antiquity of their lineage. Such nobles have estates and subjects of their own, who recognize them as their liege lords, and have a natural affection for them.

The Prince, IV

The king of France is placed in the midst of a large number of ancient nobles, who are recognized and acknowledged by their subjects as their lords, and are held in great affection by them. They have their rank and prerogatives, of which the king cannot deprive them without danger to himself.

The Prince, IV

The worst that a prince may expect of a people who are unfriendly to him is that they will desert him; but the hostile nobles he has to fear, not only lest they abandon him, but also because they will turn against him. For they, being more farsighted and astute, always save themselves in advance, and seek to secure the favor of him whom they hope may be successful. The prince also is obliged always to live with the same people; but he can do very well without the same nobles, whom he can make and unmake at will any day, and bestow upon them or deprive them of their rank whenever it pleases him.

The Prince, IX

The nobles seemed to have laid aside all their haughtiness and assumed popular manners, which made them supportable even to the lowest of the citizens. The nobility played this role so long as the Tarquins lived, without their motive being divined; for they feared the Tarquins, and also lest the ill-treated people might side with them. Their party therefore assumed all possible gentleness in their manners toward the people. But so soon as the death of the Tarquins had relieved them of their apprehensions, they began to vent upon the people all the venom they had so long retained within their breasts, and lost no opportunity to outrage them in every possible way; which is one of the proofs of the argument we have advanced, that men act right only upon compulsion; but from the moment that they have the option and liberty to commit wrong with impunity, then they never fail to carry confusion and disorder everywhere.

Discourses on Livy, I. 3

From this resulted also that the victories of the people over the nobles made Rome more virtuous, because the plebeians, in sharing with the nobles the civil, military, and judicial administration, became inspired with the same virtues that distinguished the nobles; so that Rome grew at the same time in power and in virtue. But in Florence, when the people were victors, the nobles, excluded from the magistracies, found it necessary not only to be, but also to appear, similar to the people, in their conduct, in their opinions, and in their habits of life. Thence arose the changes in their armorial bearings, and the mutations in the titles of families, to which the nobles resorted for the sake of appearing to belong to the people. So that the valor in arms and magnanimity of spirit which had existed among the nobles became extinguished, and could not be kindled among the people, who had never possessed it.

History of Florence, Preface to Book III

Do not be alarmed by the antiquity of the blood for the shedding of which they reproach us; for all men, having sprung from the same beginning, have equally ancient blood, and are by nature all alike. Strip yourselves naked, and you will see that you are the same; dress yourselves in their garments and them in yours, and doubtless you will appear noble and they ignoble; for it is only poverty and riches that make men unequal.

History of Florence, III. 14

The Army and Soldiers

Mercenary and auxiliary troops are both useless and dangerous; and if anyone attempts to found his state upon mercenaries, it will never be stable or secure; for they are disunited, ambitious, and without discipline, faithless, ... braggarts among friends but among enemies cowards, and have neither fear of God nor good faith with men; so that the ruin of the prince who depends on them will be deferred only just so long as attack is delayed; and in peace he will be despoiled by his mercenaries, and in war by his enemies. The reason of all this is that mercenary troops are not influenced by affection, or by any other consideration except their small stipend, which is not enough to make them willing to die for you. They are ready to serve you as soldiers so long as you are at peace; but when war comes, they will either run away or march off.

The Prince, XIII

No prince can ever be secure that has not an army of his own; and he will become wholly dependent upon fortune if in times of adversity he lacks the valor to defend himself. And wise men have ever held the opinion that nothing is more weak and unstable than the reputation of power when not founded upon forces of the prince's own; by which I mean armies composed of his own subjects or citizens, or of his own creation; all others are either mercenaries or auxiliaries [troops provided by an ally].

The Prince, XIII

Mercenary troops have nothing to make them fight but the small stipend they receive, which is not and cannot be sufficient to make them loyal, or so devoted as to be willing to die for you. For armies that have no such affection toward him for whom they fight as to make them his partisans, will never have bravery enough to resist an enemy who has the least courage. And as this love and devotion can only be found in your own subjects, it is necessary for the purpose of holding a government, or to maintain a republic or kingdom, to have your army composed of your own subjects, as will be seen to have been done by all those whose armies have achieved great successes.

Discourses on Livy, I. 43

In Italy, then, to know how to manage an army already formed is not enough; a general must first know how to form it and then know how to command it. Yet for this there must be princes who, having much territory and many subjects, have opportunity to do so. Among these I cannot be—I who have never commanded and can by no possibility command other than foreign armies and men obligated to others and not to myself. Whether among such men I could introduce any of these things that I have discussed today, I leave to your judgment. When can I make one of the soldiers that serve today wear more armor than is usual, and besides armor, carry food for two or three days, and a shovel? When can I make him dig or keep him every day many hours under arms in practice maneuvers, so that later I can make use of him in real ones? When will they abstain from gaming, from whoring, from cursing, from the outrages they daily commit? When can they be brought back to such discipline and such obedience and respect that a tree full of apples can stand in the middle of the camp and be left untouched, as we read many times happened in ancient armies? What can I promise them to make them respect me with love or fear if after the war is finished, they no longer will have any connection with me? What can I do to make them modest, who are born and brought up without modesty? Why should they respect me when they do not know me? By what God or by what saints can I have them take oath? By those they worship or those they blaspheme? What one they worship I do not know, but I know well that they blaspheme them all. How can I believe they will observe their promises to those for whom every hour they show contempt? How can those who feel contempt for God respect men? What sort of good form, then, can be stamped upon this matter?

The Art of War, VII

Artillery

Considering the many open field fights, or pitched battles as they are called in our day, that were fought by the Romans at various times, I have reflected upon the opinion so universally entertained, that, if artillery had existed in ancient times, the Romans would not have been allowed so easily to conquer provinces and make other peoples tributary to themselves; nor would they in any way have been able to extend their dominions so largely. It is further said, that the use of these fire-arms prevents men from displaying the same personal valor as they could in ancient times; that it is more difficult to join battle than formerly, and that the same organization and discipline of armies cannot be preserved; and that henceforth the battles will be fought mainly by artillery. I deem it, therefore, not from our purpose to examine whether these opinions are correct, and in how far the introduction of artillery has increased or diminished the strength of armies, and whether it gives or takes away from good commanders the opportunity of acting valiantly. I shall begin by examining the first proposition, that the Romans never could have carried their conquests so far if artillery had been in use in their time. To this I reply, that wars are either defensive or aggressive, and thus we must inquire first whether artillery be most useful for attack or for defense. Whatever may be said on either side of the question, I believe that it is beyond comparison more damaging to him who has to defend himself than to him who attacks. . . . Now, as to the second proposition, that, since the introduction of artillery men cannot display the same personal bravery as anciently, I maintain that, where men have to present themselves to the fire in small and scattered numbers, they are exposed to greater danger than when in ancient times they had to escalade a place, or make similar assaults, in which they had to act, not in a compact body, but singly and one after the other. It is also true that the lives of the commanders and principal officers of the armies are more exposed now than formerly; for as they can be reached everywhere by the artillery, it is of no use for them to place themselves in the rear ranks, protected by their best men. Nevertheless, we see that these dangers rarely cause any extraordinary losses; for places that are well supplied with artillery are not taken by escalade, nor are they attempted to be taken by feeble assaults, but are regularly besieged, as was done in ancient days. And even with such places as can be taken by assault, the danger is not much greater now than then; for even in those days the ancients did not lack means of defending their places by throwing projectiles upon the enemy, which, although not so noisy as cannon, yet were equally effective in the killing of men. As to the other proposition advanced, that there are nowadays no more hand-to-hand fights, and that hereafter war will be made altogether with artillery, I maintain that this opinion is wholly erroneous, and will be so regarded by all those generals who desire to manage their armies in the manner of the ancients. For whoever wishes to form a good army must, by real or sham fights, train his troops to attack the enemy sword in hand, and to seize hold of him bodily; and he must rely more upon infantry than upon cavalry, for reasons which I will explain further on. And by thus relying upon the infantry, and upon the above-indicated mode of training them, artillery will prove entirely useless. For the infantry, in engaging the enemy hand to hand, can more easily escape the effects of the artillery than it could in ancient times the rush of the elephants and the scythe chariots, and other now obsolete means of attack which the Roman infantry had to encounter, and against which they knew how to defend themselves, probably have found also the means of escaping the

effects of the artillery, as the time during which its fire is
most damaging is so much less than that during which the
elephants and the scythe chariots were dangerous. . . . I
will conclude this chapter, therefore, by saying that artillery is useful in an army when the soldiers are animated
by the same valor as that of the ancient Romans, but without that it is perfectly inefficient, especially against courageous troops.

Discourses on Livy, II. 17

Authority

The authority which is violently usurped, and not that
which is conferred by the free suffrages of the people, is
hurtful to republics. . . . And therefore, when we said that
an authority conferred by the free suffrages of the people
never harmed a republic, we presupposed that the people,
in giving that power, would limit it, as well as the time
during which it was to be exercised.

Discourses on Livy, I. 35

Cavalry

It can be clearly demonstrated by many arguments and
facts, that in all their military operations the Romans valued foot soldiers more than cavalry, and that they based
all their plans upon the former. This is proved by many
instances, one of the most striking of which occurred at
the battle with the Latins near the Lake Regillus; when the
Roman army had already begun to give way, they made

their cavalry dismount to assist the infantry, and, thus supported, they renewed the fight and carried off the victory. This shows clearly that the Romans relied more upon the same men when on foot than on horseback. They employed the same expedient in several other combats, and found it always of greatest value in moments of danger. . . . For a man on foot can go into many places where he could not penetrate on horseback; infantry can be made to preserve their ranks, and can be taught to reform them when broken; whilst it is difficult to make horses keep their ranks, and impossible to reform them when once broken. Besides this we find amongst horses (the same as amongst men) some that lack spirit and some that have too much. And it often happens that a spirited horse is ridden by a coward, or a timid horse by a man of courage; however this disparity may arise, it renders both useless, and invariably causes disorder. Well-disciplined infantry can easily break a squadron of cavalry, but it is with the greatest difficulty that cavalry can break the ranks of infantry. This opinion is corroborated not only by many examples of ancient and modern times, but is also sustained by the authority of those who study and direct the affairs of civilized societies; from which it appears that at first war was made exclusively with cavalry, because disciplined infantry had not yet been organized; but no sooner was this done than it was at once found to be more useful than cavalry, which, however, is also very necessary in armies, for the purposes of reconnaissance, to secure and ravage the country, to pursue a flying enemy, and to oppose the adversary's cavalry. But the infantry must ever be regarded and valued as the very foundation and nerve of an army.... Nothing could more conclusively prove the superiority of infantry over cavalry than this instance; for in the other cases cited, the Consuls caused the cavalry to dismount for the purpose of assisting the infantry, which was suffering and needed support, but here it was neither to help their own nor to combat the enemy's infantry, but it was a combat of cavalry against cavalry, and despairing of success the Romans judged that by dismounting victory would be more easy, and the result proved their judgment correct. I maintain further that a well-disciplined body of infantry can only be overcome with greatest difficulty, and then only by another body of infantry.

Discourses on Livy, II. 18

Cities

Those who read what the beginning of Rome was, and what her lawgivers and her organization, will not be astonished that so much virtue should have maintained itself during so many centuries; and that so great an empire should have sprung from it afterwards. To speak first of her origin, we will premise that all cities are founded either by natives of the country or by strangers. The little security which the natives found in living dispersed; the impossibility for each to resist isolated, either because of the situation or because of their small number, the attacks of any enemy that might present himself; the difficulty of uniting in time for defense at his approach, and the necessity of abandoning the greater number of their retreats, which quickly became a prize to the assailant, such were the motives that caused the first inhabitants of a country to build cities for the purpose of escaping these dangers. They resolved, of their own accord, or by the advice of someone who had most authority among them, to live together in some place of their selection that might offer them greater conveniences and greater facility of defense.

. . .

The second case is when a city is built by strangers; these may be either freemen, or subjects of a republic or of a prince, who, to relieve their states from an excessive population, or to defend a newly acquired territory which they wish to preserve without expense, send colonies there. The Romans founded many cities in this way within their empire. Sometimes cities are built by a prince, not for the purpose of living there, but merely as monuments to his glory; such was Alexandria, built by Alexander the Great. But as all these cities are at their very origin deprived of liberty, they rarely succeed in making great progress, or in being counted among the great powers.

Discourses on Livy, I. 1

We are able to appreciate the talents of the founder and the success of his work, which is more or less remarkable according as he, in founding the city, displays more or less wisdom and skill. Both the one and the other are recognized by the selection of the place where he has located the city, and by the nature of the laws which he establishes in it. And as men work either from necessity or from choice, and as it has been observed that virtue has more sway where labor is the result of necessity rather than of choice, it is a matter of consideration whether it might not be better to select for the establishment of a city a sterile region, where the people, compelled by necessity to be industrious, and therefore less given to idleness, would be more united, and less exposed by the poverty of the country to occasions for discord; as was the case with Ragusa, and several other cities that were built upon an ungrateful soil.

Discourses on Livy, I. 1

Citizenship

Sparta had a king and a senate, few in number, to govern her; Venice did not admit these distinctions, and gave the name of gentlemen to all who were entitled to have a part in the administration of the government. It was chance rather than foresight which gave to the latter this form of government; for having taken refuge on those shallows where the city now is, for the reasons mentioned above, the inhabitants soon became sufficiently numerous to require a regular system of laws. They consequently established a government and assembled frequently in council to discuss the interests of the city. When it seemed to them that they were sufficiently numerous to govern themselves, they barred the way to a share in the government to the newly arrived who came to live among them; and finding in the course of time that the number of the latter increased sufficiently to give reputation to those who held the government in their hands, they designated the latter by the title of "gentlemen," and the others were called the popular class. This form of government had no difficulty in establishing and maintaining itself without disturbances, for at the moment of its origins those who inhabited Venice had the right to participate in the government, so that no one had cause to complain. Those who afterwards came had neither the pretext nor the means to create disturbances. They had no cause, for the reason that they had not been deprived of anything; and they lacked the means, because they were kept in check by those who held the government and who did not employ them in any affairs that might tempt them to seize authority. Besides, the newcomers in Venice were not sufficiently numerous to have produced a disproportion between the governing and the governed, for the number of nobles equaled or exceeded that of the others; and thus for these reasons Venice could establish and preserve that form of government. Sparta, as I have said, being governed by a king and a limited senate, could maintain itself also for a long time, because there were but few inhabitants, and strangers were not permitted to come in; besides, the laws of Lycurgus had obtained such influence that their observance prevented even the slightest pretext for trouble.[. . .] This last advantage was due to the kings of Sparta; for being placed in this government, as it were, between the two orders, and living in the midst of the nobility, they had no better means of maintaining their authority than to protect the people against all injustice; whence these neither feared nor desired authority, and consequently there was no motive for any differences between them and the nobles, nor any cause for disturbances; and thus they could live for a long time united. Two principal causes, however, cemented this union; first, the inhabitants of Sparta were few in number, and therefore could be governed by a few; and [second], by not permitting strangers to establish themselves in the republic, they had neither opportunity of becoming corrupt, nor of increasing their population to such a degree that the burden of government became difficult to the few who were charged with it.

Discourses on Livy, I. 6

Colonies

Among other great and admirable institutions of the ancient republics and principalities that are now extinct, we must note the practice of constantly building new towns and cities. In fact, nothing is so worthy of a good prince, or of a well-organized republic, nor more useful to any province, than to build up new cities, where men may establish themselves with the conveniences for defense and habitation. It was easy for the ancients to do this, being accustomed to send new inhabitants to occupy conquered territories and vacant lands; such settlements were called colonies. This practice, besides causing new towns to be built up, rendered the conquered territory more secure to the conqueror, filled the vacant lands with inhabitants, and kept the population well distributed in the provinces.

History of Florence, II. 1

Constitution

It was necessary therefore, if Rome wished to preserve her liberty in the midst of this corruption, that she should have modified her constitution, in like manner as in the progress of her existence she had made new laws; for institutions and forms should be adapted to the subject, whether it be good or evil, inasmuch as the same form cannot suit two subjects that are essentially different. But as the constitution of a state, when once it has been discovered to be no longer suitable, should be amended, either all at once, or by degrees as each defect becomes known, I say that both of these courses are almost impossible.

Discourses on Livy, I. 18

Corruption

Princes and republics who wish to maintain themselves free from corruption must above all things preserve the purity of all religious observances, and treat them with proper reverence; for there is no greater indication of the ruin of a country than to see religion contemned.

Discourses on Livy, I. 12

The same thing happens to a people that has not been accustomed to self-government; for, ignorant of all public affairs, of all means of defense or offense, neither knowing the princes nor being known by them, it soon relapses under a yoke, oftentimes much heavier than the one which it had but just shaken off. This difficulty occurs even when the body of the people is not wholly corrupt; but when corruption has taken possession of the whole people, then it cannot preserve its free condition even for the shortest possible time, as we shall see further on; and therefore our argument has reference to a people where corruption has not yet become general, and where the good still prevails over the bad.

Discourses on Livy, I. 16

A corrupt people that becomes free can with greatest difficulty maintain its liberty.

Discourses on Livy, I. 17

It was a great good fortune for Rome, therefore, that no sooner did her kings become corrupt than they were expelled, before the corruption had time to extend to the heart of the people. This corruption caused endless disturbances in Rome; but as the intention of the people was good, these troubles, instead of harming, rather benefited the republic. And from this we may draw the conclusion that, where the mass of the people is sound, disturbances and tumults do no serious harm; but where corruption has penetrated the people, the best laws are of no avail, unless they are administered by a man of such supreme power that he may cause the laws to be observed until the mass has been restored to a healthy condition. . . . For if a state or city in decadence, in consequence of the corruption of the mass of its people, is ever raised up again, it must be through the virtue of some one man then living, and not by the people; and so soon as such a man dies, the people will relapse into their corrupt habits.

Discourses on Livy, I. 17

This was the case when the Romans instituted the Censorship, which was one of the most important provisions that helped to preserve the liberties of Rome, so long as liberty existed there. For the Censors being the supreme arbiters of the manners and customs of the Romans, they became the most potent instrument in retarding the progress of corruption in Rome.

Discourses on Livy, I. 49

And truly, where this probity does not exist, no good is to be expected, as in fact it is vain to look for anything good from those countries which we see nowadays so corrupt, as is the case above all others with Italy. France and Spain also have their share of corruption, and if we do not see so many disorders and troubles in those countries as is the case daily in Italy, it is not so much owing to the goodness of their people, in which they are greatly deficient, as to the fact that they have each a king who keeps them united not only by his virtue, but also by the institutions of those kingdoms, which are as yet preserved pure.

Discourses on Livy, I. 55

The only way to establish any kind of order there is to found a monarchical government; for where the body of the people is so thoroughly corrupt that the laws are powerless for restraint, it becomes necessary to establish some superior power which, with a royal hand, and with full and absolute powers, may put a curb upon the excessive ambition and corruption of the powerful.

Discourses on Livy, I. 55

If the government of the city is a republic, then there is no surer way of corrupting the citizens or dividing the city against itself, than to foment the spirit [of any factions] that may prevail there; for each party will strive by every means of corruption to secure friends and supporters, [and this] gives rise to two most serious evils: first, that a government which changes often, according to the caprice of the one or the other faction, can never be good, and consequently never can secure to itself the good will and attachment of its citizens; and, secondly, that such favoring of factions keeps the republic of necessity divided.

Discourses on Livy, III. 27

The general corruption of the other Italian cities, magnificent Signori, has spread to Florence and infects our city daily more and more. For ever since Italy has ceased to be subject to the Imperial authority, her cities, being without any powerful check to control them, have organized their states and governments not according to the principles of liberty, but according to the spirit of the factions that divided them. From this have sprung all the disorders and misfortunes that have afflicted this province. There is neither union nor friendship among the citizens, unless it be among such as are bound together by some villainous crime, committed either against the state or some private individual. And as all religion and the fear of God is dead in all their hearts, they value an oath or a pledge only so far as it may be useful to themselves. Men employ them, not for the purpose of observing them, but solely as means to enable them more easily to deceive; and just as this deceit succeeds more easily and securely, so much greater is the praise and glory derived from it; and therefore are dangerous men praised as being ingenious, and good men derided for being dupes. And thus do we see, in fact, all who can be corrupted, and all who can corrupt others, gather together in the cities of Italy. The young men are idle, and the old men lascivious, and every age and sex give themselves up to unbridled habits; and good laws are no remedy for this, being made useless by evil usages. Thence comes that avarice which we see so common among the citizens, and that craving, not for true glory, but for those false honors from which flow hatreds, enmities, dissensions, and factions, which, in turn, produce murders, exiles, and the afflictions of the good and the elevation of the wicked.

> Speech delivered by an anonymous citizen in
> defense of the Florentine Republic's liberty,
> *History of Florence*, III. 5

Dictatorship

The authority of the dictatorship has always proved beneficial to Rome, and never injurious; it is the authority which men usurp, and not that which is given them by the free suffrages of their fellow-citizens, that is dangerous to civil liberty.

> *Discourses on Livy*, I. 34

Hereupon the Romans resorted, among other measures which they were accustomed to employ in urgent dangers, to the creation of a dictator; that is to say, they gave the power to one man, who, without consulting anyone else, could determine upon any course, and could have it carried into effect without any appeal. This measure, which on former occasions had proved most useful in overcoming imminent perils, was equally serviceable to them in all the critical events that occurred during the growth and development of the power of the republic.

Discourses on Livy, I. 33

It is seen that the dictatorship, whenever created according to public law and not usurped by individual authority, always proved beneficial to Rome; it is the magistracies and powers that are created by illegitimate means which harm a republic, not those that are appointed in the regular way, as was the case in Rome, where in the long course of time no dictator ever failed to prove beneficial to the republic. The reason of this is perfectly evident; first, before a citizen can be in a position to usurp extraordinary powers, many things must concur, which in a republic as yet uncorrupted never can happen; for he must be exceedingly rich, and must have many adherents and partisans, which cannot be where the laws are observed; and even if he had them, he would never be supported by the free suffrages of the people, for such men are generally looked upon as dangerous. Besides this, dictators were appointed only for a limited term, and not in perpetuity, and their power to act was confined to the particular occasion for which they were created. This power consisted in being able to decide alone upon the measures to be adopted for averting the pressing danger, to do whatever he deemed proper without consultation, and to inflict punishment upon any one without appeal. But the dictator could do nothing to alter the form of the government, such as to diminish the powers of the Senate or the people, or to abrogate existing institutions and create new ones. So that, taking together the short period for which he held the office, and the limited powers which he possessed, and the fact that the Roman people were as yet uncorrupted, it is evident that it was impossible for him to exceed his powers and to harm the republic; which on the contrary, as all experience shows, was always benefited by him. And truly, of all the institutions of Rome, this one deserves to be counted among those to which she was most indebted for her greatness and dominion. For without some such an institution Rome would with difficulty have escaped the many extraordinary dangers that befell her; for the customary proceedings of republics are slow, no magistrate or council being permitted to act independently, but being in almost all instances obliged to act in concert one with the other, so that often much time is required to harmonize their several opinions; and tardy measures are most dangerous when the occasion requires prompt action. And therefore all republics should have some institution similar to the dictatorship.

Discourses on Livy, I. 34

Disorders

Being on the spot, you can quickly remedy disorders as you see them arise; but not being there, you do not hear of them until they have become so great that there is no longer any remedy for them.

The Prince, III

Having conquered the Romagna, the Duke found it under the control of a number of impotent petty tyrants, who had devoted themselves more to plundering their subjects than to governing them properly, and to encouraging discord and disorder among them rather than peace and union; so that this province was infested by brigands, torn by quarrels, and given over to every sort of violence. He saw at once that, to restore order among the inhabitants and obedience to the sovereign, it was necessary to establish a good and vigorous government there. And for this purpose he appointed as governor of that province Don Ramiro d'Orco, a man of cruelty, but at the same time of great energy, to whom he gave plenary power. In a very short time d'Orco reduced the province to peace and order, thereby gaining for himself the highest reputation.

The Prince, VII

This [the social conflicts caused by agrarian laws] shows us also how much more people value riches than honors; for the Roman nobility always yielded to the people without serious difficulties in the matter of honors, but when it came to a question of property, then they resisted with so much pertinacity that the people, to satisfy their thirst for riches, resorted to the above-described extraordinary proceedings [violent resistance]. The chief promoters of these disorders were the Gracchi, whose intentions in this matter were more praiseworthy than their prudence.

Discourses on Livy, I. 37

It would be tedious to relate how many times the Florentines, the Venetians, and the kingdom of France have bought off wars with money; and how many times they subjected themselves to an ignominy to which the Romans submitted once only. It would be equally tedious to relate how many places the Florentines and the Venetians have purchased with money, which afterwards caused great disorders; showing that what has been purchased with gold cannot be defended with iron.

Discourses on Livy, II. 30

The Fidenati, having revolted, massacred the colony which the Romans had established at Fidena. To avenge this outrage the Romans appointed four Tribunes with consular powers, one of whom remained to guard Rome, while the other three were sent against the Fidenati and Veienti. These three Tribunes gained nothing but dishonor in this expedition, in consequence of the dissensions that had arisen between them. For this dishonor they were themselves alone responsible; and it was only the valor of their soldiers that saved them from experiencing a serious check. The Romans, having perceived the cause of this disorder, resorted to the creation of a dictator; so that one man might restore that order which the three Tribunes had destroyed.

Discourses on Livy, III. 15

The city of Pistoia furnishes a most striking [proof that in order to hold a city it is not necessary to keep it divided]. Fifteen years ago that city was divided into two factions, the Panciatichi and the Cancellieri, and this division continues to the present day; but then they were in arms, whilst now they have laid them down. After many disputes, they had come to bloodshed, to the pulling down of houses, plundering each other's property, and every other kind of hostilities; and the Florentines, upon whom it devolved to restore order in that city, always employed for that purpose the third means, namely, conciliation, which, however, invariably led to greater troubles and disorders. So that, tired of this method, they resorted to the second; that is, they removed the chiefs of the factions by imprisoning some and exiling others to various places; and thus they succeeded in restoring order in a manner that could and does endure to this day.

Discourses on Livy, III. 27

For ever since Italy has ceased to be subject to the Imperial authority, her cities, being without any powerful check to control them, have organized their states and governments not according to the principles of liberty, but according to the spirit of the factions that divided them. From this have sprung all the disorders and misfortunes that have afflicted this province.

History of Florence, III. 5

If the other cities are full of such disorders, ours is more tainted by them than any of [the others]; for here the laws and civil ordinances are always made, not according to the principles of liberty, but according to the ambition of that party which for the time has the ascendency. Hence it comes that, so soon as one party is expelled and one division extinguished, another one springs up in its place; for in a city which prefers to maintain itself by factions rather than by laws, if one faction remains without opposition, it must of necessity divide against itself; for the very private measures which it had previously originated for its own promotion will now prove insufficient for its defense.

History of Florence, III. 5

For disorders increase easily after having once been started.

History of Florence, III. 10

But, as men are never satisfied with merely recovering their own, but wish also to have that which belongs to others and to satisfy their revenge, so those who hoped to profit by disorders pointed out to the artisans that they would never be secure unless a number of their enemies were expelled and crushed.

History of Florence, III. 11

Empires and Emperors

Let him also note how much more praise those emperors merited who, after Rome became an empire, conformed to the laws like good princes, than those who took the opposite course; and he will see that Titus, Nerva, Trajan, Hadrian, Antoninus, and Marcus Aurelius did not require the Praetorians nor the multitudinous legions to defend them, because they were protected by their own good conduct, the good will of the people, and by the love of the Senate. He will furthermore see that neither the Eastern nor the Western armies sufficed to save Caligula, Nero, Vitellius, and so many other wicked emperors, from the enemies which their bad conduct and evil lives had raised up against them. And if the history of these men were carefully studied, it would prove an ample guide to any prince, and serve to show him the way to glory or to infamy, to security or to perpetual apprehension. For of the twenty-six emperors who reigned from the time of Caesar to that of Maximinius, sixteen were assassinated, and ten only died a natural death; and if, among those who were killed, there were one or two good ones, like Galba and Pertinax, their death was the consequence of the corruption which their predecessors had engendered among the soldiers. And if among those who died a natural death there were some wicked ones, like Severus, it was due to their extraordinary good fortune and courage, which two qualities rarely fall to the lot of such men. He will furthermore learn from the lessons of that history how an empire should be organized properly; for all the emperors that succeeded to the throne by inheritance, except Titus, were bad, and those who became emperors by adoption were all good, such as the five from Nero to Marcus Aurelius, and when the Empire became hereditary it came to ruin. Let any prince now place himself in the times from Nerva to Marcus Aurelius, and let him compare them with those that preceded and followed that period, and let him choose in which of the two he would like to have been born, and in which he would like to have reigned. In the period under the good emperors he will see the prince secure amidst his people, who are also living in security; he will see peace and justice prevail in the world, the authority of the Senate respected, the magistrates honored, the wealthy citizens enjoying their riches, nobility and virtue exalted, and everywhere will he see tranquility and well-being. And on the other hand he will behold all animosity, license, corruption, and all noble ambition extinct. During the period of the good emperors he will see that golden age when everyone could hold and defend whatever opinion he pleased; in fine, he will see the triumph of the world, the prince surrounded with reverence and glory, and beloved by his people, who are happy in their security. If now he will but glance at the times under the other emperors, he will behold the atrocities of war, discords, and sedition, cruelty in peace as in war, many princes massacred, many civil and foreign wars, Italy afflicted and overwhelmed by fresh misfortunes, and her cities ravaged and ruined; he will see Rome in ashes, the Capitol pulled down by her own citizens, the ancient temples desolate, all religious rites and ceremonies corrupted,

and the city full of adultery; he will behold the sea covered
with ships full of fleeing exiles, and the shores stained with
blood. He will see innumerable cruelties in Rome, and nobility, riches, honor, and above all virtue, accounted capital crimes. He will see informers rewarded, servants corrupted against their masters, the freedmen arrayed against
their patrons, and those who were without enemies betrayed and oppressed by their friends. And then will he
recognize what infinite obligations Rome, Italy, and the
whole world owed to Caesar.

Discourses on Livy, I. 10

Equality

Public affairs are easily managed in a city where the body
of the people is not corrupt; and where equality exists,
there no principality can be established; nor can a republic
be established where there is no equality.

Discourses on Livy, I. 55

[T]hose republics which have . . . preserved their political
existence uncorrupted do not permit any of their citizens
to be or to live in the manner of gentlemen, but rather
maintain among them a perfect equality, and are the most
decided enemies of the lords and gentlemen that exist in
the country; so that, if by chance any of them fall into their
hands, they kill them, as being the chief promoters of all
corruption and troubles.

Discourses on Livy, I. 55

It was also the easier for the citizens to live in union, as Lycurgus had established equality in fortunes and inequality in conditions; for an equal poverty prevailed there, and the people were the less ambitious, as the offices of the government were given but to a few citizens, the people being excluded from them; and the nobles in the exercise of their functions did not treat the people sufficiently ill to excite in them the desire of exercising them themselves.

Discourses on Livy, I. 6

Errors

For to attempt to eradicate an abuse that has grown up in a republic by the enactment of retrospective laws, is a most inconsiderate proceeding, and . . . only serves to accelerate the fatal results which the abuse tends to bring about; but by temporizing, the end will either be delayed, or the evil will exhaust itself before it attains that end.

Discourses on Livy, I. 37

Expansion

As all human things are kept in perpetual movement and can never remain stable, states naturally either rise or decline, and necessity compels them to many acts to which reason will not influence them; so that, having organized a republic competent to maintain herself without expanding, still, if forced by necessity to extend her territory, in such case we shall see her foundations give way and herself quickly brought to ruin. And . . . on the other hand, if Heaven favors her so as never to be involved in war, the continued tranquility will enervate her, or provoke internal dissensions, which together, or either of them separately, will be apt to prove her ruin. Seeing then the impossibility of establishing in this respect a perfect equilibrium, and that a precise middle course cannot be maintained, it is proper in the organization of a republic to select the most honorable course, and to constitute her so that, even if necessity should oblige her to expand, she may yet be able to preserve her acquisitions.

Discourses on Livy, I. 6

Those who desire a city to achieve great empire must endeavor by all possible means to make her populous; for without an abundance of inhabitants it is impossible ever to make a city powerful. This may be done in two ways; either by attracting population by the advantages offered, or by compulsion. The first is to make it easy and secure for strangers to come and establish themselves there, and the second is to destroy the neighboring cities, and to compel their inhabitants to come and dwell in yours.

Discourses on Livy, II. 3

Whoever has studied ancient history will have found that the republics had three methods of aggrandizement. One of these was that observed by the ancient Tuscans, namely, to form a confederation of several republics, no one of which had any eminence over the others in rank or authority; and in their conquests of other cities they associated these with themselves, in a similar manner to that practiced by the Swiss nowadays, and as was done anciently in Greece by the Achaians and the Aetolians. The second method employed by the ancient republics for their aggrandizement was to make associates of other states; reserving to themselves, however, the rights of sovereignty, the seat of empire, and the glory of their enterprises. This was the method observed by the Romans. . . . The third method was to make the conquered people immediately subjects, and not associates, and was practiced by the Spartans and Athenians. Of these three methods the latter is perfectly useless, as was proved by these two republics, which perished from no other cause than from having made conquests which they could not maintain. [The most efficient was the second, which] was practiced only by the Romans; and a republic desirous of aggrandizement should adopt no other plan, for experience has proved that there is none better or surer. The first method of which we have spoken, that of forming confederations like those of the Tuscans, Achaians, and Aetolians, or the Swiss of the present day, is next best after that practiced by the Romans. But if it has seemed too difficult to imitate the example of the Romans, certainly that of the ancient Tuscans should not be deemed so, especially by the Tuscans of the present day. For if they failed to acquire that power in Italy which the Roman method of proceeding would have given them, they at least lived for a long time in security, with much glory of dominion and of arms, and high praise for their manners and religion.

Discourses on Livy, II. 4

Extraordinary Measures

A state that has freshly achieved liberty makes enemies, and no friends. And to prevent this inconvenience, and the disorders which are apt to come with it, there is no remedy more powerful, valid, healthful, and necessary than [was] the killing of the sons of Brutus, who, as history shows, had conspired with other Roman youths for no other reason than because under the Consuls they could not have the same extraordinary advantages as they had enjoyed under the kings; so that the liberty of the people seemed to have become their bondage. Whoever undertakes to govern a people under the form of either a republic or a monarchy without making sure of those who are opposed to this new order of things, establishes a government of very brief duration. It is true that I regard as unfortunate those princes who, to assure their government to which the mass of the people is hostile, are obliged to resort to extraordinary measures; for he who has but a few enemies can easily make sure of them without great scandal, but he who has the masses hostile to him can never make sure of them, and the more cruelty he employs the feebler will his authority become; so that his best remedy is to try and secure the good will of the people.

Discourses on Livy, I. 16

A gradual modification must be the work of some wise man, who has seen the evil from afar in its very beginning; but it is very likely that such a man may never rise up in the state, and even if he should he will hardly be able to persuade the others to what he proposes; for men accustomed to live after one fashion do not like to change, and the less so as they do not see the evil staring them in the face but presented to them as a mere conjecture. As to reforming these institutions all at once, when their defects have become manifest to everybody, that also is most difficult; for to do this ordinary means will not suffice; they may even be injurious under such circumstances, and therefore it becomes necessary to resort to extraordinary measures, such as violence and arms, and above all things to make one's self absolute master of the state, so as to be able to dispose of it at will.

Discourses on Livy, I. 18

And truly, of all the institutions of Rome, this one [the dictatorship] deserves to be counted among those to which she was most indebted for her greatness and dominion. For without some such an institution Rome would with difficulty have escaped the many extraordinary dangers that befell her; for the customary proceedings of republics are slow, no magistrate or council being permitted to act independently, but being in almost all instances obliged to act in concert one with the other, so that often much time is required to harmonize their several opinions; and tardy measures are most dangerous when the occasion requires prompt action. And therefore all republics should have some institution similar to the dictatorship. The republic of Venice, which is preeminent among modern ones, had reserved to a small number of citizens the power of deciding all urgent matters without referring their decisions to a larger council. And when a republic lacks some such system, a strict observance of the established laws will expose her to ruin; or, to save her from such danger, the laws will have to be disregarded. Now in a well-ordered republic it should never be necessary to resort to extra-constitutional measures; for although they may for the time be beneficial, yet the precedent is pernicious, for if the practice is once established of disregarding the laws for good objects, they will in a little while be disregarded under that pretext for evil purposes. Thus no republic will ever be perfect if she has not by law provided for everything, having a remedy for every emergency, and fixed rules for applying it. And therefore I will say, in conclusion, that those republics which in time of danger cannot resort to a dictatorship, or some similar authority, will generally be ruined when grave occasions occur.

Discourses on Livy, I. 34

Fortresses

A prince then, who can raise a good army, need not build any fortresses; and one who cannot should not build any. It is proper enough that he should fortify the city in which he resides, so as to be able to resist the first shock of an enemy and to afford himself the time to negotiate, or to obtain aid from without for his relief; but anything more is mere waste of money in time of peace, and useless in time of war.

Discourses on Livy, II. 24

The Founders and Reformers of States

I believe the greatest honor possible for men to have is that willingly given them by their native cities; I believe the greatest good to be done and the most pleasing to God is that which one does to one's native city. Besides this, no man is so much exalted by any act of his as are those men who have with laws and with institutions remodeled republics and kingdoms; these are, after those who have been gods, the first to be praised. And because they have been few who have had opportunity to do it, and very few those who have understood how to do it, small is the number who have done it. And so much has this glory been esteemed by men seeking for nothing other than glory that when unable to form a republic in reality, they have done it in writing, as Aristotle, Plato, and many others, who have wished to show the world that if they have not founded a free government, as did Solon and Lycurgus, they have failed not through their ignorance but through their impotence for putting it into practice. No greater gift, then, does Heaven give to a man, nor can Heaven show him a more glorious road than this.

Discourse on Remodeling the Government of Florence

It is necessary then . . . for men who live associated together under some kind of regulations often to be brought back to themselves, so to speak, either by external or internal occurrences. As to the latter, they are either the result of a law that obliges the citizens of the association often to examine their conduct; or some man of superior character arises among them, whose noble example and virtuous actions will produce the same effect as such a law. This good then in a republic is due either to the excellence of some one man, or to some law; and as to the latter, the institution that brought the Roman Republic back to its original principles was the creation of the Tribunes of the people, and all the other laws that tended to repress the insolence and ambition of men. But to give life and vigor to those laws requires a virtuous citizen, who will courageously aid in their execution against the power of those who transgress them.

Discourses on Livy, III. 1

There is nothing more difficult and dangerous, or more doubtful of success, than an attempt to introduce a new order of things in any state. For the innovator has for enemies all those who derived advantages from the old order of things, whilst those who expect to be benefited by the new institutions will be but lukewarm defenders. This indifference arises in part from fear of their adversaries who were favored by the existing laws, and partly from the incredulity of men who have no faith in anything new that is not the result of well-established experience. Hence it is that, whenever the opponents of the new order of things have the opportunity to attack it, they will do so with the zeal of partisans, whilst the others will defend it but feebly, so that it is dangerous to rely upon the latter.

The Prince, VI

If we desire to discuss this subject thoroughly, it will be necessary to examine whether such innovators depend upon themselves, or whether they rely upon others; that is to say, whether for the purpose of carrying out their plans they have to resort to entreaties, or whether they can accomplish it by their own force. In the first case they always succeed badly and fail to conclude anything; but when they depend upon their own strength to carry their innovations through, then they rarely incur any danger.

The Prince, VI

Neither Moses, Cyrus, Theseus, nor Romulus would have been able to ensure that their laws and institutions would be observed for any length of time, if they had not been prepared to enforce them with arms. This was the experience of Brother Girolamo Savonarola, who failed in his attempt to establish a new order of things so soon as the multitude ceased to believe in him; for he had not the means to keep his believers firm in their faith, nor to make the unbelievers believe. And yet these great men experienced great difficulties in their course, and met danger at every step, which could only be overcome by their courage and ability. But once having surmounted them, then they began to be held in veneration; and having crushed those who were jealous of their great qualities, they remained powerful, secure, honored, and happy.

The Prince, VI

Moreover, states that spring up suddenly, like other things in nature that are born and attain their growth rapidly, cannot have those roots and supports that will protect them from destruction by the first unfavorable weather. Unless indeed, as has been said, those who have suddenly become princes are gifted with such virtue that they quickly know how to prepare themselves for the preservation of that which fortune has cast into their lap, and afterwards to build up those foundations which others have laid before becoming princes.... For, as we have said above, he who does not lay the foundations for his power beforehand may be able by great ability and courage to do so afterwards; but it will be done with great trouble to the builder and with danger to the edifice.

The Prince, VII

The chiefs thus destroyed, and their adherents converted into his friends, the Duke Cesare Borgia had laid sufficiently good foundations for his power, having made himself master of the whole of the Romagna and the Duchy of Urbino, and having attached their entire population to himself, by giving them a foretaste of the new prosperity which they were to enjoy under him.

The Prince, VII

We have said how necessary it is for a prince to lay solid foundations for his power, as without such he would inevitably be ruined. The main foundations which all states must have, whether new, or old, or mixed, are good laws and good armies.

The Prince, XII

Nothing makes a prince so much esteemed as the undertaking of great enterprises and the setting of a noble example in his own person.

The Prince, XXI

If, then, your illustrious house is willing to follow the examples of those distinguished men who have redeemed their countries, you will before anything else, and as the very foundation of every enterprise, have to provide yourself with a national army.

The Prince, XXVI

Those who read what the beginning of Rome was, and what her lawgivers and her organization, will not be astonished that so much virtue should have maintained itself during so many centuries; and that so great an empire should have sprung from it afterwards. To speak first of her origin, we will premise that all cities are founded either by natives of the country or by strangers.

Discourses on Livy, I. 1

The founders of cities are independent when they are people who, under the leadership of some prince, or by themselves, have been obliged to flee from pestilence, war, or famine that was devastating their native country, and are seeking a new home. These either inhabit the cities of the country of which they take possession, as Moses did; or they build new ones, as was done by Aeneas. In such case we are able to appreciate the talents of the founder and the success of his work, which is more or less remarkable according as he, in founding the city, displays more or less wisdom and skill.

Discourses on Livy, I. 1

All those who have written upon civil institutions have demonstrated (and history is full of examples to support them) that whoever desires to found a state and give it laws, must start with assuming that all men are bad and ever ready to display their vicious nature whenever they may find occasion for it. If their evil disposition remains concealed for a time, it must be attributed to some unknown reason; and we must assume that it lacked occasion to show itself; but time, which has been said to be the father of all truth, does not fail to bring it to light.

Discourses on Livy, I. 3

We must assume, as a general rule, that it never or rarely happens that a republic or monarchy is well constituted, or its old institutions entirely reformed, unless it is done by only one individual; it is even necessary that he whose mind has conceived such a constitution should be alone in carrying it into effect. A sagacious legislator of a republic, therefore, whose object is to promote the public good and not his private interests, and who prefers his country to his own descendants, should concentrate all authority in himself; and a wise mind will never censure anyone for having employed any extraordinary means for the purpose of establishing a kingdom or constituting a republic. It is well that, when the act accuses him, the result should excuse him; and when the result is good, as in the case of Romulus, it will always absolve him from blame. For he is to be reprehended who commits violence for the purpose of destroying, and not he who employs it for beneficent purposes. The lawgiver should, however, be sufficiently wise and virtuous not to leave this authority which he has assumed either to his heirs or to anyone else; for mankind, being more prone to evil than to good, his successor might employ for evil purposes the power which he had used only for good ends. Besides, although one man alone should organize a government, yet it will not endure long if the administration of justice remains on the shoulders of a single individual; it is well then to confide this to the charge of many, for thus it will be sustained by the many. . . . Considering, then, all these things, I conclude that to found a republic, one must be alone; and that Romulus deserves to be absolved from, and not blamed for, the deaths of Remus and of Tatius.

Discourses on Livy, I. 9

The above views might be corroborated by any number of examples, such as those of Moses, Lycurgus, Solon, and other founders of monarchies and republics, who were enabled to establish laws suitable for the general good only by keeping for themselves an exclusive authority; but all these are so well known that I will not further refer to them.

Discourses on Livy, I. 9

In proportion as the founders of a republic or monarchy are entitled to praise, so do the founders of a tyranny deserve execration.

Discourses on Livy, I. 10

Although the founder of Rome was Romulus, to whom, like a daughter, she owed her birth and her education, yet the gods did not judge the laws of this prince sufficient for so great an empire, and therefore inspired the Roman Senate to elect Numa Pompilius as his successor, so that he might regulate all those things that had been omitted by Romulus. Numa, finding a very savage people and wishing to reduce them to civil obedience by the arts of peace, had recourse to religion as the most necessary and assured support of any civil society, and he established it upon such foundations that for many centuries there was nowhere more fear of the gods than in that republic, which greatly facilitated all the enterprises which the Senate or its great men attempted.

Discourses on Livy, I. 11

It is therefore the duty of princes and heads of republics to uphold the foundations of the religion of their countries, for then it is easy to keep their people religious, and consequently well conducted and united. And therefore everything that tends to favor religion (even though it were believed to be false) should be received and availed of to strengthen it; and this should be done the more the wiser the rulers are, and the better they understand the natural course of things.

Discourses on Livy, I. 12

Whoever becomes prince of a city or state and does not wish to establish there either a monarchy or a republic, especially if the foundation of his power is feeble, will find the best means for holding that principality to be organizing the government entirely anew (he being himself a new prince there); that is, he should appoint new governors with new titles, new powers, and new men, and he should make the poor rich, as David did when he became king, "who heaped riches upon the needy, and dismissed the wealthy empty-handed." Besides this, he should destroy the old cities and build new ones, and transfer the inhabitants from one place to another; in short, he should leave nothing unchanged in that province, so that there should be neither rank, nor grade, nor honor, nor wealth, that should not be recognized as coming from him. He should take Philip of Macedon, father of Alexander, for his model, who by proceeding in that manner became, from a petty king, master of all Greece. And his historian tells us that he transferred the inhabitants from one province to another, as shepherds move their flocks from place to place. Doubtless these means are cruel and destructive of all civilized life, and neither Christian nor even human, and should be avoided by everyone. In fact, the life of a private citizen would be preferable to that of a king at the expense of the ruin of so many human beings. Nevertheless, whoever is unwilling to adopt the first and humane course [preserving the old institutions] must, if he wishes to maintain his power, follow the latter evil course. But men generally decide upon a middle course, which is most hazardous; for they know neither how to be entirely good nor entirely bad.

Discourses on Livy. I. 26

Gold

The king [Philip of Macedon], by way of showing his power, and to dazzle them, displayed before them great quantities of gold and silver; whereupon the ambassadors of the Gauls, who had already as good as signed the treaty, broke off all further negotiations, excited by the intense desire to possess themselves of all this gold; and thus the very treasure which the king had accumulated for his defense brought about his spoliation.

Discourses on Livy, II. 10

Gonfalonier (Highest Magistrate of the Republic of Florence)

Salvestro de' Medici believed he had been made Gonfalonier, not to adjudicate private matters, for which there were the ordinary judges, but to guard the welfare of the state, to repress the insolence of the nobles, and to temper the rigor of those laws which were destroying the republic; and that, having diligently devoted himself to these objects, he had, as far as it was possible for him, provided for the same. But the malignity of men opposed his just efforts to that degree that they impeded the way for him to effect any good, and prevented [the nobles] from resolving upon anything and even from hearing him. Seeing, therefore, that he could be of no further use to the state or the public good, he did not know why he should continue to hold an office, which either he did not deserve, or which others thought him unworthy of. And therefore he de-

sired to retire to his home, so that the people might re-
place him by someone who had more merit or better fortune. Having spoken thus, he withdrew from the council
and returned to his house.

History of Florence, III. 9

Government

Having proposed to myself to treat of the kind of government established at Rome, and of the events that led to its
perfection, I must at the beginning observe that some of
the writers on politics distinguished three kinds of government, viz., the monarchical, the aristocratic, and the
democratic; and maintain that the legislators of a people
must choose from these three the one that seems to them
most suitable. Other authors, wiser according to the opinion of many, count six kinds of governments, three of
which are very bad, and three good in themselves, but so
liable to be corrupted that they become absolutely bad.
The three good ones are those which we have just named;
the three bad ones result from the degradation of the
other three, and each of them resembles its corresponding
original, so that the transition from the one to the other is
very easy. Thus monarchy becomes tyranny; aristocracy
degenerates into oligarchy; and the popular government
lapses readily into licentiousness. So that a legislator who
gives to a state which he founds either of these three forms
of government, constitutes it but for a brief time; for no
precautions can prevent any one of the three that are re-

puted good from degenerating into the bad form that corresponds to it; so great are in these the attractions and resemblances between the good and the evil.

Discourses on Livy, I. 2

No firm government can be devised if it is not either a true princedom or a true republic, because all the constitutions between these two are defective. The reason is entirely evident, because the princedom has just one path to dissolution, and that is to descend toward the republic. And similarly the republic has just one path toward being dissolved, and that is to rise toward the princedom. Governments of a middle sort have two ways: they can rise toward the princedom and descend toward the republic. From this comes their lack of stability.

Discourse on Remodeling the Government of Florence

They also made many other provisions for strengthening the government, which were alike unsupportable to those against whom they were aimed and odious to the good citizens of their own party, who could not regard a government good and secure that had to protect itself with so much violence.

History of Florence, III. 26

Laws

It is . . . said that poverty and hunger make men industrious, and that the law makes men good; and if fortunate circumstances cause good to be done without constraint, the law may be dispensed with. But when such happy influence is lacking, then the law immediately becomes necessary.

Discourses on Livy, I .3

I think that there can be no worse example in a republic than to make a law and not to observe it; the more so when it is disregarded by the very parties who made it.

Discourses on Livy, I. 45

In the year 1494 Florence had reformed its government with the aid of Brother Girolamo Savonarola (whose writings exhibit so much learning, prudence, and courage); and among other provisions for the security of the citizens a law had been made which permitted an appeal to the people from the decisions which the Council of Eight and the Signoria might render in cases affecting the state, which had involved great discussions and difficulties in its passage. It happened that shortly after its confirmation five citizens were condemned to death by the Signoria on account of crimes against the state; and when these men wished to appeal to the people, they were not allowed to do so, in manifest disregard of the law. This occurrence did more than anything else to diminish the influence of Savonarola; for if the appeal was useful, then the law should have been observed, and if it was not useful, then it should never have been made. And this circumstance was the more remarked as Brother Girolamo in his many subsequent preachings never condemned those who had broken the law, [but] rather excused the act in the manner of one unwilling to condemn what suited his purposes, yet was unable to excuse it wholly. He thus manifested his ambitious and partial spirit, and it cost him his reputation and much trouble.

Discourses on Livy, I. 45

Liberality

I say that it is well for a prince to be deemed liberal; and yet liberality, practiced so that you are not reputed liberal, will injure you. For liberality worthily exercised, as it should be, will not be known, and may bring upon you the reproach of the very opposite. For if you desire the reputation of being liberal, you must not stop at any degree of sumptuousness [in giving]; so that a prince will in this way generally consume his entire substance, and may in the end, if he wishes to keep up his reputation for liberality, be obliged to subject his people to extraordinary burdens, and resort to taxation, and employ all sorts of measures that will enable him to procure money. This will soon make him odious with his people and when he becomes poor, he will be contemned by everybody so that having by his prodigality injured many and benefited few, he will be the first to suffer every inconvenience and be exposed to every danger. And when he becomes conscious of this and attempts to retrench, he will at once expose himself to the imputation of being a miser. A prince then, being unable without injury to himself to practice the virtue of liberality in such manner that it may be generally recognized, should not, when he becomes aware of this and is prudent, mind incurring the charge of parsimoniousness. For after a while, when it is seen that by his prudence and economy he makes his revenues suffice him, and that he is able to provide for his defense in case of war, and engage in enterprises without burdening his people, he will be considered liberal enough by all those from whom he takes nothing, and these are the many; whilst only those to whom he does not give, and which are the few, will look upon him as parsimonious.

The Prince, XVI

Liberty and Its Safekeeping

The state that becomes free makes enemies for itself, and not friends. All those become its enemies who were benefited by the tyrannical abuses and fattened upon the treasures of the prince, and who, being now deprived of these advantages, cannot remain content, and are therefore driven to attempt to reestablish the tyranny, so as to recover their former authority and advantages. A state then, as I have said, that becomes free, makes no friends; for free governments bestow honors and rewards only according to certain honest and fixed rules, outside of which there are neither the one nor the other. And such as obtain these honors and rewards do not consider themselves under obligations to anyone, because they believe that they were entitled to them by their merits. Besides the advantages that result to the mass of the people from a free government, such as the freedom to enjoy one's own without apprehension, to have nothing to fear for the honor of one's wife and daughters, or for oneself—all these, I say, are not appreciated by any one whilst he is in the enjoyment of them; for no one will confess himself under obligation to anyone merely because he has not been injured by him.

Discourses on Livy, I. 16

And whoever becomes master of a city that has been accustomed to liberty, and does not destroy it, must himself expect to be ruined by it. For they will always resort to rebellion in the name of liberty and their ancient institutions, which will never be effaced from their memory, either by the lapse of time, or by benefits bestowed by the new master. No matter what he may do, or what precautions he may take, if he does not separate and disperse the inhabitants, they will on the first occasion invoke the name of liberty and the memory of their ancient institutions, as was done by Pisa after having been held over a hundred years in subjection by the Florentines.

The Prince, V

Thus Rome and Sparta maintained their liberties for many centuries by having armies of their own; the Swiss are most thoroughly armed, and consequently enjoy the greatest independence and liberty.

The Prince, XII

But as to the other popular desire, that of recovering their liberty, the prince, not being able to satisfy that, should examine the causes that make them desire to be free; and he will find that a small part of them wish to be free for the purpose of commanding, whilst all the others, who constitute an immense majority, desire liberty so as to be able to live in greater security. For in all republics, however organized, there are never more than forty or fifty citizens who attain a position that entitles them to command. As this is a small number, it is easy to make sure of them, either by having them put out of the way, or by giving them such a share of the public honors and offices as, according to their condition, will in great measure content them. The others, who only care to live in security, are easily satisfied by institutions and laws that confirm at the same time the general security of the people and the power of the prince.

Discourses on Livy, I. 16

It is a very true saying of political writers, that those states which have recovered their liberty treat their citizens with greater severity than such as have never lost it.

Discourses on Livy, I. 28

All the legislators that have given wise constitutions to republics have deemed it an essential precaution to establish a guard and protection to liberty; and according as this was more or less wisely placed, liberty endured a greater or less length of time. As every republic was composed of nobles and people, the question arose as to whose hands it was best to confide the protection of liberty. The Lacedaemonians, and in our day the Venetians, gave it into the hands of the nobility; but the Romans entrusted it to the people. We must examine, therefore, which of these republics made the best choice. There are strong reasons in favor of each, but, to judge by the results, we must incline in favor of the nobles, for the liberties of Sparta and Venice endured a longer space of time than those of Rome. But to come to the reasons, taking the part of Rome first, I will say that one should always confide any trust to those who have least desire of violating it; and doubtless, if we consider the objects of the nobles and of the people, we must see that the first have a great desire to dominate, whilst the latter have only the wish not to be dominated, and consequently a greater desire to live in the enjoyment of liberty; so that when the people are entrusted with the care of any privilege or liberty, being less disposed to encroach upon it, they will of necessity take better care of it; and being unable to take it away themselves, will prevent others from doing so.

Discourses on Liberty, I. 5

To come back now to the question as to which men are most dangerous in a republic, those who wish to acquire power or those who fear to lose that which they possess. . . . It seems that dangers are most frequently occasioned by those who possess; for the fear to lose stirs the same passions in men as the desire to gain, as men do not believe themselves sure of what they already possess except by acquiring still more; and, moreover, these new acquisitions are so many means of strength and power for abuses; and what is still worse is that the haughty manners and insolence of the nobles and the rich excite in the breasts of those who have neither birth nor wealth, not only the desire to possess them, but also the wish to revenge themselves by depriving the former of those riches and honors which they see them employ so badly.

Discourses on Liberty, I. 5

Ministers

The choice of his ministers is of no slight importance to a prince; they are either good or not, according as the prince himself is sagacious or otherwise; and upon the character of the persons with whom a prince surrounds himself depends the first impression that is formed of his own ability. If his ministers and counselors are competent and faithful, he will be reputed wise, because he has known how to discern their capacity and how to secure their fidelity; but if they prove otherwise, then the opinion formed of the prince will not be favorable, because of his want of judgment in their selection.

The Prince, XXII

Whenever he sees that the minister thinks more of himself than of the prince, and that in all his doings he seeks his own advantage more than that of the state, then the prince may be sure that that man will never be a good minister and is not to be trusted. For a man who has the administration of a state in his hands should never think of himself, but only of the prince, and should never bring anything to his notice that does not relate to the interest of the government.

The Prince, XXII

Mixed Government

Thus sagacious legislators, knowing the vices of each of these systems of government by itself, have chosen one that should partake of all of them, judging that to be the most stable and solid. In fact, when there is combined under the same constitution a prince, a nobility, and the power of the people, then these three powers will watch and keep each other reciprocally in check.

Discourses on Livy, I. 2

Among those justly celebrated for having established such a constitution, Lycurgus beyond doubt merits the highest praise. He organized the government of Sparta in such manner that, in giving to the king, the nobles, and the people each their portion of authority and duties, he created a government which maintained itself for over eight hundred years in the most perfect tranquility, and reflected infinite glory upon this legislator.

Discourses on Livy, I. 2

And although these kings lost their empire, for the reasons and in the manner which we have explained, yet those who expelled them appointed immediately two consuls in place of the king; and thus it was found that they had banished the title of king from Rome, but not the regal power. The government, composed of Consuls and a Senate, had but two of the three elements of which we have spoken, the monarchical and the aristocratic; the popular power was wanting. In the course of time, however, the insolence of the nobles, produced by the causes which we shall see further on, induced the people to rise against the others. The nobility, to save a portion of their power, were forced to yield a share of it to the people; but the Senate and the Consuls retained sufficient to maintain their rank in the state. It was then that the Tribunes of the people were created, which strengthened and confirmed the republic, being now composed of the three elements of which we have spoken above. Fortune favored her, so that, although the authority passed successively from the kings and nobles to the people, by the same degrees and for the same reasons that we have spoken of, yet the royal authority was never entirely abolished to bestow it upon the nobles; and these were never entirely deprived of their authority to give it to the people; but a combination was formed of the three powers, which rendered the constitution perfect, and this perfection was attained by the disunion of the Senate and the people.

Discourses on Livy, I. 2

The Multitude

A multitude without a chief is useless; and it is not well to threaten before having the power to act.

Discourses on Livy, I. 44

As the danger was pressing, All Saints' Day being near at hand, a number of people assembled in the palace; and deeming delay dangerous, they wanted the Signori to have the bell sounded, and the people called to arms. Taldo Valori was Gonfalonier at that time, and Francesco Salvi-

ati was one of the Signori; these, being relatives of the
Bardi, objected to having the alarm sounded, alleging that
it was not well to cause the people to arm for every slight
cause, as power given to the multitude and not controlled
by any check never resulted in good; that it was easy to
start tumults, but difficult to check them; and therefore it
would be better first to hear the truth of the matter, and
then to punish it legally, rather than to chastise it in a tu-
multuary manner and so risk the ruin of Florence upon a
simple denunciation.

History of Florence, II. 32

Opinion, Freedom of

At first a Tribune or any other citizen had the right to propose any law, and every citizen could speak in favor or
against it before its final adoption. This system was very
good so long as the citizens were uncorrupted, for it is always well in a state that every one may propose what he
deems for the public good; and it was equally well that
everyone should be allowed to express his opinion in rela-
tion to it, so that the people, having heard both sides, may
decide in favor of the best.

Discourses on Livy, I. 18

The People

The demands of a free people are rarely pernicious to their
liberty; they are generally inspired by oppressions, experienced or apprehended; and if their fears are ill founded,

resort is had to public assemblies, where the mere eloquence of a single good and respectable man will make
them sensible of their error. "The people," says Cicero, "although ignorant, yet are capable of appreciating the truth,"
and they yield to it readily when it is presented to them by
a man "whom they esteem worthy of their confidence."

Discourses on Livy, I. 4

And I hope it may not be accounted presumption if a man
of lowly and humble station ventures to discuss and direct
the conduct of princes; for as those who wish to delineate
countries place themselves low in the plain to observe the
form and character of mountains and high places, and for
the purpose of studying the nature of the low country
place themselves high upon an eminence, so one must be
a prince to know well the character of the people, and to
understand well the nature of a prince, one must be of the
people.

Dedicatory letter to *The Prince*

For besides the reasons given above, the dispositions of
peoples are variable; it is easy to persuade them to anything, but difficult to confirm them in that belief.

The Prince, VI

And as men, when they receive benefits from one of
whom they expected only ill treatment, will attach themselves readily to such a benefactor, so the people will become more kindly disposed to such a one than if he had
been made prince by their favor. Now a prince can secure
the good will of the people in various ways, which differ

with their character, and for which no fixed rules can be given. I will merely conclude by saying that it is essential for a prince to possess the good will and affection of his people, otherwise he will be utterly without support in time of adversity.

The Prince, IX

And let no one contravene this opinion of mine by quoting the trite saying, that "he who relies upon the people builds upon quicksand"; though this may be true when a private citizen places his reliance upon the people in the belief that they will come to his relief when he is oppressed by his enemies or the magistrates. In such a case he will often find himself deceived; as happened in Rome to the Gracchi, and in Florence to Messer Scali. But if it is a prince who places his reliance upon those whom he might command, being a man of courage and undismayed by adversity, and not having neglected to make proper preparations, and keeping all animated by his own courageous example and by his orders, he will not be deceived by the people; and it will be seen that the foundations of his state are laid solidly.

The Prince, IX

And if any one were to argue that, if the people who have possessions outside of the city were to see them ravaged and destroyed by the enemy, they would lose their patience, and that their selfish desire to protect their property would cause them to forget their attachment to the prince, I would meet this objection by saying that a powerful and valiant prince will easily overcome this difficulty by encouraging his subjects with the hope that the evil will not endure long, or by alarming them with fears of the enemy's cruelty, or by assuring himself adroitly of those who have been too forward in expressing their discontent.

The Prince, XI

The common people are always taken by appearances and by results, and it is the vulgar mass that constitutes the world.

The Prince, XVIII

Not to be hated nor contemned by the mass of the people is one of the best safeguards for a prince against conspiracies; for conspirators always believe that the death of the prince will be satisfactory to the people; but when they know that it will rather offend than conciliate the people, they will not venture upon such a course, for the difficulties that surround conspirators are infinite.

The Prince, XIX

The people love quiet, and for that reason they revere princes who are modest.

The Prince, XIX

The question may therefore be stated thus. A prince who fears his own people more than he does foreigners should build fortresses; but he who has more cause to fear strangers than his own people should do without them. The citadel of Milan, built by Francesco Sforza, has caused, and will yet cause, more trouble to the house of Sforza than any other disturbance in that state. The best fortress which a prince can possess is the affection of his people; for even if he have fortresses and is hated by his people, the fortresses will not save him; for when a people have once risen in arms against their prince, there will be no lack of strangers who will aid them.

The Prince, XX

Although the Romans happily always treated the people with liberality, yet when danger came upon them and Porsenna attacked Rome for the purpose of restoring the Tarquins, the Senate was doubtful whether the people might not rather accept the restoration of the kings than undergo a war; and to assure themselves of the people, they relieved them of the impost on salt and of all other taxes, saying that the poor did enough for the public benefit in rearing their children; and although in consequence of this liberality the people submitted to the hardships and privations of siege, famine, and war, yet let no one, trusting to this example, defer securing the good will of the people until the moment of danger; for they will never succeed in it as the Romans did. For the masses will think that they do not owe the benefits you have bestowed upon them to you, but to your adversaries; and fearing that when the danger is past you will again take from them what under the pressure of danger you conceded to them, they will feel under no obligations to you.

Discourses on Livy, I. 32

We have seen in the preceding chapter how much credit the patricians gained with the people of Rome by the apparent benefits they bestowed upon them, both by the pay granted to the soldiers and by the manner of distributing the imposts. If the nobility had understood how to maintain this feeling, all causes for further disturbances would have been removed, and the Tribunes would have lost the influence they had over the people of Rome. For in truth there is no better or easier mode in republics, and especially in such as are corrupt, for successfully opposing the ambition of any citizen, than to occupy in advance of him those ways by which he expects to attain the rank he aims at. If this mode had been employed by the adversaries of Cosimo de' Medici, it would have been much better than to expel him from Florence; for if they had adopted his plan of favoring the people, they would have succeeded without any disturbances or violence in depriving him of the weapons which he himself employed with so much skill.

Discourses on Livy, I. 52

Here we have to note two things; first, that the people often, deceived by an illusive good, desire their own ruin, and, unless they are made sensible of the evil of the one and the benefit of the other course by someone in whom they have confidence, they will expose the republic to infinite peril and damage. And if it happens that the people have no confidence in anyone, as sometimes will be the case when they have been deceived before by events or men, then it will inevitably lead to the ruin of the state. Dante says upon this point in his discourse *On Monarchy* that the people often shout, "Life to our death, and death to our life!" It is this want of confidence on the part of the people that causes good measures to be often rejected in republics, as we have related above of the Venetians, who when attacked by so many enemies could not make up their minds to conciliate some of them by giving to them what they had taken from others; it was this that brought the war upon them and caused the other powers to form a league against them before their final ruin. If we consider now what is easy and what difficult to persuade a people to, we may make this distinction: either what you wish to persuade them to represents at first sight gain or loss, or it seems brave or cowardly. And if you propose to them anything that upon its face seems profitable and courageous, though there be really a loss concealed under it which may involve the ruin of the republic, the multitude will ever be most easily persuaded to it. But if the measure proposed seems doubtful and likely to cause loss, then it will be difficult to persuade the people to it, even though the benefit and welfare of the republic were concealed under it. All this is supported by numerous examples among the Romans as well as strangers, and both in modern and in ancient times.

Discourses on Livy, I. 53

Popular Government

For a people that governs and is well regulated by laws will be stable, prudent, and grateful, as much so, and even more, according to my opinion, as a prince, although he be esteemed wise; and, on the other hand, a prince, freed from the restraints of the law, will be more ungrateful, inconstant, and imprudent than a people similarly situated. The difference in their conduct is not due to any difference in their nature (for that is the same, and if there be any difference for good, it is on the side of the people); but to the greater or lesser respect they have for the laws under which they respectively live. And whoever studies the Roman people will see that for four hundred years they have been haters of royalty and lovers of the glory and common good of their country; and he will find any number of examples that will prove both the one and the other.

Discourses on Livy, I. 58

But as regards prudence and stability, I say that the people are more prudent and stable, and have better judgment than a prince; and it is not without good reason that it is said, "The voice of the people is the voice of God"; for we see popular opinion prognosticate events in such a wonderful manner that it would almost seem as if the people had some occult virtue, which enables them to foresee the good and the evil. As to the people's capacity of judging of things, it is exceedingly rare that, when they hear two orators of equal talents advocate different measures, they do not decide in favor of the better of the two; which proves their ability to discern the truth of what they hear. And if occasionally they are misled in matters involving questions of courage or seeming utility, so is a prince also many times misled by his own passions, which are much greater than those of the people. We also see that in the election of their magistrates they make far better choice than princes; and no people will ever be persuaded to elect a man of infamous character and corrupt habits to any post of dignity, to which a prince is easily influenced in a thousand different ways.

Discourses on Livy, I. 58

I say that both governments of princes and of the people have lasted a long time, but both have required to be regulated by laws. For a prince who knows no other control but his own will is like a madman, and a people that can do as it pleases will hardly be wise. If now we compare a prince who is controlled by laws, and a people that is untrammelled by them, we shall find more virtue in the people than in the prince; and if we compare them when both are freed from such control, we shall see that the people are guilty of fewer excesses than the prince, and that the errors of the people are of less importance, and therefore more easily remedied. For a licentious and mutinous people may easily be brought back to good conduct by the influence and persuasion of a good man, but an evil-minded prince is not amenable to such influences, and therefore there is no other remedy against him but cold steel.

Discourses on Livy, I. 58

Poverty

It is this that has caused it to be said that poverty and hunger make men industrious, and that the law makes men good.

Discourses on Livy, I. 3

We have argued elsewhere that it is of the greatest advantage in a republic to have laws that keep her citizens poor. Although there does not appear to have been any special law to this effect in Rome (the agrarian law having met with the greatest opposition), yet experience shows that even so late as four hundred years after its foundation there was still great poverty in Rome. We cannot ascribe this fact to any other cause than that poverty never was allowed to stand in the way of the achievement of any rank or honor, and that virtue and merit were sought for under whatever roof they dwelt; it was this system that made riches naturally less desirable.

Discourses on Livy, III. 25

In well-regulated republics the state ought to be rich and the citizens poor.

Discourses on Livy, I. 37

The Prince

Let us come now to that other case, when a prominent citizen has become prince of his country, not by treason and violence, but by the favor of his fellow-citizens. This may be called a civil principality; and to attain it requires neither great virtue nor extraordinary good fortune, but rather a fortunate shrewdness. I say, then, that such principalities are achieved either by the favor of the people or by that of the nobles; for in every state there will be found two different dispositions, which result from this—that the people dislike being ruled and oppressed by the nobles, whilst the nobles seek to rule and oppress the people. And this diversity of feeling and interests engenders one of three effects in a state: these are either a principality, or a government of liberty, or license. A principality results either from the will of the people or from that of the nobles, according as either the one or the other prevails and has the opportunity. For the nobles, seeing that they cannot resist the people, begin to have recourse to the influence and reputation of one of their own class, and make him a prince, so that under the shadow of his power they may give free scope to their desires. The people also, seeing that they cannot resist the nobles, have recourse to the influence and reputation of one man, and make him prince, so as to be protected by his authority. He who becomes prince by the aid of the nobles will have more difficulty in maintaining himself than he who arrives at that high station by the aid of the people. For the former finds himself surrounded by many who in their own opinion are equal to him, and for that reason he can neither command nor manage them in his own way. But he who attains the principality by favor of the people stands alone, and has around him none, or very few, who will not yield him a ready obedience. Moreover, you cannot satisfy the nobles with honesty, and without wrong to others, but it is easy to satisfy the people, whose aims are ever more honest than those of the nobles; the latter wishing to oppress, and the former being unwilling to be oppressed. I will say further, that a prince can never assure himself of a people who are hostile to him, for they are too numerous; the nobles on the other hand being but few, it is easy for a prince to make himself sure of them.

The Prince, IX

A prince then should look mainly to the successful maintenance of his state. The means which he employs for this will always be accounted honorable and will be praised by everybody.

The Prince, XVIII

A prince should also show himself a lover of virtue, and should honor all who excel in any one of the arts, and should encourage his citizens quietly to pursue their vocations, whether of commerce, agriculture, or any other human industry; so that the one may not abstain from embellishing his possessions for fear of their being taken from him, nor the other from opening new sources of commerce for fear of taxes. But the prince should provide rewards for those who are willing to do these things, and for all who strive to enlarge his city or state. And besides this, he should at suitable periods amuse his people with festivities and spectacles. And as cities are generally divided into guilds and classes, he should keep account of these bodies and occasionally be present at their assemblies, and he should set an example of his affability and magnificence; preserving, however, always the majesty of his dignity, which should never be wanting on any occasion or under any circumstances.

The Prince, XXI

For the actions of a new prince are much more closely observed and scrutinized than those of an hereditary one; and when they are known to be virtuous, they will win the confidence and affections of men much more for the new prince, and make his subjects feel under greater obligations to him, than if he were of the ancient line. For men are ever more taken with the things of the present than with those of the past; and when they find their own good in the present, then they enjoy it and seek none other, and they will be ready in every way to defend the new prince, provided he be not wanting to himself in other respects.

The Prince, XXIV

Public Honors

When the city had become corrupt, this system [of allowing citizens to present their candidacy to public honors] became most pernicious; for it was no longer the most virtuous and deserving, but the most powerful who asked for the magistratures; and the less powerful, often the most meritorious, abstained from being candidates from fear. This state of things did not come all at once, but by degrees, as is generally the case with other vices. For after the Romans had subjugated Africa and Asia and had reduced nearly all Greece to their obedience, they felt assured of their liberty and saw no enemies that could cause them any apprehension. This security and the weakness of the conquered nations caused the Roman people no longer to bestow the consulate according to the merits of the candidates, but according to favor; giving that dignity to those who best knew how to entertain the people, and not to those who best knew how to conquer their enemies. After that they descended from those who were most favored to such as had most wealth and power, so that the really meritorious became wholly excluded from that dignity.

Discourses on Livy, I. 18

Although the Romans were great lovers of glory, yet they did not esteem it dishonorable to obey those whom they had at a previous time commanded, or to serve in that army of which they themselves had been chiefs. This custom is entirely contrary to the opinion, rules, and practice of our times; and in Venice they even yet hold to the error that a citizen who has once held a high post under the state would be dishonored by accepting a lower one; and the city consents to what she cannot change. However honorable this may be for a private citizen, yet for the public it is absolutely useless. A republic can and should have more hope and confidence in that citizen who from a superior grade descends to accept a less important one, than in him who from an inferior employment mounts to the exercise of a superior one; for the latter cannot reasonably be relied upon unless he is surrounded by men of such respectability and virtue that his inexperience may in some measure be compensated for by their counsel and authority.

Discourses on Livy, I. 36

Republics

Republics have more vitality, a greater spirit of resentment and desire of revenge, for the memory of their ancient liberty neither can nor will permit them to remain quiet, and therefore the surest way of holding them is either to destroy them, or for the conqueror to go and live there.

The Prince, V

Feeble republics are irresolute, and know not how to take a decided part; and whenever they do, it is more the result of necessity than of choice.

Discourses on Livy, I. 38

These examples show how dangerous it is for a republic or a prince to keep the minds of their subjects in a state of apprehension by pains and penalties constantly suspended over their heads. And certainly no more pernicious course could be pursued; for men who are kept in doubt and uncertainty as to their lives will resort to every kind of measure to secure themselves against danger, and will necessarily become more audacious and inclined to violent changes. It is important, therefore, either never to attack anyone, or to inflict punishment by a single act of rigor, and afterwards to reassure the public mind by such acts as will restore calmness and confidence.

Discourses on Livy, I. 45

In this we see one of the modes in which republics are brought to ruin, and how men rise from one ambition to another; and we recognize the truth of the sentence which

Sallust puts into the mouth of Caesar, that "all evil examples have their origin in good beginnings." The ambitious citizens of a republic seek in the first instance . . . to make themselves sure against the attacks, not only of individuals, but even of the magistrates. To enable them to do this, they seek to gain friends, either by apparently honest ways, or by assisting men with money, or by defending them against the powerful; and as this seems virtuous, almost everybody is readily deceived by it, and therefore no one opposes it, until the ambitious individual has, without hindrance, grown so powerful that private citizens fear him and the magistrates treat him with consideration. And when he has risen to that point, no one at the beginning having interfered with his greatness, it becomes in the end most dangerous to attempt to put him down, for the reasons I have given above when speaking of the danger of trying to abate an evil that has already attained a considerable growth in a city; so that in the end the matter is reduced to this, that you must endeavor to destroy the evil at the risk of sudden ruin, or, by allowing it to go on, submit to manifest servitude, unless the death of the individual or some other accident intervenes to rid the state of him. For when it has once come to that point that the citizens and the magistrates are afraid to offend him and his adherents, it will afterwards not require much effort on his part to make them render judgments and attack persons according to his will. For this reason republics should make it one of their aims to watch that none of their citizens should be allowed to do harm on pretense of doing good, and that no one should acquire an influence that would injure instead of promoting liberty.

Discourses on Livy, I. 46

It is easy to understand whence that affection for liberty arose in the people, for they had seen that cities never increased in dominion or wealth unless they were free. And certainly it is wonderful to think of the greatness which Athens attained within the space of a hundred years after having freed herself from the tyranny of Pisistratus; and still more wonderful is it to reflect upon the greatness which Rome achieved after she was rid of her kings. The cause of this is manifest, for it is not individual prosperity but the good that makes cities great; and certainly the good is regarded nowhere but in republics, because whatever they do is for the common benefit, and should it happen to prove an injury to one or more individuals, those for whose benefit the thing is done are so numerous that they can always carry the measure against the few that are injured by it.

Discourses on Livy, II. 2

Population is greater there because marriages are more free and offer more advantages to the citizen; for people will gladly have children when they know that they can support them, and that they will not be deprived of their patrimony, and where they know that their children not only are born free and not slaves, but, if they possess talents and virtue, can arrive at the highest dignities of the state. In free countries we also see wealth increase more rapidly, both that which results from the culture of the soil and that which is produced by industry and art; for everybody gladly multiplies those things and seeks to acquire those goods the possession of which he can tranquilly enjoy. Thence men vie with each other to increase both private and public wealth, which consequently increase in an extraordinary manner.

Discourses on Livy, II. 2

There is no easier way to ruin a republic where the people have power than to involve them in daring enterprises; for where the people have influence they will always be ready to engage in them, and no contrary opinion will prevent them. But if such enterprises cause the ruin of states, they still more frequently cause the ruin of the particular citizens who are placed at the head to conduct them. For when defeat comes instead of the successes which the people expected, they do not charge it upon the ill fortune or incompetence of their leaders, but upon their wickedness and ignorance; and generally either kill, imprison, or exile them, as happened to many Carthaginian and Athenian generals.

Discourses on Livy, I. 53

To explain more clearly what is meant by the term "gentlemen" [*gentiluomini*], I say that those are called gentlemen who live idly upon the proceeds of their extensive possessions, without devoting themselves to agriculture or any other useful pursuit to gain a living. Such men are pernicious to any country or republic, but more pernicious even than these are such as have, besides their other possessions, castles which they command, and subjects who obey them. This class of men abound in the kingdom of Naples, in the Roman territory, in the Romagna, and in Lombardy; whence it is that no republic has ever been able to exist in those countries, nor have they been able to preserve any regular political existence, for that class of men are everywhere enemies of all civil government. And to attempt the establishment of a republic in a country so constituted would be impossible. The only way to establish any kind of order there is to found a monarchical government; for where the body of the people is so thoroughly corrupt that the laws are powerless for restraint, it becomes necessary to establish some superior power which, with a royal hand and with full and absolute powers, may put a curb upon the excessive ambition and corruption of the powerful. This is verified by the example of Tuscany, where in a comparatively small extent of territory there have for a long time existed three republics, Florence, Sienna, and Lucca; and although the other cities of this territory are in a measure subject to these, yet we see that in spirit and by their institutions they maintain, or attempt to maintain their liberty; all of which is due to the fact that there are in that country no lords possessing castles, and exceedingly few or no gentlemen. On the contrary, there is such a general equality that it would be easy for any man of sagacity, well versed in the ancient forms of civil government, to introduce a republic there; but the misfortunes of that country have been so great that up to the present time no man has arisen who has had the power and ability to do so.

Discourses on Livy, I. 55

Upon this subject we must remark, first, that when any evil arises within a republic, or threatens it from without, that is to say from an intrinsic or extrinsic cause, and has become so great as to fill every one with apprehension, the more certain remedy by far is to temporize with it, rather than to attempt to extirpate it; for almost invariably he who attempts to crush it will rather increase its force, and will accelerate the harm apprehended from it. And such evils arise more frequently in a republic from intrinsic than extrinsic causes, as it often occurs that a citizen is allowed to acquire more authority than is proper; or that changes are permitted in a law which is the very nerve and life of liberty; and then they let this evil go so far that it becomes more hazardous to correct it than to allow it to run on. And it is the more difficult to recognize these evils at their origin, as it seems natural to men always to favor the beginning of things; and these favors are more readily accorded to such acts as seem to have some merit in them and are done by young men.

Discourses on Livy, I. 33

Revolutions and Reforms

It was necessary therefore, if Rome wished to preserve her liberty in the midst of this corruption, that she should have modified her constitution, in like manner as in the progress of her existence she had made new laws; for institutions and forms should be adapted to the subject, whether it be good or evil, inasmuch as the same form cannot suit two subjects that are essentially different. But as the constitution of a state, when once it has been discovered to be no longer suitable, should be amended, either all at once, or by degrees as each defect becomes known, I say that both of these courses are equally impossible. For a gradual modification must be the work of some wise man, who has seen the evil from afar in its very beginning; but it is very likely that such a man may never rise up in the state, and even if he should he will hardly be able to persuade the others to what he proposes; for men accustomed to live after one fashion do not like to change, and the less so as they do not see the evil staring them in the face but presented to them as a mere conjecture. As to reforming these institutions all at once, when their defects have become manifest to everybody, that also is most difficult; for to do this ordinary means will not suffice; they may even be injurious under such circumstances, and therefore it becomes necessary to resort to extraordinary measures, such as violence and arms, and above all things to make one's self absolute master of the state, so as to be able to dispose of it at will. And as the reformation of the political condition of a state presupposes a good man, whilst the making of himself prince of a republic by violence naturally presupposes a bad one, it will consequently be exceedingly rare that a good man should be found willing to employ wicked means to become prince, even though his final object be good; or that a bad man, after having become prince, should be willing to labor for good ends, and that it should enter his mind to use for good purposes that authority which he has acquired by evil means. From these combined causes arises the difficulty or impossibility of maintaining liberty in a republic that has become corrupt, or to establish it there anew. And, if it has to be introduced and maintained, then it will be necessary to reduce the state to a monarchical, rather than a republican form of government; for men whose turbulence could not be controlled by the simple force of law can be controlled in a measure only by an almost regal power. And to attempt to restore men to good conduct by any other means would be either a most cruel or an impossible undertaking.

Discourses on Livy, I. 18

He who desires or attempts to reform the government of a state and wishes to have it accepted and capable of maintaining itself to the satisfaction of everybody, must at least retain the semblance of the old forms; so that it may seem to the people that there has been no change in the institutions, even though in fact they are entirely different from the old ones. For the great majority of mankind are satisfied with appearances, as though they were realities, and are often even more influenced by the things that seem than by those that are.

Discourses on Livy, I. 25

Servitude

And the hardest of all servitudes is to be subject to a republic, and this for these reasons: first, because it is more enduring, and there is no hope of escaping from it; and secondly, because republics aim to enervate and weaken all other states so as to increase their own power. This is not the case with a prince who holds another country in subjection, unless indeed he should be a barbarous devastator of countries and a destroyer of all human civilization, such as the princes of the Orient. But if he be possessed of only ordinary humanity, he will treat all cities that are subject to him equally well, and will leave them in the enjoyment of their arts and industries and, to some measure, all their ancient institutions. So that if they cannot grow the same as if they were free, they will at least not be ruined whilst in bondage; and by this is understood that bondage into which cities fall that become subject to a stranger, for of [the bondage] to one of their own citizens we have already spoken above.

Discourses on Livy, II. 2

Social Conflicts

Nor can we regard a republic as disorderly where so many virtues were seen to shine. For good examples are the result of good education, and good education is due to good laws; and good laws in their turn spring from those very tumults which have been so inconsiderately condemned by many.

Discourses on Livy, I. 4

I maintain that those who condemn the quarrels of the Senate and the people of Rome condemn that which was the very origin of liberty, and that they were probably more impressed by the cries and noise which these distur-

bances occasioned in public places than by the good effect
which they produced; and that they do not consider that
in every republic there are two parties, that of the nobles
and that of the people, and all the laws that are favorable
to liberty result from the opposition of these parties to one
another, as may easily be seen from the events that occurred in Rome.

Discourses on Livy, I. 4

In Rome, as everybody knows, after the expulsion of the
kings a division arose between the nobles and the people,
and [with that division in place] she maintained herself
until her downfall. So did Athens, and so all the republics
that flourished in those times. But in Florence, the first
division was among the nobles, afterwards between the
nobles and the citizens, and finally between the citizens
and the underclass; and many times it happened that one
of the parties that remained in power again divided in
two. These divisions caused so many deaths, so many exiles, so much destruction in so many families as never occurred in any other city of which we have any record. And
truly no other circumstance so well illustrates the power
of our city as that which resulted from these divisions,
which would have been enough to destroy any other great
and powerful republic.

Preface to the *History of Florence*

The causes of nearly all the evils that afflict republics are to
be found in the great and natural enmities that exist between the people and the nobles, and which result from
the disposition of the one to command, and the indisposi-

tion of the other to obey. It is this diversity of disposition that supplies nourishment to all the troubles that disturb these states. This was the cause of the divisions in Rome, and it is this that kept Florence divided, if I may compare small things with great ones, although different effects were produced by it in these two republics; for the dissensions that arose in the beginning in Rome were marked by disputes, those of Florence by combats. Those of Rome were terminated by a law, those of Florence by the death and exile of many citizens. Those of Rome ever increased military valor, whilst those of Florence destroyed it entirely. Those of Rome led from an equality of citizens to the greatest inequality, and those of Florence from inequality to the most wonderful equality. This diversity of effects must have been caused by the different character of the aims which these two peoples had in view. For the people of Rome desired to enjoy the highest honors of the state equally with the nobles; the people of Florence fought for the exclusive control of the government, without any participation in it by the nobles. And as the object of the Roman people was more reasonable, so the nobles bore the wrongs inflicted upon them more readily, and yielded without coming to arms. And, after some disputes, they agreed to a law that should satisfy the people and yet leave the nobles in possession of their dignities. On the other hand, the demands of the Florentine people were injurious and unjust, and therefore did the nobility prepare itself for defense with greater energy; and thus the people resorted to bloodshed and exile. And the laws that were afterwards made were not for the common benefit, but were wholly in favor of the victor.

Preface to Book III of the *History of Florence*

The State

All states and governments that have had, and have at present, dominion over men, have been and are either republics or principalities.

The Prince, I

States thus acquired [that is, states annexed to the hereditary states of a prince] have been accustomed either to live under a prince, or to exist as free states; and they are acquired either by the arms of others, or by the conqueror's own, or by fortune or virtue.

The Prince, I

I say, then, that hereditary states, accustomed to the lineage of their prince, are maintained with much less difficulty than new states. For it is enough merely that the prince not transcend the order of things established by his predecessors, and then accommodate himself to events as they occur. So that if such a prince has but ordinary sagacity, he will always maintain himself in his state, unless some extraordinary and superior force should deprive him of it.

The Prince, II

I will say then, first, that the states which a prince acquires and annexes to his own dominions are either in the same country, speaking the same language, or they are not. When they are, it is very easy to hold them, especially if they have not been accustomed to govern themselves; for in that case it suffices to extinguish the line of the prince who, till then, has ruled over them, but otherwise to maintain their old institutions. There being no difference in their manners and customs, the inhabitants will submit quietly.... Hence, in order to retain a newly acquired state, regard must be had to two things: one, that the line of the ancient sovereign be entirely extinguished; and the other, that the laws be not changed, nor the taxes increased, so that the new may, in the least possible time, be thoroughly incorporated with the ancient state. But when states are acquired in a country differing in language, customs, and laws, then come the difficulties, and then it requires great good fortune and much sagacity to hold them, and one of the best and most efficient means is for the prince who has acquired them to go and reside there, which will make his possession more secure and durable.

The Prince, III

And thus it is in the affairs of state; for when the evils that arise in it are seen far ahead, which it is given only to a wise prince to do, then they are easily remedied; but when, in consequence of not having been foreseen, these evils are allowed to grow and assume such proportions that they become manifest to everyone, then they can no longer be remedied.

The Prince, III

Conquered states that have been accustomed to liberty and the government of their own laws can be held by the conqueror in three different ways. The first is to ruin them; the second, for the conqueror to go and reside there in person; and the third is to allow them to continue to live under their own laws, subject to a regular tribute, and to create in them a government of a few, who will keep the country friendly to the conqueror. Such a government having been established by the new prince, [the country] knows that it cannot maintain itself without the support of his power and friendship, and it becomes its interest therefore to sustain him. A city that has been accustomed to free institutions is much easier held by its own citizens than in any other way, if the conqueror desires to preserve it.

The Prince, V

It is very different with states that have been accustomed to live under a prince. When the line of the prince is once extinguished, the inhabitants, being on the one hand accustomed to obey, and on the other having lost their ancient sovereign, can neither agree to create a new one from among themselves, nor do they know how to live in liberty; and thus they will be less prompt to take up arms, and the new prince will readily be able to gain their good will and to assure himself of them.

The Prince, V

The main foundations which all states must have, whether new, or old, or mixed, are good laws and good armies.

The Prince, XII

But when a prince acquires a new state, which he annexes as an appendage to his old possessions, then it is advisable for him to disarm the inhabitants of the new state, excepting those who, upon the acquisition of the same, declared in the prince's favor. But even these it will be well for him to weaken and enervate when occasion offers; so that his armed forces shall be organized in such a way as to consist entirely of his own subjects, natives of his original state.

The Prince, XX

Tribunes of the People

Thus the nobles, after the death of the Tarquins being no longer under the influence that had restrained them, determined to establish a new order of things, which had the same effect as the misrule of the Tarquins during their existence; and therefore, after many troubles, tumults, and dangers occasioned by the excesses which both the nobles and the people committed, they came, for the security of the people, to the creation of the Tribunes, who were endowed with so many prerogatives and surrounded with so much respect that they formed a powerful barrier between the Senate and the people, which curbed the insolence of the former.

Discourses on Livy, I. 3

Tyranny

And yet nearly all men, deceived by a false good and a false glory, allow themselves voluntarily or ignorantly to be drawn toward those who deserve more blame than praise. Such as by the establishment of a republic or kingdom could earn eternal glory for themselves incline to tyranny, without perceiving how much glory, how much honor, security, satisfaction, and tranquility of mind, they forfeit; and what infamy, disgrace, blame, danger, and disquietude they incur.

Discourses on Livy, I. 10

The actions of citizens should be watched, for often such as seem virtuous conceal the beginning of tyranny.

Discourses on Livy, III. 28

Here we must note that the necessity of creating the tyranny of the Decemvirs in Rome arose from the same causes that generally produce tyrannies in cities; that is to say, the too great desire of the people to be free, and the equally too great desire of the nobles to dominate. And if the two parties do not agree to secure liberty by law, and either the one or the other throws all its influence in favor of one man, then a tyranny is the natural result.

Discourses on Livy I. 40

Although it is the nature of the nobility to desire to dominate, yet those who have no share in such domination are the enemies of the tyrant, who can never win them all over to him, because of their extreme ambition and avarice, which are so great that the tyrant can never have riches and honors enough to bestow to satisfy them all.

Discourses on Livy, I. 40

Tyranny and License

Cities that govern themselves under the name of republics, and especially such as are not well constituted, are exposed to frequent revolutions in their government, which make them pass not as is generally believed from servitude to liberty, but from servitude to license. For it is merely the name of liberty that is extolled by the ministers of license, which are the popular faction, and by the ministers of servitude, which are the nobles, neither one nor the other of these being willing to submit either to laws or to men.

History of Florence, IV. 1

And similar laws and institutions will ever be needed in all those republics that have often changed, and continue to change their governments from a state of tyranny to one of license, and from the latter to the former. For in such there is not, and cannot be, any stability, because of the violent enmities which each of them provokes; for the one does not please the good men, and the other displeases the wise ones; the one can easily work harm, and the other can only with difficulty effect any good. In the one, the insolent have too much authority, and in the other, the foolish; and both one and the other require being restrained by the virtue and good fortune of one man, who may at any moment be removed by death, or his usefulness impaired by misfortune.

History of Florence, IV. 1

War

No one should ever submit to an evil for the sake of avoiding a war. For a war is never avoided, but is only deferred to one's own disadvantage.

The Prince, III

A prince, then, should have no other thought or object so much at heart, and make no other thing so much his especial study, as the art of war and the organization and discipline of his army; for that is the only art that is expected of him who commands. And such is its power that it not only maintains in their position those who were born princes, but it often enables men born in private station to achieve the rank of princes. And . . . we have seen that princes who thought more of indulgence in pleasure than of arms have thereby lost their states. Thus the neglect of the art of war is the principal cause of the loss of your state, whilst a proficiency in it often enables you to acquire one.

The Prince, XIV

Since we have discussed above the manner in which the Romans conducted their wars, and how the Tuscans were attacked by the Gauls, it seems to me not foreign to the subject to point out that there are two different kinds of war. The one springs from the ambition of princes or republics that seek to extend their empire; such were the wars of Alexander the Great, and those of the Romans, and such are those which two hostile powers carry on against each other. These wars are dangerous, but never go so far as to drive all its inhabitants out of a province, because the conqueror is satisfied with the submission of the people and generally leaves them their dwellings and possessions, and even the enjoyment of their own institutions. The other kind of war is when an entire people, constrained by famine or war, leave their country with their families for the purpose of seeking a new home in a new country, not for the purpose of subjecting it to their dominion as in the first case, but with the intention of taking absolute possession of it themselves and driving out or killing its original inhabitants. This kind of war is most frightful and cruel.

Discourses on Livy, II. 8

VI
Machiavelli on His Contemporaries

Figure 6. Lorenzo II de' Medici, Duke of Urbino. Erich Lessing/Art Resource, NY.

Alexander VI, Pope

Afterwards Alexander VI came to the Pontificate, who, more than any of his predecessors, showed what a pope could accomplish with the money and power of the Church.* Availing himself of the opportunity of the French invasion of Italy and the instrumentality of the Duke Valentino, Alexander accomplished all those things which I have mentioned when speaking of the actions of the Duke. And although Alexander's object was not the aggrandizement of the Church, but rather that of his son, the Duke, yet all his efforts served to advance the interests of the Church, which, after his death and that of his son, fell heir to all the results of his labors.

The Prince, XI

It is necessary that the prince should know how to color this nature [that is, his faithlessness] well, and how to be a great hypocrite and dissembler. For men are so simple and yield so much to immediate necessity, that the deceiver will never lack dupes. I will mention one of the most recent examples. Alexander VI never did nor ever thought of anything but to deceive, and always found a reason for doing so. No one ever had greater skill in asseverating, nor was there anyone who affirmed his pledges with greater oaths and observed them less than Pope Alexander; and yet he was always successful in his deceits, because he knew the weakness of men in that particular.

The Prince, XVIII

---

* Pope Alexander VI, born Roderic Llançol i de Borja, was pope from August 11, 1492 until his death on August 18, 1503.

Giovanpaolo Baglioni

Sagacious men who were with the Pope observed his temerity and the cowardice of Baglioni,* and could not understand why the latter had not by a single blow rid himself of his enemy, whereby he would have secured for himself eternal fame and rich booty, for the Pope was accompanied by all the cardinals with their valuables. Nor could they believe that he had refrained from doing this either from goodness or conscientious scruples; for no sentiment of piety or respect could enter the heart of a man of such vile character as Giovanpaolo, who had dishonored his sister and murdered his nephews and cousins for the sake of obtaining possession of the state; but they concluded that mankind were neither utterly wicked nor perfectly good, and that when a crime has in itself some grandeur or magnanimity they will not know how to attempt it. Thus Giovanpaolo Baglioni, who did not mind open incest and parricide, knew not how, or, more correctly speaking, dared not, to attempt an act (although having a justifiable opportunity) for which every one would have admired his courage, and which would have secured him eternal fame, as being the first to show these prelates how little esteem those merit who live and govern as they do; and as having done an act the greatness of which would have overshadowed the infamy and all the danger that could possibly result from it.

Discourses on Livy, I. 27

* Giovanpaolo Baglioni (c. 1470–June 1520) was an Italian condottiero and lord of Perugia.

Cesare Borgia, the Duke Valentino

Upon reviewing now all the actions of the Duke, I should not know where to blame him; it seems to me that I should rather hold him up as an example . . . to be imitated by all those who have risen to sovereignty, either by the good fortune or the arms of others.* For being endowed with great courage and having a lofty ambition, he could not have acted otherwise under the circumstances; and the only thing that defeated his designs was the shortness of [Pope] Alexander's life and his own bodily infirmity. Whoever, then, in a newly acquired state, finds it necessary to secure himself against his enemies, to gain friends, to conquer by force or by cunning, to make himself feared or beloved by the people, to be followed and revered by the soldiery, to destroy all who could or might injure him, to substitute a new for the old order of things, to be severe and yet gracious, magnanimous, and liberal, to disband a disloyal army and create a new one, to preserve the friendship of kings and princes so that they may bestow benefits upon him with grace and fear to injure him—such a one, I say, cannot find more recent examples than those presented by the conduct of the Duke Valentino. The only thing we can blame him for was the election of Julius II to the Pontificate, which was a bad selection for him to make; for, as has been said, though he was not able to make a pope to his own liking, yet he could have prevented, and

* Cesare Borgia, Duke of Valentinois, was a Spanish condottiero, nobleman, politician, and cardinal. He was the illegitimate son of Pope Alexander VI.

should never have consented to, the election of one from among those cardinals whom he had offended, or who, if he had been elected, would have had occasion to fear him, for either fear or resentment makes men enemies.

The Prince, VII

Having conquered the Romagna, the Duke found it under the control of a number of impotent petty tyrants, who had devoted themselves more to plundering their subjects than to governing them properly, and to encouraging discord and disorder among them rather than peace and union; so that this province was infested by brigands, torn by quarrels, and given over to every sort of violence. He saw at once that to restore order among the inhabitants and obedience to the sovereign it was necessary to establish a good and vigorous government there. And for this purpose he appointed as governor of that province Don Ramiro d'Orco, a man of cruelty, but at the same time of great energy, to whom he gave plenary power. In a very short time d'Orco reduced the province to peace and order, thereby gaining for himself the highest reputation. After a while, the Duke found such excessive exercise of authority no longer necessary or expedient, for he feared that it might render himself odious. He therefore established a civil tribunal in the heart of the province, under an excellent president, where every city should have its own advocate. And having observed that the past rigor of Ramiro had engendered some hatred, he wished to show to the people, for the purpose of removing that feeling from their minds and to win their entire confidence, that,

if any cruelties had been practiced, they had not originated with him but had resulted altogether from the harsh
nature of his minister. He therefore took occasion to have
Messer Ramiro put to death and his body cut into two
parts and exposed in the marketplace of Cesena one
morning, with a block of wood and a bloody cutlass left
beside him. The horror of this spectacle caused the people
to remain for a time stupefied and satisfied.

The Prince, VII

Ferdinand of Aragon, King of Spain

Nothing makes a prince so much esteemed as the undertaking of great enterprises and the setting a noble example
in his own person. We have a striking instance of this in
Ferdinand of Aragon, the present king of Spain.* He may
be called, as it were, a new prince; for, from being king of
a feeble state, he has, by his fame and glory, become the
first sovereign of Christendom; and if we examine his actions we shall find them all most grand, and some of them
extraordinary. In the beginning of his reign he attacked
Granada, and it was this undertaking that was the very
foundation of his greatness. At first he carried on this war
leisurely and without fear of opposition; for he kept the
nobles of Castile occupied with this enterprise, and, their
minds being thus engaged by war, they gave no attention
to the innovations introduced by the king, who thereby
acquired a reputation and an influence over the nobles

* Ferdinand II, called "the Catholic" (1462–1516).

without their being aware of it. The money of the Church and of the people enabled him to support his armies, and by that long war he succeeded in giving a stable foundation to his military establishment, which afterwards brought him so much honor. Besides this, to be able to engage in still greater enterprises, he always availed himself of religion as a pretext, and committed a pious cruelty in spoliating and driving the Moors out of his kingdom, which certainly was a most admirable and extraordinary example. Under the same cloak of religion, he attacked Africa and made a descent upon Italy, and finally assailed France. And thus he was always planning great enterprises, which kept the minds of his subjects in a state of suspense and admiration, and occupied with their results. And these different enterprises followed so quickly one upon the other, that he never gave men a chance deliberately to make any attempt against himself.

The Prince, XXI

A certain prince of our time, whom it is well not to name, never preached anything but peace and good faith; but if he had always observed either the one or the other, it would in most instances have cost him his reputation or his state.

The Prince, XVIII

Italian Princes

Those of our princes, therefore, who have lost their dominions after having been established in them for many years, should not blame fortune, but only their own indolence and lack of energy; for in times of quiet they never thought of the possibility of a change (it being a common defect of men in fair weather to take no thought of storms), and afterwards, when adversity overtook them, their first impulse was to fly and not to defend themselves, hoping that the people, when disgusted with the insolence of the victors, would recall them.

The Prince, XXIV

The common belief of our Italian princes, before they felt the blows of Transalpine war, was that a prince needed only to think of a sharp reply in his study, to write a fine letter, to show quickness and cleverness in quotable sayings and replies, to know how to spin a fraud, to be adorned with gems and with gold, to sleep and eat with greater splendor than others, to be surrounded with wanton pleasures, to deal with subjects avariciously and proudly, to decay in laziness, to give positions in the army by favor, to despise anybody who showed them any praiseworthy course, and to expect their words to be taken as the responses of oracles. It did not enter the minds of these wretches that they were preparing themselves to be the prey of whoever attacked them. From that came in 1494 great terrors, sudden flights, and astonishing losses; and thus three of the most powerful states in Italy have been many times spoiled and plundered. But what is worse is that those who are left continue in the same error and live by the same bad system, and do not consider that those who in antiquity wished to keep their states did and caused to be done all those things that I have discussed, and that their effort was to prepare the body for hardships and the mind not to fear perils.

The Art of War, VII

Julius II, Pope

Pope Julius II was in all his actions most impetuous; and the times and circumstances happened so conformably to that mode of proceeding that he always achieved happy results.[*] Witness the first attempt he made upon Bologna, when Messer Giovanni Bentivogli was still living. This attempt gave umbrage to the Venetians, and also to the kings of Spain and France, who held a conference on the subject. But Pope Julius, with his habitual boldness and impetuosity, assumed the direction of that expedition in person; which caused the Spaniards and the Venetians to remain quiet in suspense, the latter from fear, and the others from a desire to recover the entire kingdom of Naples. On the other hand, the Pope drew the king of France after him; for that king, seeing that Julius had already started on the expedition, and wishing to gain his friendship for the purpose of humbling the Venetians, judged that he could not refuse him the assistance of his army without manifest injury to himself. Pope Julius II, then, achieved by this impetuous movement what no other Pontiff could have accomplished with all possible human prudence. For

---

[*] Born Giuliano della Rovere, was pope from November 1, 1503 until his death in 1513.

had he waited to start from Rome until all his plans were definitely arranged, and everything carefully organized, as every other Pontiff would have done, he would certainly never have succeeded; for the king would have found a thousand excuses, and the others would have caused him a thousand apprehensions.

The Prince, XXV

Soon after came Julius II, who found the Church powerful and mistress of the entire Romagna, with the Roman barons crushed and the factions destroyed by the vigorous blows of [Pope] Alexander. He also found a way prepared for the accumulation of money, which had never been employed before the time of Alexander. Julius II not only continued the system of Alexander, but carried it even further and resolved to acquire the possession of Bologna, to ruin the Venetians, and to drive the French out of Italy, in all of which he succeeded. And this was the more praiseworthy in him inasmuch as he did all these things, not for his own aggrandizement, but for that of the Church. He furthermore restrained the Orsini and the Colonna factions within the limits in which he found them upon his accession to the Pontificate; and although there were some attempts at disturbances between them, yet there were two things that kept them down: one, the power of the Church, which overawed them; and the other, the fact that neither of them had any cardinals, who were generally the fomenters of the disturbances between them. Nor will these party feuds ever cease so long as the cardinals take any part in them. For it is they who stir up

the factions in Rome as well as elsewhere, and then force
the barons to sustain them. And it is thus that the ambition of these prelates gives rise to the discord and the disturbances among the barons.

The Prince, XI

I will here cite [the example] of Pope Julius II, which is still
fresh in our minds, and whose conduct in that respect
could not well have been more imprudent than what it
was. For, wishing to take Ferrara, he placed himself entirely in the hands of a foreigner. Fortunately for him,
however, an incident occurred which saved him from the
full effect of his bad selection; for his auxiliaries having
been defeated at Ravenna, the Swiss suddenly appeared on
the field and put the victors to ignominious flight. And
thus Julius II escaped becoming prisoner either to his enemies who had fled, or to his auxiliaries; for the enemy's
defeat was not due to their assistance, but to that of
others.

The Prince, XIII

Lorenzo de' Medici (the Magnificent)

Thus Lorenzo's mode of life, his ability, and good fortune
were recognized with admiration and highly esteemed,
not only by all the princes of Italy, but also by those at a
great distance. Matthias, king of Hungary, gave him many
proofs of his affection; the Sultan of Egypt sent ambassadors to him with precious gifts; and the Grand Turk
gave up to him Bernardo Bandini, the murderer of his

brother.* These proofs of regard from foreign sovereigns caused Lorenzo to be looked upon with the greatest admiration by all Italy; and his reputation was daily increased by his rare ability, for he was eloquent and subtle in speech, wise in his resolves, and bold and prompt in their execution. Nor can he be charged with any vices that would stain his many virtues, though very fond of women, and delighting in the society of witty and sarcastic men, and even taking pleasure in puerile amusements, more so than would seem becoming to so great a man, so that he was often seen taking a part in the childish sports of his sons and daughters. Considering, then, his fondness for pleasure, and at the same time his grave character, there seemed as it were united in him two almost incompatible natures.

History of Florence, VIII. 36

Lorenzo de' Medici, Duke of Urbino

I do not want to fail to give you news of the way Lorenzo de' Medici is acting, which until now has been of such a sort that he has filled the entire city with high hopes; and it seems that everyone is beginning to recognize in him the beloved memory of his grandfather [Lorenzo the Magnificent] because His Magnificence is diligent in his work, generous and agreeable during an audience, deliberate and serious in his replies.† His way of conversing is

---

* 1449–1492, de facto ruler of Florence.
† 1492–1519, dedicatee of *The Prince*.

so different from the others that people attribute no pride to it; nor does he mingle too familiarly so that he generates too low a reputation for himself. His manner toward the young men of his class is such that he neither alienates them nor encourages them to indulge in any youthful, cheeky remarks. In sum, he makes himself both loved and revered rather than feared; the more difficult this is to achieve, the more praiseworthy in him it is. In his palace there is great magnificence and liberality, yet he does not stray from decent living. So that in all his activities, those inside and outside his palace, nobody is aware of anything offensive or reprehensible—everyone appears to be extremely satisfied with them. And although I know that you will hear all this from many people, I thought I should write you about it so that you can have the same pleasure from my account of it that we who continually experience it have; and when you have opportunity, you can attest to it on my part to His Holiness Our Lord.

Machiavelli to Francesco Vettori, February–March 1514

Louis XII, King of France

Louis XII then committed these five errors: he destroyed the weak; he increased the power of one already powerful in Italy; he established a most powerful stranger there; he did not go to reside there himself; nor did he plant any colonies there.* These errors, however, would not have injured him during his lifetime had he not committed a

---

* Born in 1462, reigned from 1498 until his death in 1515.

sixth one in attempting to deprive the Venetians of their possessions. For if Louis had not increased the power of the Church or established the Spaniards in Italy, it would have been quite reasonable, and even advisable, for him to have weakened the Venetians; but having done both those things, he ought never to have consented to their ruin; for so long as the Venetians were powerful, they would always have kept others from any attempt upon Lombardy. They would on the one hand never have permitted this unless it should have led to their becoming masters of it, and on the other hand no one would have taken it from France for the sake of giving it to the Venetians; nor would anyone have had the courage to attack the French and the Venetians combined. And should it be said that King Louis gave up the Romagna to Pope Alexander VI and divided the kingdom of Naples with the Spaniard for the sake of avoiding a war, then I reply . . . that no one should ever submit to an evil for the sake of avoiding a war. For a war is never avoided, but is only deferred to one's own disadvantage.

The Prince, III

Maximilian I, Emperor of Germany

The Emperor's good and easy nature is the cause why all persons whom he has about him deceive him.* One of the men attached to his person has told me that he can be

---

* Maximilian I, born in 1459, was Holy Roman Emperor from 1508 until his death in 1519.

deceived once by everybody and everything, until he has found them out. But there are so many men and so many things that he is exposed every day to being deceived, [and would be] even if he were constantly on his guard. He has endless good qualities, and if he could overcome his two qualities of weakness and an easy nature, he would be a most perfect man; for he is a good commander, governs his country with great justice, is affable and gracious in his audiences, and has many other qualities of a most excellent prince; and to conclude, if he could modify the two above-mentioned defects, it is judged that he would succeed in everything he undertakes.

Second Report on the Affairs of Germany

I will cite one modern example to this effect. Padre Luca, in the service of the present Emperor Maximilian, in speaking of his Majesty, says that he "counsels with no one, and yet never does anything in his own way"; which results from his following the very opposite course to that above indicated; for the Emperor is a reserved man, who never communicates his secrets to anyone, nor takes advice from anybody. But when he attempts to carry his plans into execution and they begin to be known, then also do they begin to be opposed by those whom he has around him; and being easily influenced, he is diverted from his own resolves. And thence it comes that he undoes one day what he has done the day before, and that one never knows what he wants or designs to do; and therefore his conclusions cannot be depended upon.

The Prince, XXIII

Girolamo Savonarola (Friar)

Since the Signoria has written to the pope in his behalf and he [Savonarola] realizes that he no longer needs to be afraid of his adversaries in Florence, instead of trying as he once had solely to unite his party through hatred of his adversaries and through frightening them with the word "tyrant," he has changed coats, [for he now] understands that he no longer needs to act in this way.* So, he urges them to the union that was initiated, and he no longer mentions either the tyrant or the wickedness of the people; he seeks to set all of them at odds with the Supreme Pontiff and, turning toward him and his attacks, says of the pope what could be said of the wickedest person you might imagine. Thus, in my judgment, he acts in accordance with the times and colors his lies accordingly.

Niccolò Machiavelli to Ricciardo Becchi, March 9, 1498

The people of Florence are far from considering themselves ignorant and benighted, and yet Brother Girolamo Savonarola succeeded in persuading them that he held converse with God. I will not pretend to judge whether it was true or not, for we must speak with all respect of so great a man; but I may well say that an immense number believed it, without having seen any extraordinary manifestations that should have made them believe it; . . . the purity of his life, the doctrines he preached, and the sub-

---

* Girolamo Savonarola (1452–1498) was an Italian Dominican friar and preacher active in Renaissance Florence, known for his prophecies of civic glory, the destruction of secular art and culture, and calls for Christian renewal.

jects he selected for his discourses . . . sufficed to make the people have faith in him. Let no one, then, fear not to be able to accomplish what others have done, for all men (as we have said in our preface) are born and live and die in the same way, and therefore resemble each other.

Discourses on Livy, I. 11

Savonarola, however, could not put it [the maxim that you must first suppress all feelings of envy if you want to pursue the public good] into practice for want of power and authority; still, he was not remiss in doing all he could, for his sermons abound with accusations and invectives against the wise of this world, for it was thus he styled the jealous opponents of his doctrines.

Discourses on Livy, III. 30

Caterina Sforza, Countess of Forlì

Some conspirators of Forlì killed the Count Girolamo, their lord, and took his wife and children, who were of tender age, prisoners. Believing, however, that they could not be secure if they did not obtain possession of the castle, which the castellan refused to surrender, the Lady Catharine, as the Countess was called, promised to the conspirators to procure its surrender if they would allow her to enter it, leaving them her children as hostages.* Upon this pledge the conspirators consented to let her enter the castle; but no sooner was she within than she

---

* Caterina Sforza, 1463–1509, was an Italian noblewoman, Countess of Forlì and Lady of Imola.

reproached them for the murder of the Count, and threatened them with every kind of vengeance. And to prove to them that she cared not for her children, she pointed to her sexual parts, calling out to them that she had wherewith to have more children. Thus the conspirators discovered their error too late, and suffered the penalty of their imprudence in perpetual exile.

Discourses on Livy, III. 6

Piero Soderini

Having already in another place treated this subject at length, I refer to what I have there said, and confine myself now to citing a single and most remarkable example, taken from the history of our own country. It is that of Piero Soderini, who believed that he would be able by patience and gentleness to overcome the determination of the new sons of Brutus to return to another form of government; in which, however, he greatly deceived himself.[*] And although his natural sagacity recognized the necessity of destroying them, and although the quality and ambition of his adversaries afforded him the opportunity, yet he had not the courage to do it. For he thought, and several times acknowledged it to his friends, that boldly to strike down his adversaries and all opposition would oblige him to assume extraordinary authority, and even legally to destroy civil equality; and that, even if he should

[*] Born in 1452, he was Gonfalonier of the Republic of Florence between 1503 and 1512. He died in 1522.

not afterwards use this power tyrannically, this course would so alarm the masses that after his death they would never again consent to the election of another Gonfalonier for life, which he deemed essential for the strengthening and maintaining of the government. This respect for the laws was most praiseworthy and wise on the part of Soderini. Still one should never allow an evil to run on out of respect for the law, especially when the law itself might easily be destroyed by the evil; and he should have borne in mind that as his acts and motives would have to be judged by the result, [for] in case he had been fortunate enough to succeed and live, everybody would have attested that what he had done was for the good of his country, and not for the advancement of any ambitious purposes of his own. Moreover, he could have regulated matters so that his successors could not have employed for evil the means which he had used for beneficent purposes. But Soderini was the dupe of his opinions, not knowing that malignity is neither effaced by time nor placated by gifts. So that by failing to imitate Brutus he lost at the same time his country, his state, and his reputation.

Discourses on Livy, III. 3

For any man accustomed to a certain mode of proceeding will never change it, . . . and consequently when time and circumstances change, so that his ways are no longer in harmony with them, he must of necessity succumb. Piero Soderini, whom we have mentioned several times already, was in all his actions governed by humanity and patience. He and his country prospered so long as the times favored this mode of proceeding; but when afterwards circumstances arose that demanded a course of conduct the opposite to that of patience and humanity, he was unfit for the occasion, and his own and his country's ruin were the consequence.

Discourses on Livy, III. 9

Soderini believed that he would be able in time to silence envy by his affability and good fortune, and by bestowing benefits upon some of his adversaries. Feeling himself young, and being loaded with public favors on account of his conduct, he hoped to triumph over the jealousy of his rivals without any violence or public disturbance. But he forgot that in such matters nothing is to be expected from time, that goodness does not suffice, and that benefits will not placate envious malignity.

Discourses on Livy, III. 30

The night when Piero Soderini died, His soul for entrance into Hell applied. / But Pluto shouted: Hence, thou simple soul! This is no place for you. Go to the infants' Limbo, fool!

Epigram on Piero Soderini

VII
Past and Present

Figure 7. Desk at Machiavelli's summer cottage. Courtesy of Don MacDonald.

Achilles

It is told of Alexander [the Great] that he imitated Achilles, and of Caesar that he had taken Alexander for his model, as Scipio had done with Cyrus.

The Prince, XIV

Agathocles of Syracuse

Agathocles, a Sicilian, rose to be king of Syracuse, not only from being a mere private citizen, but from the lowest and most abject condition. He was the son of a potter and led a vicious life through all the various phases of his career. But his wickedness was coupled with so much moral and physical courage, that, having joined the army, he rose by successive steps until he became Praetor of Syracuse. Having attained that rank he resolved to make himself sovereign, and to retain by violence, and regardless of others, that which had been entrusted to him by public consent. For this purpose he came to an understanding with Hamilcar the Carthaginian, who was at that time carrying on war with his army in Sicily; and having one morning called an assembly of the people and the Senate of Syracuse, as though he wished to confer with them about public affairs, he made his soldiers, at a given signal, slay all the Senators and the richest of the people, and then he seized the sovereignty of that city without any resistance on the part of the citizens. Although afterwards twice defeated by the Carthaginians, and finally besieged by them in Syracuse, he not only defended that city, but, leaving a portion of his forces to sustain the siege, he crossed the sea with the other part and attacked Africa, thus raising the siege of Syracuse in a short time and driving the Carthaginians to the most extreme necessity, compelling them to make terms with him and to remain content with the possession of Africa and leave Sicily to him. Whoever now reflects upon the conduct and valor of Agathocles will find in them little or nothing that can be attributed to fortune; for, as I have said, he achieved sovereignty not by the favor of any one, but through his high rank in the army, which he had won by a thousand efforts and dangers, and he afterwards maintained his sovereignty with great courage, and even temerity. And yet we cannot call it virtue to massacre one's fellow-citizens, to betray one's friends, and to be devoid of good faith, mercy, and religion; such means may enable a man to achieve empire, but not glory. Still, if we consider the valor of Agathocles in encountering and overcoming dangers, and his invincible courage in supporting and mastering adversity, we shall find no reason why he should be regarded inferior to any of the most celebrated captains. But with all this, his outrageous cruelty and inhumanity, together with his infinite crimes, will not permit him to be classed with the most celebrated men. We cannot therefore ascribe to either virtue or fortune the achievements of Agathocles, which he accomplished without either the one or the other.

The Prince, VIII

Alexander the Great

If now we consider the nature of the government of Darius, we shall find that it resembled that of the Turk, and therefore it was necessary for Alexander to attack him in full force and drive him from the field. After this victory and the death of Darius, Alexander remained in secure possession of the kingdom for the reasons above explained. And if his successors had remained united, they might also have enjoyed possession at their ease; for no other disturbances occurred in that empire, except such as they created themselves.

The Prince, IV

When Alexander the Great wished to build a city that should serve as a monument to his glory, his architect, Dinocrates, pointed out to him how he could build a city on Mount Athos, which place he said, besides being very strong, could be so arranged as to give the city the appearance of the human form, which would make it a wonder worthy of the greatness of its founder. Alexander having asked him what the inhabitants were to live upon, he replied, "that I have not thought of"; at which Alexander smiled, and, leaving Mount Athos as it was, he built Alexandria, where the inhabitants would be glad to remain on account of the richness of the country and the advantages which the proximity of the Nile and the sea afforded them.

Discourses on Livy, I. 1

Aristotle

I do not know what Aristotle says about confederated republics, but I certainly can say what might reasonably exist, what exists, and what has existed.

Machiavelli to Francesco Vettori, August 26, 1513

Aristotle mentions as one of the first causes of the ruin of tyrants the outrages committed by them upon the wives and daughters of others, either by violence or seduction; and we have discussed this subject at length when treating of conspiracies.

Discourses on Livy, III. 26

Athens and Sparta

[The] constitution given by Solon to the Athenians, by which he established only a popular government, was of such short duration that before his death he saw the tyranny of Pisistratus arise. And although forty years afterwards the heirs of the tyrant were expelled, so that Athens recovered her liberties and restored the popular government according to the laws of Solon, yet it did not last over a hundred years; although a number of laws that had been overlooked by Solon were adopted to maintain the government against the insolence of the nobles and the license of the populace. The fault he had committed in not tempering the power of the people and that of the prince and his nobles made the duration of the government of Athens very short as compared with that of Sparta.

Discourses on Livy, I. 2

Sparta, as I have said, being governed by a king and a limited senate, could maintain itself also for a long time, because there were but few inhabitants, and strangers were not permitted to come in; besides, the laws of Lycurgus had obtained such influence that their observance prevented even the slightest pretext for trouble. It was also the easier for the citizens to live in union, as Lycurgus had established equality in fortunes and inequality in conditions; for an equal poverty prevailed there, and the people were the less ambitious, as the offices of the government were given but to a few citizens, the people being excluded from them; and the nobles in the exercise of their functions did not treat the people sufficiently ill to excite in them the desire of exercising them themselves. This last advantage was due to the kings of Sparta; for being placed in this government, as it were, between the two orders, and living in the midst of the nobility, they had no better means of maintaining their authority than to protect the people against all injustice; whence these neither feared nor desired authority, and consequently there was no motive for any differences between them and the nobles, nor any cause for disturbances; and thus they could live for a long time united. Two principal causes, however, cemented this union: first the inhabitants of Sparta were few in number, and therefore could be governed by a few; and the other was that, by not permitting strangers to establish themselves in the republic, they had neither opportunity of becoming corrupt, nor of increasing their population to such a degree that the burden of government became difficult to the few who were charged with it. [Sparta,] having subjected to her rule nearly all Greece, exposed its feeble foundations at the slightest accident, for when the rebellion of Thebes occurred, which was led by Pelopidas, the other cities of Greece also rose up and almost ruined Sparta.

Discourses on Livy I. 6

Cicero

Before deciding upon any course, therefore, men should well consider the objections and dangers which it presents; and if its perils exceed its advantages, they should avoid it, even though it is in accord with their previous determination; for to do otherwise would expose them to an experience similar to that of Cicero, who, wishing to destroy the credit and power of Mark Antony, only increased it. For Antony, having been declared an enemy of the Senate, had collected a large army, composed in great part of soldiers who had served under Caesar; Cicero, wishing to withdraw these soldiers from him, advised the Senate to employ Octavian and to send him with the army and the Consuls against Antony, alleging that so soon as the soldiers of Antony should hear the name of Octavian, who was the nephew of Caesar and who had himself called by the name of Caesar, they would leave the former and join Octavian; and that Antony, thus bereft of support, would easily be crushed. But the result was just the opposite, for Antony managed to win Octavian over to himself, who, abandoning Cicero and the Senate, allied himself with the former, which brought about the complete ruin of the party of the patricians. This might easily have been foreseen, and therefore they should not have followed the advice of Cicero, but should have borne in mind the name and character of him who had vanquished his enemies with so much glory and seized for himself the sovereignty of Rome; and then they might have known that they could not expect from his adherents anything favorable to liberty.

Discourses on Livy, I. 52

Constantinople

Many of you can remember when Constantinople was taken by the Turks. That Emperor foresaw his ruin. He called upon his citizens, not being able with his organized forces to make proper provision. He showed them their dangers, showed them the preventives; and they ridiculed him. The siege came on. Those citizens who had before had no respect for the exhortations of their lord, when they heard within their walls the thunder of artillery and the yells of the army of their enemies, ran weeping to the Emperor with their bosoms full of money; but he drove them away, saying: "Go to die with this money, since you have not wished to live without it."

Words to Be Spoken on the Law for Appropriating Money,
after giving a little introduction and excuse

Cyrus, King of Persia

If we consider Cyrus and others who have conquered or founded empires, we shall find them all worthy of admiration.

The Prince, VI

It was necessary for Cyrus to find the Persians dissatisfied with the rule of the Medes, and the Medes effeminate and enfeebled by long peace.

The Prince, VI

[It was necessary that] the Persians should be opposed to the Medes, so as to bring to light the greatness and courage of Cyrus.

The Prince, XXVI

That which belongs neither to him nor to his own subjects, a prince may spend most lavishly, as was done by Cyrus, Caesar, and Alexander. The spending of other people's substance will not diminish, but rather increase, his reputation; it is only the spending of his own that is injurious to a prince.

The Prince, XVI

I have heard men of much practical experience in the art of war discuss the question whether, supposing there to be two princes of nearly equal power, one of whom, being the more spirited, has declared war against the other, it be better for the latter to await the attack within his own territory, or to march directly into the country of the former and attack him; and I have heard them give good reasons in favor of either proceeding. Those favoring the latter course cited the advice given by Croesus to Cyrus, to whom, upon arriving at the confines of the Messagetes, their queen Tamiris sent to ask which course he preferred, whether to come into her kingdom and attack her there, in which case she would await him, or that she should come out to meet him beyond her confines. When the matter was under discussion, Croesus, contrary to the opinion of the others, advised Cyrus to attack Tamiris within her own possessions, alleging that, if he were to defeat her away from her country, he would not be able to take her kingdom from her, as she would in that case have time to recover; but if he vanquished her within her dominions, he would be able to follow her in her flight, and thus, without giving her time to recover, he could deprive her of her state.

Discourses on Livy, II. 12

Xenophon shows in his life of Cyrus the necessity of deception to success: the first expedition of Cyrus against the king of Armenia is replete with fraud, and it was deceit alone, and not force, that enabled him to seize that kingdom. And Xenophon draws no other conclusion from this than that a prince who wishes to achieve great things must learn to deceive. Cyrus also practiced a variety of deceptions upon Cyaxares, king of the Medes, his maternal uncle; and Xenophon shows that without these frauds

Cyrus would never have achieved the greatness which he did attain.

Discourses on Livy, II. 13

. . . Xenophon takes great pains to show how many victories, how much honor and fame, Cyrus gained by his humanity and affability, and by his not having exhibited a single instance of pride, cruelty, or luxuriousness, nor of any other of the vices that are apt to stain the lives of men.

Discourses on Livy, III. 20

Dante Alighieri

Whence it comes that kingdoms which depend entirely upon the virtue of one man endure but for a brief time, for his virtue passes away with his life, and it rarely happens that it is renewed in his successor, as Dante so wisely says: "'Tis seldom human wisdom descends from sire to son; / Such is the will of Him who gave it, / That at his hands alone we may implore the boon."

Discourses on Livy, I. 11

If it happens that the people have no confidence in anyone, as sometimes will be the case when they have been deceived before by events or men, then it will inevitably lead to the ruin of the state. Dante says upon this point in his discourse *On Monarchy* that "the people often shout, 'Life to our death, and death to our life!'"

Discourses on Livy, I. 53

Upon leaving the woods, I go to a spring; from there to one of the places where I hang my bird nets. I have a book under my arm: Dante, Petrarch, or one of the minor poets like Tibullus, Ovid, or some such. I read about their amorous passions and their loves, remember my own, and these reflections make me happy for a while.

Machiavelli to Francesco Vettori, December 10, 1513

As the infirmities of our bodies are dangerous in proportion as their progress is slow, so Florence, being slower in following the factions of Italy, was also afterwards the more sorely afflicted by them. The cause of the first division is most noteworthy; and although it has been mentioned by Dante and many other writers, it seems to me proper briefly to relate it here.

History of Florence, II. 2

King David (Old Testament)

I will also recall to memory an illustration from the Old Testament applicable to this subject. David had offered to go and fight the Philistine bully Goliath, and Saul, by way of encouraging David, gave him his own arms and armor, which David however declined, after having tried them, saying that he could not make the most of his strength if he used those arms; and therefore he preferred to meet the enemy with no other arms but his sling and his knife. In short, the armor of another never suits you entirely; it is either too large and falls off your back, or weighs you down, or it is too tight.

The Prince, XII

David was beyond doubt a most extraordinary man in war, in learning, and in superior judgment; and such was his virtue that, having conquered and crushed his neighbors, he left a peaceful kingdom to his son Solomon.

Discourses on Livy, I. 19

Cosimo de' Medici

Cosimo de' Medici, to whom the house of Medici owes the beginning of its greatness, obtained such reputation and authority through his own sagacity and the ignorance of his fellow-citizens that he became a cause of apprehension to the government, so that the other citizens judged it hazardous to offend him, but more dangerous still to allow him to go on.* At that time there lived in Florence Niccolò Uzzano, reputed a man of consummate ability in matters of state, who, having committed the first error of not foreseeing the danger that might result from the great influence of Cosimo, would never permit the Florentines, so long as he lived, to commit the second error of trying to destroy Cosimo, judging that any such attempt would lead to the ruin of the state, as in fact proved to be the case after his death. For the citizens, regardless of the counsels of Uzzano, combined against Cosimo and drove him from Florence. The consequence was that the partisans of Cosimo, resenting this insult, shortly afterwards recalled him and made him prince of the republic, which position he

---

* Founder of the Medici regime, also known as "Cosimo the Elder" (1389–1464).

never would have attained but for the previous hostility manifested toward him.

Discourses on Livy, I. 33

Cosimo de' Medici, after the death of his father, displayed more zeal in public affairs, and even more devotion and liberality towards his friends than his father had done; so that those who had rejoiced at Giovanni's death became greatly depressed when they saw what Cosimo was. For Cosimo was a man of rare prudence, of grave but agreeable presence, and most liberal and humane. He never attempted anything against the party opposed to him, or against the state, but endeavored to do good to all; and by his generosity he won the attachment of a great many citizens who became his partisans, so that his example increased the cares of those who held the government, whilst he judged that in this way he would be able to live in Florence as securely, and exercise as much power, as anyone else; or if his adversaries from motives of ambition should attempt to resort to extraordinary measures against him, that he would be superior to them both in force of arms and by the support of his friends.

History of Florence, IV. 26

Cosimo died full of glory and great renown, and the city of Florence, as well as all Christian princes, condoled with his son Piero upon his loss. His funeral was attended by all the citizens with greatest pomp; and being interred in the church of San Lorenzo, there was, by public decree, inscribed over his tomb, "FATHER OF THIS COUNTRY."

History of Florence, VII. 6

Giovanni de' Medici

About this time Giovanni de' Medici* fell sick, and, feeling his illness to be mortal, he called his two sons, Cosimo and Lorenzo, to him, and said to them: "I believe I have lived to the time appointed for me by God and nature at my birth. I die content, for I leave you rich and healthy, and of such quality that, if you will follow in my footsteps, you can live in Florence honored and beloved by everyone. Nothing makes me die so content as the reflection that I have never injured anyone, but that rather, according to my ability, I have benefited all. I advise you to do the same; and if you desire to live securely, take only such share of the government as the laws and the citizens may choose to bestow upon you, which will never expose you to envy or danger. For it is that which a man takes, not that which is given to him, that renders him odious to others; and thus you will always have much more than those who, wishing to take the share of others, lose their own, and who, before losing it live in constant anxiety. In this way have I, in the midst of so many enemies and divisions, not only maintained but increased my influence in the city; and thus, if you follow my example, will you maintain and increase yours. But if you do otherwise, re-

* Father of Cosimo, banker, 1360–1389.

member that your fate will not be different from that of those who within our memory have ruined themselves and their families."

Soon after this he died, in 1429, greatly regretted by everyone in Florence, as he deserved to be because of his admirable qualities. Giovanni was most charitable, and not only gave alms to whomever asked them, but often succored the poor without being solicited. He loved all mankind; he praised the good and had compassion upon the wicked. He never asked for honors, but had them all. He never went to the palace unless called there. He loved peace and avoided war; he remembered men in their adversity, and aided them in prosperity. He was a stranger to public rapine, and only aimed to increase the wealth of the state. As a magistrate he was courteous; his eloquence was moderate, but his prudence very great. The expression of his countenance was sad, but his conversation was cheerful, and even witty. He died rich in treasure, but richer in good fame and the general affection. The heritage he left both in wealth of fortune and of character was not only maintained, but increased, by his son Cosimo.

History of Florence, IV. 16

Florence

Such was the origin of Florence; for it was built either by the soldiers of Sylla, or perhaps by the inhabitants of Mount Fiesole, who, trusting to the long peace that prevailed in the reign of Octavian, were attracted to the plains along the Arno. Florence, thus built under the Roman Empire, could in the beginning have no growth except what depended on the will of its master.

Discourses on Livy, I. 1

It is undoubtedly true, as has been shown by Dante and Villani, that the city of Fiesole, being situated on the summit of a mountain and wishing to make its markets more frequented and accessible to those who desired to come there with their merchandise, established a place for this purpose in the plain, between the foot of the mountain and the river Arno. This market, I judge, caused the first buildings to be erected at that place, owing to the desire of the merchants to have convenient places for receiving and delivering their goods, and these buildings in the course of time became permanent structures. Afterwards, when the Romans, by the conquest of the Carthaginians, had rendered Italy secure from foreign attacks, these buildings were multiplied in great numbers; for men do not select inconvenient places to dwell in, except from necessity; so that if the fear of attack constrains them to live in rude and inaccessible places, they will naturally be attracted to inhabit agreeable and convenient localities whenever that fear of attack ceases. Security, then, which sprang from the reputation of the Roman Republic, caused the increase of those habitations (which were already commenced in the manner above stated) in such numbers that they assumed the form of a settlement, which at first was called Villa Arnina. Afterwards civil wars arose in Rome, first between Marius and Sylla, subsequently between Caesar and

Pompey, and then between the murderers of Caesar and those who wished to avenge his death. Sylla first, and after him those other three Roman citizens, who, after having avenged Caesar, divided the Empire between them, sent colonies to Fiesole, and these established their dwellings, in whole or in part in the plain, near the settlement which had already been commenced. And thus by this increase that place became filled with habitations and men, which by its civil organization could soon be counted among the cities of Italy. As to the origin of the name of Florentia, however, there are various opinions. Some claim that it was so called after Florino, one of the chiefs of the colony; others maintain that it was at first called, not Florentia, but Fluentia, from being situated near the river Arno, and they adduce the testimony of Pliny, who says: "The Fluentines dwell near the river Arno." This opinion may, however, be erroneous; for the text quoted from Pliny tells where the Florentines dwelt, not how they were called. And most probably the word "Fluentines" is a corruption; for both Frontinus and Cornelius Tacitus, who wrote in the times of Pliny, call the place Florentia and the people Florentines. Already at the time of Tiberius (in the year 17 after Christ), the Florentines governed themselves, according to the custom of the other cities of Italy. And Cornelius Tacitus refers to the coming of Florentine ambassadors to the Emperor to request that the waters of the river Chiana might not be discharged into the Arno above their settlement. It is not reasonable to suppose that that city should in those days have had two names, and I am inclined to believe that it was always called Florentia, whatever the reason may have been why it was so named. And to whatever cause its origin may be due, it came into existence under the Roman Empire, and began to be mentioned by writers at the time of the first Emperors.

History of Florence, II. 2

If the divisions of any republic were ever noteworthy, then those of Florence most certainly are, because the greater part of the other republics of which we have any knowledge were content with one division, by which, according to chance, they either increased or ruined their city. But Florence, not content with one division, had many. In Rome, as everybody knows, after the expulsion of the kings, a division arose between the nobles and the people, and with that [division in place] she maintained herself until her downfall. So did Athens, and so all the republics that flourished in those times. But in Florence, the first division was among the nobles, afterwards between the nobles and the citizens, and finally between the citizens and the underclass; and many times it happened that one of the parties that remained in power again divided in two. These divisions caused so many deaths, so many exiles, so much destruction of so many families as never occurred in any other city of which we have any record. And truly no other circumstance so well illustrates the power of our city as that which resulted from these divisions, which would have been enough to destroy any other great and powerful republic. Ours, nevertheless, seems always to have increased in power; such was the virtue of her citizens and the strength of their genius and courage to make themselves and their country great, that the many who remained untouched by so many evils could by their virtues exalt their city more than the malignity of those events that diminished her greatness could have oppressed her. And doubtless if Florence had had so much good fortune that, after having freed herself from the Empire, she could have adopted a form of government that would have kept her united, I know not what republic, modern or ancient, would have been her superior, such abundance of power of arms and industry would she in that case have possessed.

Preface to the *History of Florence*

The reason why Florence throughout her history has frequently varied her methods of government is that she has never been either a republic or a princedom having the qualities each requires, because we cannot call that republic well established in which things are done according to the will of one man yet are decided with the approval of many; nor can we believe a republic fitted to last, in which there is no content for those elements that must be contented if republics are not to fall.

Discourse on Remodeling the Government of Florence

This, as will be seen, was the case with the city of Florence, which from her first beginning had been subject to the Roman Empire, and, having always existed under a foreign government, remained for a long time in this subject condition without ever attempting to free herself. And when afterwards the opportunity occurred for her to gain her liberty in a measure, she began by making a constitution that was a mixture of her old and bad institutions with new ones, and consequently could not be good. And thus she has gone on for the two hundred years of which we have any reliable account, without ever having a government that could really be called a republic.

Discourses on Livy, I. 49

That constitution [of 1393] also suffered from a failing not of slight importance: that men in private station took part in deliberations on public business. This kept up the prestige of the men in private stations and took it away from those in official ones, and it had the effect of taking away power and prestige from the magistrates, a thing opposed to every sort of well-ordered government. To these failings of that constitution was added another, which amounted to as much as all the rest: the people did not have their share. These conditions, altogether, caused countless injustices, and if, as I have said, external wars had not kept that government solid, it would have fallen sooner than it did.

Discourse on Remodeling the Government of Florence

After [the regime of Cosimo de' Medici between 1434 and 1464], the city decided to resume the form of a republic, but did not apply herself to adopting it in a form that would be lasting, because the ordinances then made did not satisfy all the parties among the citizens; and on the other hand, the government could not inflict punishment. And it was so defective and remote from a true republic that a Gonfalonier for life, if he was intelligent and wicked, easily could make himself prince; if he was good and weak, he could easily be driven out, with the ruin of the whole government. Since it would be a long matter to set forth all the reasons, I will tell just one: the Gonfalonier did not have those around him who could protect him, if he were good; nor anyone who, if he were bad, could restrain him or set him right. The reason why all these governments have been defective is that the alterations in them have been made not for the fulfilment of the common good, but for the strengthening and security of the party. Such security has not yet been attained, because there has always been in the city a party that was discontented, which has been a very powerful tool for anybody who wished to make a change.

Discourse on Remodeling the Government of Florence

In all cities where the citizens are accustomed to equality, a princedom cannot be set up except with the utmost difficulty, and in those cities where the citizens are accustomed to inequality, a republic cannot be set up except with the utmost difficulty. In order to form a republic in Milan, where inequality among the citizens is great, necessarily all the nobility must be destroyed and brought to an equality with the others, because among them are men so above all rules that the laws are not enough to hold them down, but there must be a living voice and a kingly power to hold them down. On the contrary, in order to have a princedom in Florence, where equality is great, the establishment of inequality would be necessary; noble lords of walled towns and boroughs would have to be set up, who in support of the prince would with their arms and their followers stifle the city and the whole province. A prince alone, lacking a nobility, cannot support the weight of a princedom; for that reason it is necessary that between him and the generality of the people there should be a middle group that will help him support it. This can be seen in all the states with a prince, and especially in the kingdom of France, where the gentlemen rule the people, the princes the gentlemen, and the king the princes. But because to form a princedom where a republic would go well is a difficult thing and, through being difficult, inhumane and unworthy of whoever hopes to be considered merciful and good, I shall pass over any further treatment of the princedom and speak of the republic, . . . because Florence is a subject very suitable for taking this form.

Discourse on Remodeling the Government of Florence

Without satisfying the generality of the citizens, to set up a stable government is always impossible. Never will the generality of the Florentine citizens be satisfied if the Hall [of the great Council, symbol of republican government] is not reopened.

Discourse on Remodeling the Government of Florence

France and the French

The contrary takes place in kingdoms governed like that of France; for [once a potential conqueror has] gained over some of the great nobles of the realm, there will be no difficulty in entering it, there being always malcontents and others who desire a change. These, for the reasons stated, can open the way into the country for the assailant and facilitate his success. But for the conqueror to maintain himself there afterwards will involve infinite difficulties, both with the conquered and with those who have aided him in his conquest. Nor will it suffice to extinguish the line of the sovereign, because the great nobles remain, who will place themselves at the head of new movements; and the conqueror, not being able either to satisfy or to crush them, will lose the country again on the first occasion that presents itself.

The Prince, IV

Among the well-organized and well-governed kingdoms of our time is that of France, which has a great many excellent institutions that secure the liberty and safety of the king. The most important of these is the Parliament and its authority; for the founder of that kingdom knew the ambition and insolence of the nobles, and judged it necessary to put a bit into their mouths with which to curb them. He knew at the same time the hatred of the mass of the people towards the nobles, based upon their fears. Wishing to secure both, and yet unwilling to make this the special care of the king, so as to relieve him of the responsibility to the nobles of seeming to favor the people, and to the people of favoring the nobles, he instituted the Parliament to act as a judge, which might, without reference to the king, keep down the great, and favor the weak. Nor could there be a wiser system, or one that affords more security to the king and his realm.

The Prince, XIX

The kingdom of France shows us the good effects of such renewals; for this monarchy more than any other is governed by laws and ordinances. The Parliaments, and mainly that of Paris, are the conservators of these laws and institutions, which are renewed by them from time to time by executions against some of the princes of the realm, and at times even by decisions against the king himself. And thus this kingdom has maintained itself up to the present time by its determined constancy in repressing the ambition of the nobles; for if it were to leave them unpunished, the disorders would quickly multiply, and the end would doubtless be either that the guilty could no longer be punished without danger, or that the kingdom itself would be broken up.

Discourses on Livy, III. 1

The French are by nature more ferocious than vigorous and adroit; and if you can resist the fury of their first onset, you will find them so depressed and so entirely discouraged that they become cowardly like women. They do not support fatigue or discomforts, and soon become neglectful of everything, so that it is easy to surprise them in disorder, and to overcome them. . . . Whoever, therefore, wishes to defeat the French must beware of their first onset; whilst keeping them at bay for a time will defeat them, for the above-stated reasons. And therefore Caesar said that "at the beginning the French were more than men, but in the end less than women."

Report on the Affairs of France

By the extent of her territory and the advantages derived from her large rivers, France is very productive and opulent; but the abundant productions of the soil, as well as manual labor, have little or no value, owing to the scarcity of money among the people, who can scarcely get enough together to pay their dues to the lord proprietor, although the amounts are but very small. This arises from their not having an outlet for the productions of the soil, for every man gathers enough to sell some; so that if in any one place a man wanted to sell a bushel of grain, he would not find a purchaser, everybody having grain to sell. And of the money which the gentlemen draw from their tenants, they spend nothing except for their clothing; for they have cattle enough to give them meat, innumerable fowls, lakes full of fish, and parks with an abundance of every variety of game; and thus almost every gentleman lives upon his estates. In this way all the money accumulates in the hands of the proprietors, and their wealth is accordingly great; whilst the people, when they have a florin, deem themselves rich.

Report on the Affairs of France

The Frenchman is naturally covetous of other people's goods, of which, together with his own, he is afterwards prodigal. Thus, the Frenchman will rob most skillfully to eat, or to waste what he has robbed, or even to enjoy it together with the very person whom he has robbed; entirely different from the Spaniard, who will never let you see again what he has taken from you.

Report on the Affairs of France

The French people are submissive and most obedient, and they hold their king in great veneration. They live at a very small expense, owing to the great abundance of the products of the soil; and everyone has a small property to himself. They dress coarsely, in cheap cloth, and neither the men nor the women use silk in any way, for it would at once be noted by the nobles.

Report on the Affairs of France

On that occasion the Cardinal [of Rouen] said to me that the Italians did not understand the art of war. To which I replied that the French did not understand the art of the state; for if they had understood it, they would never have allowed the Church to attain such greatness and power.

The Prince, III

Germany and the German Free Cities

No one can doubt the power of Germany, for she abounds in population, wealth, and troops. As to riches, there is not a community that has not a considerable amount in the public treasury; it is said that Strasburg alone has several millions of florins so placed. This arises from the fact that they have no expenses for which they draw money from the treasury, except to keep up their munitions, which, when once provided require very little to keep them up. The order established in these matters is really admirable; for they always keep in the public magazines grain, drink, and fuel enough for one year. They also keep a supply of the raw material for their industries, so that in case of siege they can feed the people and supply those who live by the labor of their hands with the necessary materials for an entire year without any loss. They spend nothing for soldiers, for they keep all their men armed and exercised, and on holidays these men, instead of amusing themselves with idle play, exercise themselves, some with the gun, some with the pike, and some with one or another kind of arms; for which exercises they have established prizes of honor and other rewards. These are their only expenses, for in other matters they spend very little; and thus every community is rich in public treasure. The reason why the private citizens are rich is that they live as if they were poor; they do not build, and spend nothing on dress or costly furniture in their houses. They are satisfied with having plenty of bread and meat, and a stove where they can take refuge from the cold; and those who have no other things are satisfied to do without them, and do not seek after them. They spend two florins in ten years for clothing to put on their backs; all live in this proportion, according to their rank, caring little for what they have not, but only for that which is strictly necessary; and their necessities are much fewer than ours. With such habits, it is natural that the money does not go out of the country, the people being content with what their country produces. But money is always being brought into the country by those who come to purchase the products of their industry, with which they supply almost all Italy. And the profit which they make is so much the greater, as the larger part of the money which they receive is for the labor of their hands only, and but little is for the raw material employed. And thus they enjoy their rough life and liberty, and for that reason they will not take service to go to war, unless they are exorbitantly paid; and this alone will not satisfy them, unless they are ordered by their communities.

Report on the Affairs of Germany

The cities of Germany enjoy great liberties; they own little land outside of the walls, and obey the Emperor at their pleasure, fearing neither him nor any other neighboring power; for they are so well fortified that their capture would manifestly be tedious and difficult. They all have suitable walls and ditches, and are amply supplied with artillery, and always keep in their public magazines a year's supply of provisions, drink, and fuel. Moreover, by way of feeding the people without expense to the public, they always keep on hand a common stock of raw materials to last for one year, so as to give employment in those branches of industry by which the people are accustomed to gain their living, and which are the nerves and life of the city. They also attach much importance to military exercises, and have established many regulations for their proper practice.

The Prince, X

In Germany alone do we see that a large measure of probity and religion still survives among the people, in consequence of which many republics exist there in the full enjoyment of liberty, observing their laws in such manner that no one from within or without dare venture to master them. And in proof that the ancient virtue still prevails there, I will cite an example similar to that given above of the Senate and people of Rome. When these republics have occasion to spend any considerable amount of money for public account, their magistrates or councils, who have authority in these matters, impose upon all the inhabitants a tax of one or two per cent of their possessions. When such a resolution has been passed according to the laws of the country, every citizen presents himself before the collectors of this impost, and, after having taken an oath to pay the just amount, deposits in a strongbox provided for the purpose the sum which according to his conscience he ought to pay, without anyone's witnessing what he pays. From this we may judge of the extent of the probity and religion that still exists among those people. And we must presume that everyone pays the true amount, for if this were not the case the impost would not yield the amount intended according to the estimates based upon former impositions; the fraud would thus be discovered, and other means would be employed to collect the amount required. This honesty is the more to be admired as it is so very rare that it is found only in that country and this results from two causes. The one is that the Germans have no great commerce with their neighbors, few strangers coming among them, and they rarely visiting foreign countries, being content to remain at home and to live on what their country produces and to clothe themselves with the wool from their own flocks, which takes away all occasion for intimate intercourse with strangers and all opportunity of corruption. Thus they have been prevented from adopting either French,

Spanish, or Italian customs, and these nations are the great corrupters of the world. The other cause is that those republics which have thus preserved their political existence uncorrupted do not permit any of their citizens to be or to live in the manner of nobles, but rather maintain among them a perfect equality, and are the most decided enemies of the lords and nobles that exist in the country; so that, if by chance any of them fall into their hands, they kill them as being the chief promoters of all corruption and troubles.

Discourses on Livy, I. 55

Italy

There is no difficulty in demonstrating the truth of this; for the present ruin of Italy can be attributed to nothing else but to the fact that she has for many years depended upon mercenary armies, who for a time had some success, and seemed brave enough among themselves, but so soon as a foreign enemy came they showed what stuff they were made of. This was the reason why Charles VIII, king of France, was allowed to take Italy with scarcely an effort, and as it were with merely a piece of chalk. Those who assert that our misfortunes were caused by our own faults speak the truth; but these faults were not such as are generally supposed to have been the cause, but those rather which I have pointed out; and as it was the princes who committed these faults, so they also suffered the penalties. This expression of taking Italy "as it were with merely a piece of chalk" (*col gesso*) was used by Alexander VI, and it means that Charles VIII had merely to send a quarter-master ahead with a piece of chalk to mark the houses in which the French troops were to be quartered.

The Prince, XII

If now you examine Italy, which is the seat of the changes under consideration and has occasioned their occurrence, you will see that she is like an open country, without dikes or any other protection against inundations; and that if she had been protected with proper valor and wisdom, as is the case in Germany, Spain, and France, these inundations would either not have caused the great changes which they did, or they would not have occurred at all.

The Prince, XXV

If, as I have said, it was necessary for the purpose of displaying the virtue of Moses that the people of Israel should be held in bondage in Egypt; and that the Persians should be opposed to the Medes, so as to bring to light the greatness and courage of Cyrus; and that the Athenians should be dispersed for the purpose of illustrating the excellence of Theseus; so at present, for the purpose of making manifest the virtues of one Italian spirit, it was necessary that Italy should have been brought to her present condition of being in a worse bondage than that of the Jews, more enslaved than the Persians, more scattered than the Athenians, without a head, without order, vanquished and despoiled, lacerated, overrun by her enemies, and subjected to every kind of devastation.

The Prince, XXVI

Although, up to the present time, there may have been someone who received a gleam of hope that he was ordained by Heaven to redeem Italy, yet have we seen how, in the very zenith of his career, he was so checked by fortune that poor Italy remained as it were lifeless, waiting to see who might be chosen to heal her wounds—to put an end to her devastation, to the sacking of Lombardy, to the spoliation and ruinous taxation of the kingdom of Naples and of Tuscany—and who should heal her sores that have festered so long. You see how she prays God that he may send someone who shall redeem her from this cruelty and barbarous insolence. You see her eagerly disposed to follow any banner, provided there be someone to bear it aloft.

The Prince, XXVI

The people have great courage, provided it be not wanting in their leaders. Look but at their single combats and their encounters when there are but a few on either side, and see how superior the Italians have shown themselves in strength, dexterity, and ability. But when it comes to their armies, then these qualities do not appear, because of the incapacity of the chiefs, who cannot enforce obedience from those who are versed in the art of war, and everyone believes himself to be so; for up to the present time there has been none so decidedly superior in valor and good fortune that the others have yielded him obedience. Thence it comes that in so great a length of time, and in the many wars that have occurred within the past twenty years, the armies, whenever wholly composed of Italians,

have given but poor account of themselves. Witness first
Taro, then Alessandria, Capua, Genoa, Vailà, Bologna,
and Mestri.

The Prince, XXVI

You must not, then, allow this opportunity to pass, so that
Italy, after waiting so long, may at last see her deliverer
appear. Nor can I possibly express with what affection he
would be received in all those provinces that have suffered
so long from this inundation of foreign foes! With what
thirst for vengeance, with what persistent faith, with what
devotion, and with what tears! What door would be closed
to him? Who would refuse him obedience? What envy
would dare oppose him? What Italian would refuse him
homage? This barbarous dominion of the foreigner of-
fends the very nostrils.

The Prince, XXVI

We Italians then owe to the Church of Rome and to her
priests our having become irreligious and bad; but we owe
her a still greater debt, and one that will be the cause of
our ruin, namely, that the Church has kept and still keeps
our country divided.

Discourses on Livy, I. 12

As for the state of affairs in the world, I derive this conclusion from them. The sort of princes who govern us possess, whether by nature or by chance, the following qualities: we have a wise pope, and therefore a serious and
scrupulous one; an unstable and capricious emperor; a
haughty, timorous king of France; a niggardly and avari-

cious king of Spain; a rich, impetuous, and glory-hungry king of England; the brutish, victorious, and insolent Swiss; and we Italians [are] poverty-stricken, ambitious, and cowardly.

Niccolò Machiavelli to Francesco Vettori,
August 26, 1513

Julius Caesar

Should it be alleged that Gaius Julius Caesar attained the Empire by means of his liberality, and that many others by the same reputation have achieved the highest rank, then I reply that you are either already a prince or are in the way of becoming one; in the first case liberality would be injurious to you, but in the second it certainly is necessary to be reputed liberal. Now Caesar was aiming to attain the Empire of Rome; but having achieved it, had he lived and not moderated his expenditures, he would assuredly have ruined the Empire by his prodigality.

The Prince, XVI

It is impossible that those who have lived as private citizens in a republic, or those who by fortune or courage have risen to be princes of the same, if they were to read history and take the records of antiquity for an example, should not prefer Scipio to Caesar; and that those who were (originally) princes should not rather choose to be like Agesilaus, Timoleon, and Dion than Nabis, Phalaris, and Dionysius; for they would then see how thoroughly the latter were despised, and how highly the former were appreciated. They would furthermore see that Timoleon and the others had no less authority in their country than Dionysius and Phalaris, but that they enjoyed far more security, and for a much greater length of time. Nor let anyone be deceived by the glory of that Caesar who has been so much celebrated by writers; for those who praised him were corrupted by his fortune, and frightened by the long duration of the empire that was maintained under his name and which did not permit writers to speak of him with freedom. And if anyone wishes to know what would have been said of him if writers had been free to speak their minds, let them read what Catiline said of him. Caesar is as much more to be condemned as he who commits an evil deed is more guilty than he who merely has the evil intention. He will also see how highly Brutus was eulogized; for, not being allowed to blame Caesar on account of his power, they extolled his enemy.

Discourses on Livy, I. 10

For as a free city is generally influenced by two principal objects, the one to aggrandize herself, and the other to preserve her liberties, it is natural that she should occasionally be betrayed into faults by excessive eagerness in the pursuit of either of these objects. As to the faults that result from the desire for aggrandizement, we shall speak of those elsewhere. Those that result from the desire to preserve her liberty are among others the following: to injure those citizens whom she should reward, and to hold in suspicion those in whom she should most place confidence. And although the effects of such conduct occasion great evils in a republic that is already corrupt, such as often lead to despotism—as was seen under Caesar in Rome, who took for himself by force what ingratitude had refused him—still, in a republic not yet entirely corrupt, they may be productive of great good in preserving her freedom for a greater length of time; as the dread of punishment will keep men better, and less ambitious.

Discourses on Livy, I. 29

The same thing happened in Rome with regard to Caesar, who by his courage and merits at first won the favor of Pompey and of other prominent citizens, but this was a favor that shortly after changed into fear; to which Cicero testifies, saying that Pompey had begun too late to fear Caesar: "This fear caused them to think of measures of safety, which however only accelerated the ruin of the republic."

Discourses on Livy, I. 33

Thus civil war was provoked, and after much bloodshed and varied fortunes the nobility retained the upper hand. In the time of Caesar and Pompey these troubles were revived, Caesar placing himself at the head of the party of Marius, and Pompey upholding that of Sylla; conflicts of arms ensued, and Caesar remained master and became the first tyrant of Rome, so that that city never afterwards recovered her liberty.

Discourses on Livy, I. 37

Livy (Roman Historian)

Wishing, therefore, so far as in me lies, to draw mankind from this error, I have thought it proper to write upon those books of Titus Livius that have come to us entire despite the malice of time; touching upon all those matters which, after a comparison between ancient and modern events, may seem to me necessary to facilitate their proper understanding.

Preface to Book I of the *Discourses on Livy*

The great things which Rome achieved, and of which Titus Livius has preserved the memory, have been the work either of the government or of private individuals; and as they relate either to the affairs of the interior or of the exterior, I shall begin to discourse of those internal operations of the government which I believe to be most noteworthy, and shall point out their results.

Discourses on Livy, I. 1

Moses

[It] was necessary for the purpose of displaying the virtue of Moses that the people of Israel should be held in bondage in Egypt.

The Prince, XXVI

The founders of cities are independent when they are people who, under the leadership of some prince, or by themselves, have been obliged to flee from pestilence, war, or famine that was devastating their native country, and are seeking a new home. These either inhabit the cities of the country of which they take possession, as Moses did, or they build new ones, as was done by Aeneas.

Discourses on Livy, I. 1

The above views might be corroborated by any number of examples, such as those of Moses, Lycurgus, Solon, and other founders of monarchies and republics, who were enabled to establish laws suitable for the common good only by keeping for themselves an exclusive authority; but all these are so well known that I will not further refer to them.

Discourses on Livy, I. 9

Whoever reads the Bible attentively will find that Moses, for the purpose of insuring the observance of his laws and institutions, was obliged to have a great many persons put to death who opposed his designs under the instigation of no other feelings than those of envy and jealousy.

Discourses on Livy, III. 30

Plutarch

Many authors, among them that most serious writer Plutarch, have held the opinion that the people of Rome were more indebted in the acquisition of their empire to the favors of Fortune than to their own merits. And among other reasons adduced by Plutarch is that it appears by their own confession that the Roman people ascribed all their victories to Fortune, because they built more temples to that goddess than to any other deity. It seems that Livius accepts that opinion, for he rarely makes a Roman speak of valor without coupling fortune with it. Now I do not share that opinion at all, and I do not believe that it can be sustained; for if no other republic has ever been known to make such conquests, it is acknowledged that none other was so well organized for that purpose as Rome. It was the valor of her armies that achieved those conquests, but it was the wisdom of her conduct and the nature of her institutions, as established by her first legislator, that enabled her to preserve these acquisitions. . . .

Discourses on Livy, II. 1

Rome and the Roman People

Those who read what the beginning of Rome was, and what her lawgivers and her organization, will not be astonished that so much virtue should have maintained itself during so many centuries; and that so great an empire should have sprung from it afterwards.

Discourses on Livy, I. 1

If we accept the opinion that Aeneas was the founder of Rome, then we must count that city as one of those built by strangers; but if Romulus is taken as its founder, then must it be classed with those built by the natives of the country. Either way it will be seen that Rome was from the first free and independent, and we shall also see (as we shall show further on) to how many privations the laws of Romulus, of Numa, and of others subjected its inhabitants; so that neither the fertility of the soil, nor proximity

of the sea, nor their many victories, nor the greatness of
the Empire, could corrupt them during several centuries,
and they maintained there more virtues than have ever
been seen in any other republic.

Discourses on Livy, I. 1

Although Rome had no legislator like Lycurgus, who constituted her government at her very origin in such a way
as to secure her liberty for a length of time, yet the disunion that existed between the Senate and the people produced such extraordinary events that chance did for her
what the laws had failed to do.

Discourses on Livy, I. 2

This was seen when Rome became free, after the expulsion of the Tarquins, when there was no other innovation
made upon the existing order of things than the substitu-
tion of two Consuls, appointed annually, in place of an
hereditary king; which proves clearly that all the original
institutions of that city were more in conformity with the
requirements of a free and civil society than with an absolute and tyrannical government.

Discourses on Livy, I. 9

The Roman people, then, admiring the wisdom and goodness of Numa, yielded in all things to his advice. It is true
that those were very religious times, and the people with
whom Numa had to deal were very untutored and super-
stitious, which made it easy for him to carry out his designs, being able to impress upon them any new form.
Considering, then, all these things, I conclude that the

religion introduced by Numa into Rome was one of the chief causes of the prosperity of that city; for this religion gave rise to good laws, and good laws bring good fortune, and from good fortune results happy success in all enterprises.

Discourses on Livy, I. 11

But there is not a more striking example of this than Rome itself, which after the expulsion of the Tarquins was enabled quickly to resume and maintain her liberty; but after the death of Caesar, Caligula, and Nero, and after the extinction of the entire Caesarean line, she could not even begin to reestablish her liberty, much less preserve it. And this great difference in the condition of things in one and the same city resulted entirely from this fact, that at the time of the Tarquins the Roman people was not yet corrupt, whilst under the Caesars it became corrupt to the lowest degree. For to preserve her sound and ready to expel the kings in the time of the Tarquins, it sufficed merely that they should take an oath never to permit any of them ever to reign again in Rome; but in the time of the Caesars the authority of Brutus with all the Eastern legions was insufficient to keep her disposed to preserve that liberty which he, in imitation of the first Brutus, had restored to her. This was the result of that corruption which had been spread among the people by the faction of Marius, at the head of which was Caesar, who had so blinded the people that they did not perceive the yoke they were imposing upon themselves.

Discourses on Livy, I. 17

Such were the people of Rome, who, so long as that republic remained uncorrupted, neither obeyed basely nor ruled insolently, but rather held its rank honorably, supporting the laws and their magistrates. And when the unrighteous ambition of some noble made it necessary for them to rise up in self-defense, they did so, as in the case of Manlius, the Decemvirs, and others who attempted to oppress them; and so when the public good required them to obey the dictators and Consuls, they promptly yielded obedience.

Discourses on Livy, I. 58

FABRIZIO: I shall never depart, in giving examples of anything, from my Romans. If we consider their life and the organization of their republic, we shall see there many things not impossible for introduction into any state in which there is still left something good.

COSIMO: What are these things you would like to introduce that are like the ancient ones?

FABRIZIO: To honor and reward excellence, not to despise poverty, to esteem the methods and regulations of military discipline, to oblige the citizens to love one another, to live without factions, to esteem private less than public good, and other like things that could easily fit in with our times. About these customs, it is not difficult to be persuaded when one thinks about them enough and takes them up in the right way, because in them so plainly can be seen the

truth that every public-spirited nature is capable
of receiving. He who accomplishes such a thing
plants trees beneath the shade of which
mankind lives more prosperously and more
happily than beneath this shade.

The Art of War, I

Romulus

For Romulus and all the other kings gave her many and
good laws, well suited even to a free people; but as the
object of these princes was to found a monarchy, and not
a republic, Rome, upon becoming free, found herself lacking all those institutions that are most essential to liberty,
and which her kings had not established.

Discourses on Livy, I. 2

Many will perhaps consider it an evil example that the
founder of a civil society, as Romulus was, should first
have killed his brother and then have consented to the
death of Titus Tatius, who had been elected to share the
royal authority with him; from which it might be concluded that the citizens, according to the example of their
prince, might, from ambition and the desire to rule, destroy those who attempt to oppose their authority. This
opinion would be correct, if we do not take into consideration the object that Romulus had in view in committing
that homicide. . . . That Romulus deserves to be excused
for the death of his brother and that of his associate, and
that what he did was for the general good and not for the

gratification of his own ambition, is proved by the fact that he immediately instituted a Senate with which to consult, and according to the opinions of which he might form his resolutions. And on carefully considering the authority which Romulus reserved for himself, we see that all he kept was the command of the army in case of war, and the power of convening the Senate.

Discourses on Livy, I. 9

Turks and the Turkish Empire

When states are acquired in a country differing in language, customs, and laws, then come the difficulties, and then it requires great good fortune and much sagacity to hold them; and one of the best and most efficient means is for the prince who has acquired them to go and reside there, which will make his possession more secure and durable. Such was the course adopted by the Turk in Greece, who even if he had respected all the institutions of that country, yet could not possibly have succeeded in holding it, if he had not gone to reside there. For being on the spot, you can quickly remedy disorders as you see them arise; but not being there, you do not hear of them until they have become so great that there is no longer any remedy for them. Besides this, the country will not be despoiled by your officials, and the subjects will be satisfied by the easy recourse they have to the prince who is near them, which contributes to win their affections, if they are well disposed, and to inspire them with fear, if otherwise. And other powers will hesitate to assail a state where the prince himself resides, as they would find it very difficult to dispossess him.

The Prince, III

In those states that are governed by an absolute prince and slaves, the prince has far more power and authority; for in his entire dominion no one recognizes any other superior but him; and if they obey anyone else, they do it as though to his minister and officer, and without any particular affection for such an official. Turkey and France furnish us examples of these two different systems of government at the present time. . . . The whole country of the Turk is governed by one master; all the rest are his slaves; and having divided the country into Sanjacs, or districts, he appoints governors for each of these, whom he changes and replaces at his pleasure.

The Prince, IV

The reasons that make the conquest of the Turkish empire so difficult are that the conqueror cannot be called into the country by any of the great nobles of the state; nor can he hope that his attempt might be facilitated by a revolt of those who surround the sovereign; which arises from the above given reasons. For being all slaves and dependents of their sovereign, it is more difficult to corrupt them; and even if they were corrupted, but little advantage could be hoped for from them, because they cannot carry the people along with them. Whoever therefore attacks the Turks must expect to find them united, and must depend wholly upon his own forces and not upon any internal disturbances. But once having defeated and driven the Turk from the field so that he cannot reorganize his army, then he will have nothing to fear but the line of the sovereign. This however once extinguished, the conqueror has nothing to apprehend from anyone else, as none other has any influence with the people; and thus, having had nothing to hope from them before the victory, he will have nothing to fear from them afterwards.

The Prince, IV

Venice

[It] is said, in favor of the course adopted by Sparta and Venice, that the preference given to the nobility, as guardians of public liberty, has two advantages: the first, to yield something to the ambition of those who, being more engaged in the management of public affairs, find, so to say, in the weapon which the office places in their hands, a means of power that satisfies them; the other, to deprive the restless spirit of the masses of an authority calculated from its very nature to produce trouble and dissensions, and apt to drive the nobles to some act of desperation, which in time may cause the greatest misfortunes.

Discourses on Livy, I. 5

In Sparta we have an example amongst the ancients, and in Venice amongst the moderns; to both these states I have already referred above. Sparta had a king and a senate, few in number, to govern her; Venice did not admit these distinctions, and gave the name of gentlemen to all who were entitled to have a part in the administration of the government. It was chance rather than foresight which gave to the latter this form of government; for having taken refuge on those shallows where the city now is, for the reasons mentioned above, the inhabitants soon became sufficiently numerous to require a regular system of laws. They consequently established a government, and assembled frequently in council to discuss the interests of the city. When it seemed to them that they were sufficiently numerous to govern themselves, they barred the way to a share in the government to the newly arrived who came to live amongst them; and finding in the course of time that the number of the latter increased sufficiently to give reputation to those who held the government in their hands, they designated the latter by the title of "gentlemen," and the others were called the popular class. This form of government had no difficulty in establishing and maintaining itself without disturbances; for at the moment of its origin all those who inhabited Venice had the right to participate in the government so that no one had cause to complain. Those who afterwards came to live there, finding the government firmly established, had neither a pretext for, nor the means of, creating disturbances. They had no cause, for the reason that they had not been deprived of anything; and they lacked the means, because they were kept in check by those who held the government, and who did not employ them in any affairs that might tempt them to seize authority. Besides, the new-comers in Venice were not sufficiently numerous to have produced a disproportion between the governing and the governed, for the number of nobles equaled or exceeded that of the others; and thus for these reasons Venice could establish and preserve that form of government. . . . In like manner, Venice, having obtained possession of a great part of Italy, and the most of it not by war, but by means of money and fraud, when occasion came for her to give proof of her strength, she lost everything in a single battle [the battle of Agnadello, March 14, 1509].

Discourses on Livy, I. 6

The republic of Venice, which is pre-eminent amongst modern ones, had reserved to a small number of citizens the power of deciding all urgent matters without referring their decisions to a larger council. And when a republic lacks some such system, a strict observance of the established laws will expose her to ruin; or, to save her from such danger, the laws will have to be disregarded.

Discourses on Livy, I. 34

Selected Bibliography

Anglo, Sydney. 2002. "'Le plus gentil esprit qui soit apparu au monde depuis les derniers siècles': The Popularity of Machiavelli in Sixteenth-Century France," in *Renaissance Reflections: Essays in Memory of C. A. Mayer*, ed. Pauline Smith and Trevor Peach, pp. 195–212. Paris: Champion.

———. 2005. *Machiavelli, the First Century: Studies in Enthusiasm, Hostility and Irrelevance*. Oxford: Oxford University Press.

Arienzo, Alessandro, and Borrelli Gianfranco, eds. 2009. *Anglo-American Faces of Machiavelli. Machiavelli e machiavellismi nella cultura anglo-americana (secoli XVI-XX). Atti del Convegno di Napoli, febbraio, 2007.* Monza: Polimetrica.

Aron, Raymond. 1993. *Machiavel et les tyrannies modernes.* Paris: Fallois.

Ascoli, Albert Russell, and Victoria Kahn, eds. 1993. *Machiavelli and the Discourses of Literature.* Ithaca: Cornell University Press.

Atkinson, Catherine. 2002. "Debts, Dowries, Donkeys: The Diary of Niccolò Machiavelli's father, Messer Bernardo," in *Quattrocento Florence.* Frankfurt am Main: Lang.

Barbuto, Gennaro Maria. 2013. *Machiavelli.* Roma: Salerno Editrice.

Bardazzi, Giovanni. 2007. "Da Cesena a Ginevra: la lettera di Machiavelli del 19 dicembre 1502 (Seconda Legazione al Valentino)," *Interpres: rivista di studi quattrocenteschi* 26: 325–53.

Baron, Hans. 1961. "Machiavelli: The Republican Citizen and the Author of *The Prince*," *English Historical Review* 76:217–53.

———. 1966. *The Crisis of the Early Italian Renaissance.* Princeton: Princeton University Press.

Barthas, Jérémie. 2001. "Au fondement intellectuel de l'irréligion machiavélienne, Lucrèce? Controverses, notes et considerations," in *Sources antiques de l'irréligion moderne: le relais italien XVe-XVIIIe siècles*, ed. D. Foucault and J.-P. Cavaillé, pp. 67–90. Toulouse: Collection de l'E.C.R.I.T.

Bassani, Luigi Marco and Vivanti Corrado, eds. 2006. *Machiavelli nella storiografia e nel pensiero politico del XX secolo*. Milano: Giuffrè.

Bausi Francesco. 2002. "Politica e poesia. Ancora sulla cultura di Machiavelli," *Intersezioni: rivista di storia delle idee* 23:377–93.

———. 2005. *Machiavelli*. Rome: Salerno Editrice.

———. 2010. "Tipologia degli autografi machiavelliani," in *Atti del convegno, Di mano propria. Gli autografi dei letterati italiani, Forlì, 24–27 novembre, 2008*, pp. 287–318. Rome: Salerno Editrice.

———. 2014. "Da Bernardo a Niccolò Machiavelli. Sui legislatori che fecero ricorso alla religione (*Discorsi* I, 11)," *Bruniana & Campanelliana* XX, 1:25–33.

Benner, Erica. 2009. *Machiavelli's Ethics*. Princeton: Princeton University Press.

———. 2013. *Machiavelli's Prince: A New Reading*. Oxford: Oxford University Press.

Berlin, Isaiah. 1980. "The Originality of Machiavelli," in *Against the Current*, ed. Isaiah Berlin, pp. 25–79. New York: Viking Press.

Black, Robert. 2011. "Notes on the Date and Genesis of Machiavelli's *De principatibus*," in *Europe and Italy. Studies in Honour of Giorgio Chittolini*, ed. P. Guglielmotti, I. Lazzarini, and G. M. Varanini, pp. 29–41. Firenze: Firenze University Press.

———. 2012. "Machiavelli: Some Recent Biographies and Studies," *English Historical Review* 127, 524:110–25.

———. 2014. "Machiavelli and the Militia: New Thoughts," *Italian Studies* 69, 1:41–50.

Bobbitt, Philip. 2013. *The Garments of Court and Palace: Machiavelli and the World That He Made*. New York: Grove Press.

Bock, Gisela, Quentin Skinner, and Maurizio Viroli, eds. 1990. *Machiavelli and Republicanism*. Cambridge: Cambridge University Press.

Breiner, Peter. 2008. "Machiavelli's 'New Prince' and the Primordial Moment of Acquisition," *Political Theory* 36, 1:66–92.

Brown, Alison. 2010. *The Return of Lucretius to Renaissance Florence*. Cambridge (Mass.) and London: Harvard University Press.

Burckhardt, Jacob. [1860] 1990. *The Civilization of the Renaissance in Italy*. New York: Penguin Books.

Cadoni, Giorgio. 2001. "Il 'profeta disarmato.' Intorno al giudizio di Machiavelli su Girolamo Savonarola," *La Cultura* 2:239–66.

Chabod, Federico. 1958. *Machiavelli and the Renaissance*. London: Bowes and Bowes.

Chiappelli, Fredi. 1952. *Studi sul linguaggio del Machiavelli*. Florence: Le Monnier.

Colish, Marcia. 1971. "The Idea of Liberty in Machiavelli," *Journal of the History of Ideas* 32:323–51.

Connell, William J. 2001. "Machiavelli on Growth as an End," in *Historians and Ideologues: Essays in Honor of Donald R. Kelley*, ed. Anthony Grafton and J.H.M. Salmon. Rochester, NY: University of Rochester Press, pp. 259–77.

———. 2003. "Repubblicanesimo e Rinascimento (nella storiografia anglofona del secondo Novecento)," *Archivio storico italiano* 161:343–62.

———. 2005. *Niccolò Machiavelli: The Prince with Related Documents*. Boston: Bedford/St. Martin's.

———. 2011. "New Light on Machiavelli's Letter to Vettori, 10 December 1513," in *Europe and Italy: Studies in Honour of Giorgio Chittolini*, ed. P. Guglielmotti, I. Lazzarini, and G. M. Varanini, pp. 93–127. Firenze: Firenze University Press.

De Grazia, Sebastian. 1989. *Machiavelli in Hell*. Princeton: Princeton University Press.

Donaldson, Peter S. 1988. *Machiavelli and Mystery of State*. Cambridge: Cambridge University Press.

Femia, Joseph. 2004. "Machiavelli and Italian Fascism," *History of Political Thought* 25, 1:1–15.

———. 2005. "Gramsci, Machiavelli and International Relations," *Political Quarterly* 76, 3:341–49.

Fleisher, Martin, ed. 1972. *Machiavelli and the Nature of Political Thought*. New York: Atheneum.

Fontana, Alessandro, Jean-Louis Fournel, Xavier Tabet, and Jean-Claude Zancarini, eds. 2004. *Language et écritures de la république et de la guerre. Études sur Machiavel*. Genova: Name.

Fontana, Benedetto. 2003. "Sallust and the Politics of Machiavelli," *History of Political Thought* 24, 1:86–108.

Fournel, Jean-Louis, and Grossi Paolo, eds. 2007. *Governare a Firenze: Savonarola, Machiavelli, Guicciardini. Atti della giornata di studi, 20 novembre 2006*. Paris: Istituto italiano di Cultura.

Fournel, Jean-Luc. 2000. "De l'acquisition par le crime: le Temps des cruautés (Lecture du chapitre VIII du 'Prince' de Machiavel)," *Quaderni di Italianistica* 21:127–40.

Frigorilli, Maria Cristina. 2006. *Machiavelli moralista. Ricerche su fonti, lessico e fortuna*. Napoli: Liguori.

Garver, Eugene. 1987. *Machiavelli and the History of Prudence*. Madison: University of Wisconsin Press.

Gilbert, Allan H. 1938. *Machiavelli's* Prince *and Its Forerunners: "The Prince" as a Typical Book* de Regimine Principum. Durham, N.C.: Duke University Press.

Gilbert, Felix. 1965. *Machiavelli and Guicciardini: Politics and History in Sixteenth-Century Florence*. Princeton: Princeton University Press.

———. 1977. *History: Choice and Commitment*. Cambridge, Mass.: Harvard University Press.

Ginzburg, Carlo. 2003. "Machiavelli, l'eccezione e la regola," *Quaderni Storici* 38:195–213.

Guidi, Andrea. 2005. "L'esperienza cancelleresca nella formazione politica di Niccolò Machiavelli," *Il Pensiero Politico* 38:3–23.

———. 2006. "Machiavelli al tempo del sacco di Prato alla luce di sei lettere inedite a lui inviate," *Filologia e Critica* May–August:274–87.

———. 2009. *Un segretario militante. Politica, diplomazia e armi nel Cancelliere Machiavelli*. Bologna: Il Mulino.

Hale, J. R. 1961. *Machiavelli and Renaissance Italy*. London: English Universities Press.

Hanasz, Waldemar. 2010. "The Common Good in Machiavelli," *History of Political Thought* 31, 1:57–85.

Hankins, James ed. 2000. *Renaissance Civic Humanism: Reappraisal and Reflections*. Cambridge: Cambridge University Press.

Haslam, Jonathan. 2002. *No Virtue Like Necessity: Realist Thought in International Relations since Machiavelli*. New Haven and London: Yale University Press.

Hörnqvist, Mikael. 2004. *Machiavelli and Empire*. Cambridge: Cambridge University Press.

Hulliung, Mark. 1983. *Citizen Machiavelli*. Princeton: Princeton University Press.

Hunsicker, Jacqueline R. 2013. "The Two Cyruses: Models of Machiavellian Humanity and Harshness for Republican Leaders," *History of Political Thought* 34, 1:19–34.

Inglese, Giorgio. 2014. "Sul testo del *Principe*," *La Cultura* 1:47–76.

Jackson, Michael. 2000. "Imagined Republics: Machiavelli, Utopia, and 'Utopia,'" *Journal of Value Inquiry* 34, 4:427–37.

Jurdjevic, Mark. 2007. "Machiavelli's Hybrid Republicanism," *English Historical Review* 122, 499:1228–57.

———. 2014. *A Great and Wretched City: Promise and Failure in Machiavelli's Florentine Political Thought*. Cambridge (Mass.): Harvard University Press.

Kahn, Victoria. 1994. *Machiavellian Rhetoric: From the Counter-Reformation to Milton*. Princeton: Princeton University Press.

Kane, Thomas M. 2006. *Theoretical Roots of US Foreign Policy: Machiavelli and American Unilateralism*. London: Routledge.

Kapust, Daniel J. 2010. "Acting the Princely Style: Ethos and Pathos in Cicero's 'On the Ideal Orator' and Machiavelli's *The Prince*," *Political Studies* 58, 3:590–608.

Krause, Sharon R., and Mary Ann McGrail, eds. 2009. *The Arts of Rule. Essays in Honor of Harvey Mansfield*. New York and Toronto: Lexington Books.

Lamberton, Harper John. 2007. *American Machiavelli: Alexan-*

der Hamilton and the Origins of U.S. Foreign Policy. Cambridge: Cambridge University Press.

Landi, Sandro. 2014. "'Per purgare li animi di quelli populi.' Metafore del vincolo politico e religioso in Machiavelli," *Storia del Pensiero Politico* 2:187–212.

Landon, William J. 2005. *Politics, Patriotism and Language: Niccolò Machiavelli's 'Secular patria' and the Creation of an Italian National Identity*. New York and Oxford: Peter Lang.

Larivaille, Paul. 1982. *La pensée politique de Machiavel: les discours sur la première décade de Tite-Live*. Nancy: Presses Universitaries de Nancy.

Lefort, Claude. 1972. *Le travail de l'oeuvre Machiavel*. Paris: Gallimard.

Lynch, Christopher. 2012. "War and Foreign Affairs in Machiavelli's 'Florentine Histories,'" *Review of Politics* 74, 1:1–26.

Mansfield, Harvey C. J. 1979. *Machiavelli's New Modes and Orders: A Study of the Discourses on Livy*. Ithaca, N.Y.: Cornell University Press.

———. 1996. *Machiavelli's Virtue*. Chicago: University of Chicago Press.

———. 2001. *Machiavelli's New Modes and Orders: A Study of the Discourses on Livy*. Chicago and London: University of Chicago Press.

———. 2013. "Strauss on *The Prince*," *Review of Politics* 75, 4: 641–65.

Marchand, Jean-Jacques, ed. 2004. *Machiavelli senza i Medici (1498–1512): Scrittura del potere, potere della scrittura. Convegno di Losanna, 18–20 novembre 2004*. Rome: Salerno Editrice.

Martelli, Mario. 2009. *Otto studi machiavelliani*, ed. F. Bausi. Rome: Salerno Editrice.

McCormick, John P. 2001. "Addressing the Political Exception: Machiavelli's 'Accidents' and the Mixed Regime," *American Political Science Review* 87, 4:888–900.

———. 2003. "Machiavelli against Republicanism: On the Cambridge School's 'Guicciardinian Moments,'" *Political Theory* 31, 5:615–43.

———. 2007. "Machiavelli's Political Trials and 'The Free Way of Life,'" *Political Theory* 35, 4:385–411.

———. 2007. *Machiavellian Democracy*. Cambridge: Cambridge University Press.

———. 2009. "Machiavelli and the Gracchi: Prudence, Violence and Redistribution," *Global Crime* 10, 4:298–305.

———. 2009. "Machiavelli, Weber and Cesare Borgia: The science of Politics and Exemplary Statebuilding," *Storia e Politica* 1, 1:7–33.

———. 2011. "Prophetic Statebuilding: Machiavelli and the Passion of the Duke," *Representations* 115, 1:1–19.

———. 2012. "Subdue the Senate: Machiavelli's 'Way of Freedom' or Path to Tyranny?" *Political Theory* 40, 6:714–35.

———, ed. 2014. "Machiavelli's The Prince, 500 Years," *Social Research: An International Quarterly* special issue 81, 1.

Murari, Pires Francisco. 2008. "Machiavel, la cour des Antiques et (le dialogue) avec Thucydide," *Dialogues d'histoire ancienne* 34, 1:59–84.

Najemy, John M. 2006. *A History of Florence, 1200–1575*. Oxford: Oxford University Press.

———. 2013. "Machiavelli and Cesare Borgia: A Reconsideration of Chapter 7 of *The Prince*," *Review Of Politics* 75, 4:539–56.

———, ed. 2010. *The Cambridge Companion to Machiavelli*. Cambridge: Cambridge University Press.

Nelson, Eric. 2004. *The Greek Tradition in Republican Thought*. Cambridge: Cambridge University Press.

———. 2007. "The Problem of the Prince," in *The Cambridge Companion to Renaissance Philosophy*, ed. J. Hankins, pp. 319–37. Cambridge: Cambridge University Press.

O'Brien, Conor Cruise. 1972. "The Ferocious Wisdom of Machiavelli," in *The Suspecting Glance*, ed. Conor Cruise O'Brien. London: Faber and Faber.

Orwin, Clifford. 1978. "Machiavelli's Unchristian Charity," *American Political Science Review* 72:1217–28.

Parel, Anthony, ed. 1972. *The Political Calculus: Essays on Machiavelli's Philosophy*. Toronto: University of Toronto Press.

Parel, Anthony, ed. 2006. *The Machiavellian Cosmos*. New Haven: Yale University Press, 1992.

Patapan, Haig. 2006. *Machiavelli in Love: The Modern Politics of Love and Fear*. Oxford: Lexington Books.

Perini, Leandro. 2007. "Postfazione," in *Bernardo Machiavelli. Libro di ricordi*, ed. Cesare Olschki, pp. 263–323. Rome: Edizioni di Storia e Letteratura.

Pincin, Carlo. 1966. "La prefazione e la dedicatoria dei *Discorsi* di Machiavelli," *Giornale storico della letteratura italiana* 143:72–83.

———. 1971. "Osservazioni sul modo di procedere di Machiavelli nei *Discorsi*," in *Renaissance Studies in Honor of Hans Baron*, ed. Anthony Molho and John A. Tedeschi, pp. 385–408. DeKalb: Northern Illinois University Press.

Pitkin, Hanna Fenichel. 1984. *Fortune Is a Woman: Gender and Politics in the Thought of Niccolò Machiavelli*. Berkeley and Los Angeles: University of California Press.

Pocock, J.G.A. 1975. *The Machiavellian Moment: Florentine Political Thought and the Atlantic Republican Tradition*. Princeton: Princeton University Press.

Price, Russell. 1977. "The Theme of *Gloria* in Machiavelli," *Renaissance Quarterly* 30: 588–632.

Rahe, Paul A., ed. 2006. *Machiavelli's Liberal Republican Legacy*. Cambridge: Cambridge University Press.

Rebhorn, Wayne A. 1988. *Foxes and Lions: Machiavelli's Confidence*. Ithaca: Cornell University Press.

Ridolfi, Roberto. 1963. *The Life of Niccolò Machiavelli*, trans. Cecil Grayson. London: Routledge & K. Paul.

Ruggiero, Guido. 2007. *Machiavelli in Love: Sex, Self, and Society in the Italian Renaissance*. Baltimore: The John Hopkins University Press.

Sasso, Gennaro. 1980. *Niccolò Machiavelli: storia del suo pensiero politico*. Bologna: il Mulino.

———. 1987. *Machiavelli e gli antichi e altri saggi*. 3 vols. Milano: R. Ricciardi.

Saxonhouse, Arlene. 1985. *Women in the History of Political Thought, Ancient Greece to Machiavelli*. New York: Praeger.

Scott, Jonathan. 2004. *Commonwealth Principles: Republican Writing of the English Revolution.* Cambridge: Cambridge University Press.

Simonetta, Marcello. 2004. *Rinascimento segreto: Il mondo del segretario da Petrarca a Machiavelli.* Milano: Franco Angeli.

Skinner, Quentin. 1978. *The Foundations of Modern Political Thought,* 2 vols. Cambridge: Cambridge University Press.

———. 1981. *Machiavelli.* New York: Hill and Wang.

———. 2002. *Visions of Politics,* 3 vols. Cambridge: Cambridge University Press.

Strauss, Leo. 1958. *Thoughts on Machiavelli.* Glencoe, Ill.: The Free Press.

———. 1970. "Machiavelli and Classical Literature," *Review of National Literatures* 1:7–25.

———. 1983. "Niccolò Machiavelli," in *History of Political Philosophy,* ed. Leo Strauss and Joseph Cropsey. Chicago: University of Chicago Press.

Sullivan, Vickie B. 1996. *Machiavelli's Three Romes: Religion, Human Liberty, and Politics Reformed.* De Kalb: Northern Illinois University Press.

Tarcov, Nathan. 1982. "Quentin Skinner's Method and Machiavelli's *Prince,*" *Ethics* 92: 692–709.

———. 2003. "Arms and Politics in Machiavelli's *Prince,*" in *Entre Kant et Kosovo: Études offertés à Pierre Hassner,* ed. A.-M. Le Gloannec and A. Smolar, pp. 109–21. Paris: Presses de Sciences Po.

———. 2007. "Freedom, Republics, and People in Machiavelli's *Prince,*" in *Freedom and the Human Person,* ed. R. Velkley, pp. 122–42. Washington D.C.: Catholic University of America Press.

———. 2013. "Belief and Opinion in Machiavelli's *Prince,*" *Review of Politics* 75, 4: 573–86.

Vasoli, Cesare. 2001. "Machiavelli, la religione 'civile' degli antichi e le 'armi,'" *Il Pensiero Politico* 34, 3:337–52.

———. 2007. *Ficino, Savonarola, Machiavelli.* Torino: Aragno.

Vatter, Miguel E. 2000. *Between Form and Event: Machiavelli's*

Theory of Political Freedom. Dordrecht, Boston, and London: Kluwer.

———. 2005. "Machiavelli after Marx: The Self-Overcoming of Marxism in the Late Althusser," *Theory & Event* 7,4.

———. 2012. "The Quarrel between Populism and Republicanism: Machiavelli and the Antinomies of Plebeian Politics," *Contemporary Political Theory* 11, 3:242–63.

Viroli, Maurizio. 2007. "Machiavelli's Realism," *Constellations: An International Journal Of Critical And Democratic Theory* 14, 4:466–82.

———. 2008. *How to Read Machiavelli*. London: Granta.

———. 2010. *Machiavelli's God*. Princeton: Princeton University Press.

———. 2013. *Redeeming* The Prince: *The Meaning of Machiavelli's Masterpiece*. Princeton: Princeton University Press.

Vivanti, Corrado. 2008. *Niccolò Machiavelli. I tempi della politica*. Rome: Donzelli.

Whitfield, J. H. 1966. *Machiavelli*. New York: Russell & Russell.

———. 1969. *Discourses on Machiavelli*. Cambridge: Heffer.

Zmora, Hillay. 2004. "Love of Country and Love of Party: Patriotism and Human Nature in Machiavelli," *History of Political Thought* 25, 3:424–45.

Zuckert, Catherine. 2014. "Machiavelli's Democratic Republic," *History of Political Thought* 35, 2:262–94.

Credits

Machiavelli and His Friends: Their Personal Correspondence,
trans. and ed. James B. Atkinson and David Sices,
DeKalb: Northern Illinois University Press, 1996.

Page 7. My poverty, he proudly proclaimed . . . (265)

Page 13. because never did I disappoint that republic . . . (336)

Page 241. I do not know what Aristotle says about confederated republics . . . (258)

The Art of War, in *Machiavelli: The Chief Works and Others,*
trans. Allan Gilbert, Durham and London,
Duke University Press, 1989, vol. 2.

Page 16. And I repine at Nature . . . (VII)

Page 101. By Italy's condition I do not wish you to be dismayed or terrified . . . (VII)

Page 132-33. In Italy, then, to know how to manage an army already formed is not enough . . . (VII)

Page 224. The common belief of our Italian princes . . . (VII)

Page 280. I shall never depart, in giving examples of anything, from my Romans. . . . (I)

Page 280. COSIMO. What are these things you would like to introduce . . . (I)

Belfagor, the Devil Who Married, in *Machiavelli: The Chief Works and Others,* trans. Allan Gilbert, Durham and London, Duke University Press, 1989, vol. 2.

Page 26. Calling them therefore to council . . . (869-70)

Discourse on Remodeling the Government of Florence, in *Machiavelli: The Chief Works and Others,* trans. Allan Gilbert, Durham and London, Duke University Press, 1989, vol. 1.

Page 32. No greater gift, then, does Heaven give to a man . . . (114)

Page 163. I believe the greatest honor ...

Page 256. The reason why Florence throughout her history has frequently varied her methods of government ... (101)

Page 257. That constitution [of 1393] also suffered ... (102)

Page 257. After that [after the regime of Cosimo de' Medici between 1434 and 1464], the city ... (103)

Page 258. In all cities where the citizens are accustomed ... (106)

Page 259. Without satisfying the generality of the citizens ... (110)

An Exhortation to Penitence, in *Machiavelli: The Chief Works and Others*, trans. Allan Gilbert, Durham and London, Duke University Press, 1989, vol. 1.

Page 32. Since this evening, honored fathers and superior brothers ... (171)

The [Golden] Ass, in *Machiavelli: The Chief Works and Others*, trans. Allan Gilbert, Durham and London: Duke University Press, 1989, vol. 2.

Page 30. Not yet has Heaven altered its opinion ... (lines 100–110)

Page 33. Observe the stars above, the moon ... (lines 94–104)

Mandragola, in *Machiavelli: The Chief Works and Others*, trans. Allan Gilbert, Durham and London: Duke University Press, 1989, vol. 2.

Page 2. The story is called *Mandragola.* You will see ... (Prologue)

Page 26. But then on the other hand, the worst that can happen to you ... (Act 4, Scene 1)

Page 34. WOMAN: Take this florin, then ... (Act 3, Scene 3)

Page 45. Women are the most compassionate creatures ... (Act 3, Scene 4)

Pages 46–47. FRATE TIMOTEO: If you want to confess, I'm at your service. ... (Act 3, Scene 3)

Page 47. I have already told you, and I'll say it again . . . (Act 3, Scene 10)

Page 48. As far as conscience is concerned, you must follow this rule . . . (Act 3 , Scene 11)

Page 48. I swear to you, my lady, by this consecrated breast . . . (Act 3, Scene 11)

Page 56. CALLIMACO: I realize you're right. But what can I do? . . . (Act 1, Scene 3)

Page 56. CALLIMACO: Oh God! What have I done to deserve such a reward? . . . (Act 4, Scene 2)

Page 66. Besides that, we must always consider the end result . . . (Act 3, Scene 11)

Page 107. FATHER TIMOTEO: I want to go back to what I said earlier . . . (Act 3, Scene 11)

Page 109. Everybody knows how happy he is . . . (Following Act 2)

Page 118. NICEA: In this town [Florence] there's nothing . . . (Act 2, Scene 3)

Page 118. SOSTRATA: Listen to him, my dear. Don't you see . . . (Act 3, Scene 11)

Page 118. MESSER NICIA: And I'm going to give them the key . . . (Act 5, Scene 6)

Tercets on Ambition, in *Machiavelli: The Chief Works and Others*, trans. Allan Gilbert, Durham and London, Duke University Press, 1989, vol. 2.

Page 36. Hardly had God created stars and light . . . (16–29, 735)

Page 127. You will see how Ambition results in two kinds of action . . . (127–161, 738)

Tercets on Fortune, in *Machiavelli: The Chief Works and Others*, trans. Allan Gilbert, Durham and London, Duke University Press, 1989, vol. 2.

Page 28. By many this goddess is called omnipotent . . . (25–30, 749)

Tercets on Ingratitude or Envy, in *Machiavelli: The Chief Works and Others*, trans. Allan Gilbert, Durham and London: Duke University Press, 1989, vol. 2.

Pages 84–85. When the stars, when the heavens were indignant . . . (740–741)

Index

Page numbers in **bold** indicate the primary discussion of a person or topic.